Esteban Alterman

About the Author

Yossi Klein Halevi is the Israel correspondent for *The New Republic* and senior writer for *The Jerusalem Report*. He is a regular commentator on Middle Eastern and religious affairs for the *Los Angeles Times* and has written for the *New York Times*, the *Washi[...]* and other publications. The document[...] focuses on his relationship [...] survivor, was named b[...] the ten best films of 1985.

ALSO BY
YOSSI KLEIN HALEVI

Memoirs of a Jewish Extremist: An American Story

AT THE
ENTRANCE
TO THE
GARDEN
OF EDEN

A Jew's Search for Hope with Christians and

Muslims in the Holy Land

YOSSI KLEIN HALEVI

Perennial

An Imprint of HarperCollinsPublishers

A hardcover edition of this book was published in 2001 by William Morrow, an imprint of
HarperCollins Publishers.

HarperCollins books may be purchased for educational, business, or sales promotional use.
For information please write: Special Markets Department, HarperCollins Publishers Inc.,
10 East 53rd Street, New York, NY 10022.

First Perennial edition published 2002.

Designed by Shubhani Sarkar

Library of Congress Cataloging-in-Publication Data is available.

ISBN 0-06-050582-6

02 03 04 05 06 RRD 10 9 8 7 6 5 4 3 2

For SARAH, a reciprocal gesture

Rabbi Judah said, "Abraham . . . saw Adam and Eve buried
there. . . . As he was gazing, an opening to the Garden of Eden
opened for him. . . . He saw a light shining in the cave and
a single lamp burning. Then Abraham yearned to dwell
in that site; his heart and will focused
constantly on the cave."

ZOHAR 1:127a

CONTENTS

ACKNOWLEDGMENTS

This project was blessed with devoted supporters. My editor, Claire Wachtel, was generous, wise, and ironic, as the situation called for. Pam Bernstein has become, over the years, more friend than agent. The support of Alan Slifka, founder of the visionary Abraham Fund, which encourages Arab-Jewish coexistence in Israel, freed me from journalistic deadlines. My editors, David Horovitz at the *Jerusalem Report* and Peter Beinart at the *New Republic,* were accommodating and sympathetic.

Sam Freedman, Yoel Glick, and Daniel Rossing provided invaluable literary and spiritual advice.

I am grateful for the insights of Rabbi Alon Goshen-Gottstein, Dr. Muhammad Hourani, Rabbi David Rosen, Rabbi Ron Kronish, Rev. Petra Heldt, Father Francesco Rossi de Gasperis, Brother Jack Driscoll, Sister Maureena Fritz, Rabbi Irving Greenberg, and Bishop Krister Stendhal—all heroes of the interfaith adventure.

In addition, help in various forms was provided by Esteban Alterman, Sima Levy, Jennifer Pooley, Dee Dee DeBartlo, Yehezkel Landau, Yaakov Maoz, Carl Perkal, Sharon Ashley, Richard Bardenstein, Isabel Kershner, and Chava Naeh.

Thanks to Daniel Matt for providing translation from the Zohar, and to Paul Lakeland for permission to quote from his essay on faith that appeared in *Cross Currents* magazine.

The late Benedictine monk and lover of Jerusalem Vincent

Martin offered crucial emotional support. My friends at Jerusalem's Melkite monastery, Saint Jean du Desert—Father Jacob, Father Elisha, and Father Samuel—opened their home to me for retreats.

The inspiration for this journey was implanted many years ago by *The Wild Goats of Ein Gedi*, Herbert Weiner's account of religious life among Christians, Muslims, and Jews during Israel's early years. Weiner's loving narrative was my introduction to the religious diversity of this land.

Finally, my deep gratitude to all those who allowed me to enter their spiritual lives. I hope I have justified their trust.

FOREWORD

On the morning of September 11, 2001, I was waiting in a restaurant in midtown Manhattan for my editor, Claire Wachtel, to arrive for breakfast. I'd come to New York from my home in Jerusalem for the launching party of the hardcover edition of this book, which was scheduled for that evening.

As I waited for Claire, I read a day-old Israeli newspaper and felt very far from home. Almost the entire news section focused on the suicide bombing at the train station in the northern Israeli town of Nahariya two days before, claiming three lives and wounding nearly a hundred. My sixteen-year-old daughter, Moriah, who'd spent the weekend at a friend's house near the Lebanon border, had been at the Nahariya station and had boarded a train for Tel Aviv just before the bomber blew himself up. And so I was desperate for real news, the names and faces of the dead and the details that get misplaced in the broad strokes of American reporting from abroad. One of the reasons I'd left my native New York for Jerusalem nineteen years earlier was to know Israel not just from the headlines but also from the back pages, to immerse myself in the details of the story that engaged me most—the return of the Jews home.

The unbearable intimacy of Israel intruded. One of the Nahariya dead, I read, was a teenage soldier who'd graduated from the elementary school my children had attended. I tried to conceal my weeping from the other diners. At that moment, my alienation from America felt complete. Since arriving in New York two weeks earlier, I'd been trying, with little success, to explain to people what it now meant to be an Israeli living with the constant threat of terrorism. My disorientation was embodied by ambulance sirens: When an Israeli hears a siren, he waits for the second one, and when he hears the third, he turns on the television. In America, though, a siren was just—a siren.

Claire appeared a little before nine A.M. Just as our breakfasts arrived, the maître d' approached our table and discreetly mentioned that a plane had crashed into the World Trade Center. His tone—half stunned, half bemused—seemed to say, Isn't this a bizarre world? "It's terrorism," said Claire, with the grim instinct of a Jew from Brooklyn and a child of Holocaust survivors, the background we share.

The horizon at the lower end of Fifth Avenue was dominated by a pillar of smoke, a demonic play on the biblical image of divine protection. Strangers gathered around radios, a familiar Israeli image. "Now it's war," one man with a Spanish accent said to me when I paused to listen to his radio. An ambulance went by, and all sound seemed subsumed in its siren; everyone paused, as if waiting for the next ambulance. For the first time since I'd moved to Jerusalem, New York City felt like home.

Later that morning, I was scheduled to address religious leaders at the Interfaith Center of New York, on East 30th Street. I phoned the center and suggested the obvious: Let's cancel. To my surprise, the director insisted on proceeding. Even if no one shows up but you and us, he said, at least we'll be together.

And so I found myself walking south, toward the inferno, while thousands of people rushed in the opposite direction, desperate for a way out of Manhattan. As soon as I entered the Interfaith Center, its walls covered with symbols of the world's faiths, I felt relief. Here was the antidote to the terrorists' desecration of God's name, a reminder that the real war wasn't being fought between secularism and fundamentalism but within religion itself, between those who insist that one God means one way and those who believe that God is vast enough to receive multiple paths.

Several people actually showed up—a Catholic theologian who'd come from Connecticut and was now stranded, a Japanese Buddhist leader who knew no English and brought his own translator. We sat together, listening to news updates and then lapsing into silence. I was expected to offer Israeli expertise on how to emotionally absorb terrorism, but the scale of this disaster reduced me to shaking my head and mumbling inadequate exclamations. We were so stunned that we forgot to pray for the victims, for ourselves. Or perhaps our sitting together was itself a form of prayer.

In the months following September 11, as America gradually emerged from its initial trauma, Israel descended into fear and despair. Suicide bombers—perhaps the most monstrous deviance ever produced by religion—targeted our buses and cafés and wedding halls. Dread accompanied the most mundane foray into public space; daily life itself became a threat. The routinization of terrorism turned the inconceivable into a blur, and one atrocity supplanted the next with such rapidity that we even lost the ability to mourn. Few countries had ever faced such a sustained campaign of terrorism, small acts of mass murder that are preenactments of the genocidal impulse. We were in the grip of an experiment testing how long a society can endure under relentless terror before it begins to disintegrate. Gradually, we became a nation of agoraphobics, restricting our movements to essential functions.

I am part of the Israeli majority that is ready to offer almost any concessions for real peace, to end the pathological hundred-year war between Arabs and Jews that threatens to draw the world into cataclysm. The journey described in this book—my attempt, as a religious Israeli Jew, to encounter the devotions of my Christian and Muslim neighbors—was the ultimate gesture I was capable of offering for peace. My experiences with Palestinians in their intimate moments of prayer reinforced my belief that both sides share ample rights and wrongs, and that both have been indispensable in prolonging this conflict.

Still, I am equally certain that Israel isn't to blame for the current war. At the crucial moment, at Camp David in July 2000, Israel proposed almost full withdrawal from the territories and the uprooting of most settlements. And it became the first country ever to offer shared sovereignty over its capital city. That offer had previously been inconceivable, and so was the Palestinians' response to it: Yasser Arafat declared a terrorist war against the most left-wing government in Israel's history. The willingness of so many young Palestinians to turn themselves into human bombs wasn't the result of desperation as much as of hate education in the mosques, media, and schools of Palestine. While a majority of Israelis finally acknowledged that the Middle East conflict was a struggle between two legitimate national movements, most Palestinians continued to insist that all justice belongs to them and all blame to Israel.

In Manhattan in early September, a few days before the attack on the Towers, I met an Arab American woman, daughter of a well-known spokesman for the Palestinian cause, whom I'll call Nadia. She was moved by my effort to experience and respect Islam, and we became friends. The day after the World Trade Center was destroyed, as I was trying to determine the fate of my flight back to Israel, Nadia called. "I'm praying for your safe return home," she said.

Back in Israel, I wrote her, "I don't know whether you intended to use the word 'home' when you wished me a safe trip. But I was moved by the notion of an Arab woman acknowledging that an Israeli flying to Tel Aviv was on his way home."

"I was very conscious of using that word," she replied. "I've certainly come a long way!" I wrote back, "When Israelis hear those simple words from the Arab world, 'You've come home,' there will be peace in the Middle East."

The despair so many Israelis feel today has been deepened by the religiously inspired hysteria against the Jewish people now spreading through much of the Muslim world. As a Jew who learned to love Islam and its choreographed prayers of surrender, this has been a particularly devastating time. Shamefully few Muslim clerics have denounced the ritual mass murder committed in the name of God and Islam. Instead, the Arab world has indulged in a frenzy of Jew-hatred unprecedented anywhere since Nazi Germany. Government-controlled media deny the reality of the Holocaust and resurrect medieval libels accusing Jews of using the blood of gentile children for religious observance. Much of the Muslim world seems intent on reviving the demonization of the Jews abandoned by the Christian world after the Holocaust. The Muslim-Jewish relationship, which has known glorious moments in the past, seems to be descending into an abyss. It is, to say the least, hardly a propitious time to be publishing a book about a Jew's love for Islam.

Still, in my better moments, when I manage to overcome the desperation that surrounds and often overwhelms me, I realize that this is precisely the time to try to counter the pathological alienation growing between our two faiths, which risks turning the Arab-Israeli conflict into a Muslim-Jewish war.

Understandably, most of the attention on this book has focused on my encounters with moderate Islam, in particular the Sufi mystical stream. Given the post–September 11 urgency for dialogue with pluralistic elements in Islam, it was inevitable that the sections of this book dealing with my Christian encounters would be neglected. Yet an essential motive for this journey was my desire to offer a reciprocal Jewish gesture of respect to Christianity, in recognition of the heroic effort of many Christians to confront their negative theology toward Judaism and the Jewish people. Leading churches have not only repudiated but to some extent reversed their anti-Jewish theology, no longer seeing the Jews as cursed but blessed. Perhaps the most powerful moment of that transformation occurred during

Pope John Paul II's pilgrimage to the Holy Land in March 2000, when he bent before the Western Wall and inserted a note asking forgiveness for Christian sins toward "the people of the covenant." While the media focused on the Pope's request for forgiveness, the truly remarkable phrase was the one reaffirming the ongoing validity of God's covenant with the Jews, repudiating the Church's insistence that it had replaced the Jews as God's beloved people. Implicit in the Pope's new formulation was a Creator generous enough to accommodate more than one covenant.

That transformation gives me hope for an eventual reconciliation with Islam. It is depressingly true that mainstream Islam hasn't yet accepted the legitimacy of Jewish sovereignty over any part of the Holy Land. Muslim theologians continue to insist that Jews (and Christians) must ultimately be brought under "protected" Islamic status—allowed to practice their faiths so long as they surrender to Muslim rule. In the Middle Ages, that doctrine was a marked advance over the Crusaders' "convert or die" approach to interfaith dialogue; but in a pluralistic world, "protected status" is an insult. Still, the Christian precedent proves that, at crucial moments, religions are capable of adjusting their theologies to new insights. What Jew, after all, would have believed, even fifty years ago, that the Catholic Church would be capable of reversing its enmity?

In my daily life I am a journalist, dealing with concrete events in the material world. Given the vehement anti-Jewish hatred emanating from the Arab world, I often find myself questioning the value of my encounters with the Sufis, who are hardly representative of Palestinian Islam. So what if we danced together, even in a Gaza refugee camp? Rereading parts of this book is sometimes disorienting for me, as if I'm encountering someone else's experiences. But when I stop being a journalist and become instead a spiritual seeker, I recall another reality. The laws of faith, after all, operate differently than the laws of politics. In mundane reality, numbers count; but, as the history of religion repeatedly proves, God doesn't need multitudes to effect spiritual change, only a few individuals determined to become portals for divine will. I met people who aspire to be such instruments, and their presence here gives me hope that God will find His entry points into this despairing land.

In its essence, this journey was an experiment in what could be called "radical monotheism." Taken to its ultimate conclusion, monotheism is frightening in its uncompromising inclusivism: If God is literally one, and all of creation is a projection of that unified will, then every living thing exists within the same organism, is in effect a cell in the divine "body," as mystics insist. I am implicated in all of creation; nothing alive is extraneous to me. And so all love is ultimately self-love; all hatred, self-hate. For the radical monotheist, empathy is the only possible state of being: Human oneness isn't a philosophical notion or a moral imperative but simply a fact.

I wish I could say that I've maintained, or even recalled, that state through this bitter conflict with my neighbors. Instead, I've often been so enraged at Arafat's betrayal of peace and so caught up with the urgency of resisting the terrorist evil, that I've forgotten the suffering on the other side—even forgotten that, for a monotheist, there is no "other side." At best, I can say that I long for that elusive awareness.

As I write, peace seems more distant than ever. But even as we brace for more terrible conflict, I believe that this war will ultimately exhaust itself, and the beauty of Islam that I glimpsed will become manifest. Islam, after all, contains those qualities necessary for peacemaking—humility before God and an acute awareness of mortality. Some day, Jews, Muslims, and Christians will be able to share wisdom, if not doctrine. And so I offer, for the future, this account of one pilgrim's journey into an alternative Middle East. A gesture of hope. A prayer.

Jerusalem,
April 2002

AT THE ENTRANCE TO THE GARDEN OF EDEN

Introduction

In early winter 1998, I set out to discover my country, the Holy Land. My pilgrimage was an attempt at religious empathy: I was hoping to encounter, as an Israeli Jew, my Christian and Muslim neighbors in their intimate devotions. For the next two years, through the turn of the millennium, I visited monasteries and mosques and holy sites, discovering hidden corners of this land. My sense of sacred time expanded to include Christian and Muslim holidays, which I tried to experience in the company of monks and nuns and Islamic Sufi mystics.

My intention wasn't to blur the differences between the faiths but to discover points of commonality. Nor was I seeking complex theological exchanges, which in any case were beyond my expertise as a journalist. Instead, I wanted to test whether faith could be a means of healing rather than intensifying the conflicts in this land. My hope was to pray and meditate with my Christian and Muslim fellow believers. That approach was a conscious refutation of the way we religious people of different faiths have always judged each other— by what we believe about God, rather than how we experience God's presence. Theology distinguishes between truth and untruth; prayer knows only different measures of depth.

I approached this journey with two spiritual commitments. I am a religious Jew for whom the Jewish story, from the ancient exodus from Egypt to the modern return to Israel, is the context in which I try to encounter the miraculous. And I am a religious pluralist who believes that all the great religions are in effect denominations in one great religion, which teaches the primacy of the unseen over the visible and of unity over fragmentation. For me, the test of whether a religion is true is in its capacity to turn ordinary people into decent believers and extraordinary people into saints whose presence affirms the reality of God. By that measure, Christianity, Islam, and Judaism—and Hinduism and Buddhism—are all true faiths, regardless of their conflicting theologies.

In part, I owe my commitment to Judaism to an interfaith experience. Though raised in an Orthodox Jewish home, I abandoned ritual as a teenager, having been shocked out of religious complacency by biblical criticism. Then, sometime in my mid-twenties, I discovered a little book that offered first-person mystical testimonies from various traditions. I no longer recall which mystics appeared there, only that I was struck by their commonality, how Hindus and Christians and Muslims and Jews from across the generations all experienced a universe functioning within a unified "mind" and animated by light and love. That multiplicity of mystical voices reporting the same basic insights suggested to me that God might indeed be real and that it was possible for human beings to know Him.

My eventual decision to return to Jewish observance wasn't inspired by any sudden realization that Judaism was the "true" faith after all; Judaism simply was my language of intimacy with God. My Jewish spiritual heroes became the kabbalists and the early Hasidim, theosophists and ecstatics who perceived the human being as fashioned from divine qualities like will, wisdom, and love and who saw each soul as a kind of cell in the "body" of God, which was evolving toward greater states of perfection, at least partly through the evolution of its human components. So when I began my journey into Christian and Muslim communities, I inevitably turned to their mystics, for whom monotheism isn't a theology but an experience of oneness.

My upbringing hardly prepared me for the interfaith encounter. I was raised in the heartland of Jewish isolationism, a Brooklyn neighborhood called Borough Park, populated mostly by Orthodox Holocaust survivors. My father, a survivor from Hungary, taught me that the non-Jewish world was divided between those who actively wanted to kill the Jews and those who were indifferent to our fate. Auschwitz, after all, had been allowed to run unimpeded for four years, and even the Allies couldn't spare a few bombs to destroy the train tracks leading to the death camps. No less than the actual killing, the great Jewish wound of the Holocaust was that sense of total abandonment. I grew up seeing myself as a stranger in a hostile world, a member of a people related only formally to humanity, in effect a separate species.

My father reserved a special rage for Christianity, which he blamed for preparing the ground of the Holocaust by demonizing the Jews. No phrase struck him as more ironic than "Christian love." When Christians spoke of love, he said, they meant "everyone but Jews." The church leaders my father and his friends remembered from Hungary and Poland were Jew-haters and pogromists; for survivors, Hitler wasn't a pagan but a Christian.

The centuries of martyrdom and forced conversions imposed on Jews by the church instilled in me, an American child born in the interfaith era, an inherited dread toward Christianity. Religious custom forbade Jews from entering a church, but the formal restriction was unnecessary. As a boy, I was reluctant even to walk past a church, fearing that grasping hands might emerge from the massive doors and drag me into the basement, where priests would kidnap me and force me to become a Christian.

Interfaith, partly inspired, ironically, by Christian guilt over the Holocaust, was an unknown concept in Borough Park. When Nostra Aetate, the Vatican II declaration on the Jews, was released in 1965, our local Orthodox Jewish newspaper responded with contempt. The Vatican, an editorial raged, had dared to "forgive" the Jews for the crucifixion, instead of begging our forgiveness for all it had done to us. Only years later did I learn that Nostra Aetate hadn't "forgiven" the Jews at all but absolved them. And it went far beyond the issue of deicide to embrace the Jewish people spiritually, beginning an educational process among Catholics to regard the Jews as blessed by God, rather than cursed. But that news didn't penetrate my corner of Brooklyn.

In a previous book, *Memoirs of a Jewish Extremist,* I told of my struggle to overcome the mentality of Jewish isolationism. The high point of that process was falling in love with Sarah, a former Episcopalian who eventually converted to Judaism and became my wife. Sarah and her family helped me realize that it was possible for Jews and Christians to begin a new relationship, based on love and mutual respect.

Sarah and I left New York and moved to Israel in 1982. In the joy of homecoming, the grudges of exile became less urgent, more remote. My Jewish present became so vital that it held little place for inherited wounds. I immersed myself in an ethnic Jewish diversity that was far more exhilarating and bewildering than the constricted Ashkenazi remnant of my childhood, and in a frenetic Hebrew culture that sanctified the mundane and scandalized the sacred. I learned to relax into a Jewish majority and gradually forgot the self-consciousness of Diaspora.

The disillusionments of homecoming were no less essential in turning me from an insecure and self-righteous victim into an Israeli. There was the humbling experience of Jewish power: I was drafted into the army during the Intifada, the Palestinian uprising against the Israeli occupation in the late 1980s and early '90s, and for one month a year served in West Bank towns and in Gaza refugee camps, policing a hostile civilian population. The dilemmas of Jewish power, along with the pleasures of Jewish sovereignty, reinforced the same message: We were no longer victims. Zionism's hard gift to the Jews was to force us to assume our place among the morally ambiguous nations, pry us from the comfortable self-image of a helpless people to accept responsibility for our fate. Overcoming the victim's compensatory sense of superiority was a kind of initiation for me into Israeli identity. The goal of Zionism, after all, hadn't been to return us only to the land of Israel but also to the community of nations, to end the exile of the Jewish people from humanity. Thanks to Zionism's healing effects on the Jewish psyche, I could now approach other peoples and faiths with the curiosity and self-confidence of a free person.

Becoming an Israeli made my journey into Christianity and Islam possible. Had I remained a Diaspora Jew, I may well have lacked the self-confidence to explore the two faiths that had long subjected us to humiliation and worse. Being an Israeli also made this journey necessary. For the first time, a sovereign Jewish majority had its own Muslim and Christian minorities. (Judea at the time of early Christianity wasn't sovereign, and the Christians then were fellow Jews.) Our role reversal demanded of Jews a new psychological and theological maturity. The spiritual analogue to Zionism's normalization of the Jews as a nation among nations was the normalization of Judaism as a faith among faiths, neither superior nor outcast. That transformation remained the key missing component in our return home. We had taken the necessary steps toward political and military empowerment, but in our religious lives we retained the insecurity of a minority.

For Diaspora Jews, maintaining distance from Christianity and Islam was crucial to preserving their besieged identity. For me, though, Islam and Christianity were somehow part of my identity as an Israeli. However uneasily, I shared the name "Israel" with 800,000 Muslims and 200,000 (mostly Arab) Christians. Encountering Islam and Christianity, then, was an attempt to become more at home in this land and in my Israeliness.

But being an Israeli rather than a Diaspora Jew also complicated this journey, especially into Islam, with which Judaism now competed for control of the Holy Land. As much as I wanted to avoid politics and simply regard Muslims and Christians as fellow spiritual seekers, that proved impossible. I, too, couldn't help implicating God in politics. The very existence of the state of Israel, after all, was essential to my own Jewish faith, affirmation after Auschwitz of a good God and a purposeful universe. I couldn't conveniently avoid "politics" and focus on "spirituality." A Muslim who denied the right of Jewish sovereignty over even a part of this land threatened me spiritually as well as physically. Nor was I particularly mindful of the spiritual attachment of Christians and Muslims to the Holy Land.

In fact, I knew almost nothing about Christianity and Islam. I couldn't distinguish between the Muslim holy days of Id el-Fitr and Id el-Adha or between the Assumption and the Annunciation. I knew hardly any Christians and even fewer Muslims. That typical majority disinterest in its minorities was intensified by fear: Israel's Christians and Muslims are peculiar minorities, belonging to outside majorities that have, at various times, been hostile to Jewish existence. And so we Israeli Jews simply tried to forget them. Besides, our own Jewish problems, trying to re-create a people while fighting an endless war of survival, were so compelling that they left little room to deal with the outsiders among us, especially Israeli Arab citizens, who identifed emotionally if not tangibly with the country's enemies. I too had been drawn into our self-obsession. As a journalist, I'd written almost exclusively about Jewish Israel. Now, I was about to discover the religious worlds of Christians and Muslims, some of whom lived mere minutes from my home in Jerusalem.

Like many Jews of my generation, I have learned much from Hinduism and Buddhism. I've practiced meditation and yoga and been inspired by the unsentimental clarity of Buddhist teachers and the loving detachment of Hindu saints. I wanted to treat Judaism's sister faiths with the same reverence and curiosity with which I approached the religions of the East. But trying to relate to Christianity and Islam as spiritual paths rather than as devouring forces that had tried to displace the Jews proved even more difficult than I'd imagined. Inevitably, my journey into the faiths of my neighbors became an attempt to overcome history, theology, politics, psychological taboos, and, at times, concern for my physical safety—a confrontation with my own limitations and fears.

My relationships with Christianity and Islam each contained its own distinct ambivalence. I shared with Christianity a shattering past but a promising present. The brave Christian-Jewish dialogue begun after the Holocaust, and the profound theological changes toward the Jews adopted especially by the Catholic Church over the last forty years, allowed me to struggle with the past. My relationship with Islam was essentially the reverse. The past offered inspiring examples of Muslim-Jewish cooperation, especially among mystics, but the present state of dialogue was abysmal. Jews and Christians had learned to treat each other more or less with civility, if not intimacy; Jews and Muslims, having known intimacy at certain periods, could no longer manage even civility. The existence of a Jewish-Christian dialogue made my encounter with Christianity possible; the absence of a Jewish-Muslim dialogue made an encounter with Islam essential.

When I began this journey in 1998, the Oslo peace process was in its fifth year and approaching its disastrous conclusion. I was part of the Israeli majority that accepted the need for painful concessions. But I didn't trust Yasser Arafat as a credible partner, and I didn't believe that, in exchange for land, we'd get peace. I opposed the occupation because Jewish history forbade us to be oppressors; but I opposed the Oslo process because Jewish history also forbade us to be fools. Although peace education was promoted intensively by Israeli schools and media, no attempt was made by the Palestinian Authority to teach its people that the war was over. Arafat invoked "the peace of the brave" while speaking in English, but in Arabic he preached holy war and lauded the fundamentalist suicide bombers as *shaheed*, holy martyrs. My children returned from kindergarten waving peace flags, Stars of David entwined with doves, but on official Palestinian TV, six-year-olds announced their dream of becoming suicide bombers, while their teachers applauded.

Precisely because I doubted the peace being negotiated with Arafat, I sought more genuine acts of reconciliation with Palestinians. I joined a support group for Open House, an interreligious meeting place for children, parents, and teachers in the mixed Arab-Jewish Israeli town of Ramle. And I was active in efforts at dialogue between Israeli and Palestinian journalists. My journey into Christianity and Islam, then, was an extension of that search for alternative forms of peacemaking. If the political peace had betrayed us, perhaps we believers could create religious peace, a peace not yet of this world.

I made life easy for myself in this sense: I avoided the fanatics and even the decent but closed-minded Orthodox. Instead, I sought out Christians and Muslims who combined depth and width, that is, rootedness in their own faith but openness to others. I had no illusions about the nature of established religion in the Holy Land. Official Islam and Christianity, like official Judaism, fear intimacy between the faiths and engage in only the most formal dialogue. (Official Islam usually refuses to participate even in that limited encounter.) Because I sought out the best representatives of each religion, I can make no claim for the wider relevance of this journey. In the end, my effort remains an experiment, testing the border crossings between faiths.

The tenuousness of my interfaith encounters, especially with Islam, became evident in the fall of 2000, with Arafat's violent rejection of Israel's unprecedented offer to share sovereignty over Jerusalem and to withdraw to nearly the 1967 borders. My forays into the West Bank and Gaza became impossible; Israeli Jews who ventured into Palestinian-controlled territory were shot or lynched. The physical and even spiritual borders closed; the interfaith experiment in this land seemed at times not just peripheral but hopeless.

Still, if peace is ever to come to the Middle East, religion must be an integral part of the process. The Oslo Accords tried to impose a peace of secular elites on a region whose language and instincts are religious. This book, then, is an attempt at helping to begin to redress that fateful omission. It is an offering to the future, one scenario for avoiding holy war and interreligious apocalypse.

Religious pluralism is the great spiritual adventure of our generation. For the first time, believers can experience something of the inner life of other religions while remaining faithful to their own. This journey allowed me to search for wisdom and holiness in places that are usually off-limits to outsiders from other faiths. Because some of the Holy Land's mystics work in anonymity and silence, as demanded by spiritual practice, their generous visions rarely draw attention, leaving the intolerant and the shrill to represent God in His land. Extraordinary people admitted me into their inner sanctums; there were moments, in their presence, when I thought I glimpsed the shadow of God crossing this land of light and stone.

PART I

one

Ramadan

I

I lived on the border of Jerusalem. My apartment was in the last row of buildings just before the desert hills of the West Bank. In the distance lay the quiescent Dead Sea, in summer only a blurred extension of an indecisive sky, but emerging in the winter light as a distinct patch of blue, transforming the desert into an extended shore.

Between my porch and the sea, a handful of Arab villages were scattered through the hills. The tallest structures in every village were spare white minarets, bridges of longing from the desert toward heaven. The three monotheistic peoples all loved this land for the same reason: This was the place where heaven and earth mingled. The Divine Presence descending on the Temple Mount, Muhammad ascending from the Temple Mount, Jesus transcending death at nearby Golgotha—for me, those weren't competing claims but mutual reinforcements of the same insight. Islam and Christianity strengthened my Jewish faith in the holiness of this land, and I was grateful for living at this fitful place where God had repeatedly tried to contact humanity and would, perhaps, try again.

When I first moved to the edge of the desert in 1986, I would awaken at dawn to pray. I sat cross-legged on a rug, covered my head in a prayer shawl, and wound the tefillin strap around my arm, trying to bind myself to God's will. As I began the prayers thanking God for invigorating the weary and straightening the bent—avoiding the unbearably archaic prayers thanking God for not making me a gentile or a woman—the call of the muezzin would rise from the minaret in the village of Anata just across from my porch. Though amplified, it was a soft, melodic voice, gently nudging the faithful awake. And though the muezzin certainly didn't intend to include me among the faithful, his call couldn't be confined to his hill alone, and it urged me not to squander this moment of intimacy with God. I didn't understand the words of his chant, but I came to know its melody so well that, even if I tried to sleep in, it would penetrate my dreams and stir me.

Through the day I tried to note the muezzin's periodic call, cutting through the cacophony of daily life to affirm a purposeful creation. Each new call seemed to grow less melodic and more emphatic, a spare voice from the desert urgently intruding on my city obtuseness: "Brother! Have you forgotten God so quickly? At any moment this dream can end!" Responding to his call, I would suspend activity and try to evoke God's presence, closing my eyes and visualizing the four Hebrew letters of His name imprinted on my forehead until they throbbed. Even without his consent, the muezzin became my partner in prayer.

For me, connecting to the muezzin was an expression of becoming an oleh, literally an "ascender," an immigrant to the Land of Israel. At those moments when my devotion merged with the muezzin's, I knew that I, an exile by way of New York and Hungary and places beyond that I couldn't even name, was a returning son, and that this landscape of prayer recognized me and welcomed me home.

Those were the only moments of intimacy I experienced with my Arab neighbors. The Jews of my neighborhood, French Hill, and the Arabs of nearby Anata and Isawiyah never visited each other's homes. We lived in estranged cultures with conflicting histories and saw each other's daily lives as a threat to our very existence. When we built new houses, our Palestinian neighbors feared us as usurpers intent on expelling them. When groups of white-kerchiefed women from Isawiyah strolled through French Hill and teenage Arab boys gathered in our parks, we wondered whether they were demonstratively staking a future claim.

Our only common language was devotion. Real peace, I felt, depended on reconciliation among the region's believers, however improbable that might be; religion, after all, was the Middle East's language of extremism. Despite the peace process, the Arab world still didn't respect the legitimacy of the Jewish return, while Israel hadn't learned to respect the culture of the Middle East. Both insults, it seemed to me, could be eased by an encounter between Judaism and Islam. I fantasized about entering a mosque and joining the prayer line in prostration to the one God, that confession of ultimate human helplessness. But mosques were off-limits to non-Muslims during prayer time, so I had to settle for my illicit dialogue of prayer.

For many of my neighbors, the muezzin was relegated to background noise, an unpleasant reminder that we lived in the Middle East, with its frightening passions and implacable feuds. Once, while walking along the French Hill promenade overlooking Anata, I overheard an Israeli woman, probably an academic, explain to a foreign visitor that the minaret on the next hill was obviously a phallic symbol. In her easy dismissal of centuries of Islamic devotion, I felt my own faith being mocked. I belonged to that woman's world of democratic values and voted for secular parties because I opposed theocracy and saw Israel's role as protecting the Holy Land from fundamentalist madness. Yet at that moment, I felt more connected to the muezzin than to my fellow Israeli. In her spiritual ignorance, she was condemning herself to foreignness, exile in the Middle East. Ultimately, it was not our Jewishness but our intransigent Westernness that would prevent our acceptance by the Arab world. I wanted a Jewish state that was politically Western but culturally hybrid, nurtured by both West and East. I feared a Jewish version of Iran, but I also feared for an Israel that would become like Tel Aviv, the secular city on the sands, without roots, facing the sea with longing.

The Intifada began in late 1987. On the opposite hill, within easy view from my porch, teenagers gathered around the mosque, throwing stones at soldiers. Often the minaret was obscured by the white smoke of tear gas and the black smoke of burning tires. On the mosque's loudspeakers, voices hoarse with shouting would be heard outside of prayer time. Even the muezzin's call lost its delicacy, becoming shrill and coarse. It was the voice of jihad, holy war, and it was aimed against the occupation not only of his hill but of mine.

For one month each year I served as a reservist soldier, chasing stone throwers in Gaza and the West Bank. But watching them as a civilian from my porch, I couldn't help admiring their courage, and I knew that, in their place, I would do the same. Still, I refused to understand the muezzin. Unlike the rock-throwers, he seemed an unworthy opponent, manipulating faith for hatred. Even when the rioting began to ease, his voice continued to leap with hate. Like most of my Israeli neighbors, I came to fear his call as a reminder of the chaos of the Middle East. I stopped imagining us praying together, and gradually his voice receded into background noise, like the cars on the road that separated French Hill from Anata. I'd deceived myself with romanticism. The Arab world couldn't live with itself, let alone with a non-Muslim state in its midst. My poetic longings only undermined my political savvy, essential for survival in the Middle East.

Stones turned to knives. Muslim terrorists went on stabbing sprees in Israeli streets, shouting *Allahu akbar!* "God is great!" as they slashed. For Israelis, those wonderful words became the murderers' cry. When I heard them in the muezzin's call, it seemed he was trying to destroy me with prayer.

The Oslo peace process that began in 1993 intensified the holy war. Inspired in equal measure by hatred of Jews and longing for paradise, young men strapped explosives to their bodies and blew themselves up in Israeli crowds. The ultimate logic of fundamentalism: You entered heaven by sending heretics to hell. Only Islam had the power to turn the Arab world into a storm uprooting us from the Middle East. Islam now threatened me in the most personal way possible: It endangered the lives of my children. And so, like other Israelis, I too tried to ignore the Muslim devotion around me, because admitting that we lived in the heart of Islam meant conceding the impossibility of a normal life.

I knew there must be another Islam, cringing from the fanatics who desecrated its name. More in desperation than hope, I attended an interfaith gathering of Muslims and Jews, held in a kibbutz guest house overlooking the wooded Judean hills. The Muslims were all Israeli Arabs; we spoke in Hebrew. A scholar in Muslim law who lectured at a local Islamic college spoke of the long history of friendship between Muslims and Jews: Maimonides had been influenced by Islamic philosophers; Muslim and Jewish mystics in medieval Egypt had learned from each other's devotions. Afterward I asked him whether Islam could reconcile theologically with Jewish sovereignty in any part of the Holy Land. "Forget about it!" he said. "It will never happen! Islam commands me to destroy the Jewish state." He explained that Islam divided the world into *Dar el-Islam,* the House of Islam, and *Dar el-Harb,* the House of War, or the territory controlled by non-Muslims. Any land, especially the Holy Land, that had once been controlled by *Dar el-Islam* and had passed into the hands of *Dar el-Harb* must revert to Muslim rule. Muslims, he continued, were obliged to treat Jews and Christians—the "peoples of the Book," as Islam called them—with kindness and respect; still, they had to be brought under Islamic rule.

"But"—and he smiled like a man about to reveal a secret—"Islam doesn't obligate me to try to destroy the Jewish state immediately. There is time. Right now Israel is strong. We can wait fifty years, a hundred years. What's the hurry? Meanwhile, you and I can live in peace."

Was he hinting at a pragmatic Islam, able indefinitely to defer to reality? Or was he warning me: Any territorial concessions will only weaken you and hasten that time when we feel strong enough to destroy you.

Sometimes, across the barrier of fear, Islam revealed to me glimpses of its beauty. Walking around Jerusalem, I would see a lone Muslim street sweeper or gardener fall to his knees, responding to an invisible call to prayer. I would watch from a respectful distance, trying not to pry, envying his lack of self-consciousness, the Muslim ability to ignore human judgment in the presence of God. Once I saw a Muslim atop a crane at a construction site prostrate himself in prayer, as if blessing the city below.

But those were rare moments, reminders of a lost link. As Muslim terrorism intensified, Islam slipped away, untouchable in its separatism and rage.

2

In early December 1998, Ramadan suddenly arrived. Because it was based on Islam's lunar calendar, the month-long fast always seemed to come unexpectedly, like an ambush. I knew it was Ramadan only because of the usual security alert about suicide bombers that coincided with Muslim festivals. For Israeli Jews, Muslim holidays had become what Christian holidays were to Eastern European Jews a century ago: a time of menace, when religious zeal could turn lethal. Every Friday of Ramadan, tens of thousands of worshipers converged on the Temple Mount, creating vast traffic jams on the roads around French Hill. Border police and helicopters monitored their movement. A Ramadan without rioting or bombed buses was considered by Israelis an achievement. When it was over, we relaxed. We'd survived another Ramadan.

No matter how many times I read about the Islamic holidays, I kept forgetting the most basic facts, blocked by fear of intimacy with the force that threatened my permanence in the Middle East. Why exactly were they fasting a whole month? Is this when they went on the hajj, or pilgrimage to Mecca? Which *id* came at the end of Ramadan, Id el-Fitr or Id el-Adha? And which *id* was it again when they claim that Abraham tried to sacrifice Ishmael?

But this year was supposed to be different. I had set myself the goal of experiencing Islam along with Christianity, and with its month-long devotions and festivities, Ramadan offered an unmatched opportunity. Yet the days were passing and I couldn't find a way into the holiday. The mosques were obviously off-limits, but so were the family feasts that began every day at sundown. Like most Israeli Jews, I had no religious Muslim friends. The colleagues I knew from the Palestinian media were hardly fasters; it was precisely their secularism that seemed to make a relationship between us possible at all. One Palestinian journalist I knew did have an interest in Sufism, Islam's mystical movement, and he offered to take me to late-night prayers in a Sufi mosque in Jerusalem's Old City. But each time we set a date he abruptly canceled, and each excuse sounded more improbable than the last.

I called Israeli friends who were active in efforts at dialogue with Palestinians, and the consensus was I was wasting my time. "I've been meeting with Palestinians for twenty years," said one friend, a religious Jew. "And I've never been able to shift the dialogue from politics to religion." Another friend, with long experience in interfaith relations, added, "I can't even get Muslims to show up to a meeting. You want to *pray* with them?"

A Christian friend said to me, "Maybe you should concentrate on Christian-Jewish relations. There is so much that we have to do together; why confuse it by bringing in another religion?"

I explained to her that I had to learn to live with Islam. Making peace with Christianity was an urgent opportunity for Jews, but making peace with Islam was a life-and-death necessity.

Still, was she right? If I couldn't find a way of touching Islam during an entire holiday month, maybe my intended journey into Islam was premature. After all, the Jewish-Christian dialogue had matured over the last fifty years. For all the ongoing tensions between Jews and Christians—with evangelicals over missionizing, with liberal Protestants over anti-Zionism, with Catholics over the church's role in the Holocaust—we had learned the habit of dialogue. The hard work had been done by theologians on both sides who had explored their own traditions for ways to validate the other's faith. But there was no comparable Muslim-Jewish dialogue. Whatever intimacy existed between Jewish and Muslim philosophers and mystics a thousand years ago seemed irretrievable.

This year, Ramadan coincided with the Tenth of Tevet, a minor Jewish fast, which meant that the fast began at dawn rather than, like Yom Kippur, with sundown the night before; therefore, it was a fast like Ramadan itself. However briefly, I felt bound with Muslim devotion. The discomfort of my little fast renewed my appreciation for the discipline of Islam: Imagine doing this for an entire month. Yet even that fragile link with Ramadan quickly passed. In fact, the Tenth of Tevet only emphasized the abyss between Muslim and Jew. It marked the beginning of the Roman siege of Jerusalem and was a time to pray for the protection of the holy city from those who would once again deny it to the Jews—protection, in other words, from the jihad of Islam.

And then, just as I was about to despair of experiencing Ramadan, Sheykh Ishak Idriss Sakouta appeared in Jerusalem on a one-man mission of religious peace. Not even his sponsors seemed to know much about him. He was believed to be a member of a Sufi order, but no one knew which. It was said that he divided his time between Cairo, where he owned substantial land, and Mecca, where he helped organize provisions for pilgrims. He was said to be close to the Saudi royal family, which had awarded him the title of "religious counselor" to the World Muslim League, the royal family's charitable foundation. That title, however mysterious, had been impressive enough to win him audiences with the Israeli president and chief rabbi. A spiritual leader from the heartland of Islam—the forbidden city of Mecca, no less—was actually willing to talk to us; it was best not to examine his credentials too closely. That way, we could imagine that a major religious figure had broken the Muslim boycott on contact with Israel and that peace with Islam was possible after all.

This much could be said definitively about Sheykh Ishak: He had courage. Rabbi David Rosen, an interfaith leader and former chief rabbi of Ireland, had met Sheykh Ishak at an interreligious conference in Malta. Rosen invited all the participating Muslim clerics to visit Israel. "Some admitted to me privately that they were afraid for their lives," Rosen told me, referring to the danger posed by Muslim extremists. "Only Sheykh Ishak immediately agreed to come."

Like the late Egyptian president Anwar Sadat, the sheykh simply appeared in Jerusalem. But the sheykh's journey was more moving because it was more lonely. He came without an entourage, without protection, speaking in the name of God alone. Islam had a genius for fearlessness; the dark side was the suicide bombers. But here was another expression of Muslim contempt for death, a sheykh ready to die for peace with the Jews.

I went to hear the sheykh address a small gathering of Jerusalem's interfaith activists at Yakar, a center for liberal Orthodox Judaism that taught kabbalah and Jewish spirituality while reaching out to other traditions. On one wall of its synagogue-turned-meeting-hall hung a calligraphic text called "The Four-Fold Song," written by Israel's first chief rabbi, Abraham Isaac Hacohen Kook, and which was a kind of manifesto for Yakar's version of Judaism. Rabbi Kook described four levels of song of the soul: the song of the self, the song of the nation, the song of humanity, the song of creation. The highest level, he concluded, was to embrace all songs simultaneously: "And then there is one who rises with all these songs in one ensemble, and they all join their voices. Together they sing their songs with beauty, each one lends vitality and life to the other. . . . It is the song of the King Who contains wholeness."

I sat beside my friend, Maureena Fritz, a nun in her early seventies who had just returned from a motorcycle trip across Europe. Maureena, a former Canadian, ran a center in Jerusalem that taught Judaism to Christians. She spoke curtly from the corner of her mouth, like a hipster, and had short gray hair and black eyebrows, which accentuated the austerity of her face. That severity, though, was aimed at theological smugness; she treated religious authority with the fearlessness of a rebellious teenager.

Maureena told me about a conference she'd attended in the Vatican, where she delivered a paper promoting her latest idea: the need to replace the Son with the Father as the central object of Christian devotion. Only a theocentric Christianity, she said, could truly embrace the new pluralistic paradigm. Christians, she insisted, should see Jesus not as the ultimate address for all intercessions but as a role model for how to fulfill the divine potential of a human being. Rather than seeing God becoming man, Maureena preferred to see Jesus as man becoming God. Not surprisingly, her Vatican audience had been unenthusiastic.

"They're going to put you in Vatican prison, Maureena," joked her friend Jack Driscoll, a member of a Catholic monastic teaching order and retired president of Iona College in New York, who now codirected Maureena's institute.

She wasn't amused. "Let them try and stop me," she replied, in the flat accent of the Canadian prairies. Maureena's good fortune was that she belonged to the Sisters of Sion, an order that had once prayed for the conversion of the Jews but was now committed to bringing love for Judaism into the church. The Sisters of Sion appreciated Maureena's theological restlessness. Like the Orthodox Jews of Yakar, Maureena and her fellow nuns loved their tradition even as they resisted its limitations.

In this room, with its easy mingling of faiths, was a vision of the possible Jerusalem. We were so engaged in conversation that few noticed the sheykh enter. *"Salaam aleikum,"* he said, and he raised his hands in greeting. It didn't seem to matter to him whether or not he was acknowledged; he was welcoming us. He took a seat at the table in front and smiled with joy, as if to say: How wonderful to be together with my fellow believers in the holy city of Jerusalem. Suddenly, the room became focused on his extraordinary presence. He was very tall, dressed in a white turban and gold-embroidered brown robe. He was dark-skinned, with a trim white beard, a thick nose gracefully sloped, and lips spread flat as though caught in a kiss. His feminine eyes were startling in such a strong masculine presence. Elongated at the edges, they seemed painted, as if lines ran from the corner of the eyes toward the temples. He looked around the room, smiling and nodding, without self-consciousness. He was too busy watching us to notice that we were watching him.

Rabbi Mickey Rosen, director of Yakar, introduced the sheykh as a courageous man of God who had come to Jerusalem to challenge the misuse of faith for hate. The sheykh held his hands up in mock triumph and laughed.

Speaking through a translator, the sheykh began, "Some say I am a courageous man. But when faith in God is great, there is no room for fear. Courage comes from faith. I asked God to let me come to Jerusalem before I died, and He has answered my prayers. I am a Sudanese from Khartoum, but my roots are in the Prophet's family. My ancestors were men of faith and property. For twenty years I lived among the great sheykhs of Khartoum. And then I moved to Mecca. For forty years I'm in the Great Mosque. From the Kaaba to the Mosque, from the Mosque to the Kaaba." In establishing his credentials, he was asserting his right to speak for Islam.

As a boy, he continued, he'd studied with a Sufi sheykh. Once the Jews of Khartoum complained to his sheykh that they'd been mistreated by Muslims. The Jews, announced the sheykh to his followers, are my children, and he forbade anyone to harass them.

Still, Sheykh Ishak admitted, he himself had grown up with anti-Jewish misconceptions. But then, ten years ago, he met Jews for the first time at an interfaith conference in Rome. "I was surprised to meet such cultured and refined people. It broke all my stereotypes."

He told us that Moses had appeared to him recently in a dream. He'd asked the prophet for a knife; instead, Moses gave him his staff. The sheykh didn't interpret the dream for us, but I thought he meant: I come bearing the staff of the prophet whom both Jews and Muslims revere, the staff that performed miracles of redemption.

He concluded with the usual affirmations of religious brotherhood, backed by quotes from the Koran. There was nothing startling or profound in his comments, but he conveyed a combination of strength and calm that made me want to remain in his presence. He didn't just speak about peace but seemed to embody it.

Yet it was precisely the sheykh's equilibrium that troubled Rabbi Rosen, who appeared restless and anguished, pulling at his thick gray beard. "Since the sheykh is a man of truth," he began, "allow me to ask a blunt question. How is it that, in our part of the world, religion has been so debased that it has become an instrument of violence and hatred, and people like yourself are so rare? Doesn't that indicate the complete failure of our religious traditions?"

This was the time for angry prophets, Rosen was insisting, not serene mystics. Those of us who loved Judaism and Islam must cry out in pain and despair, join in a partnership of outrage against the fanatics who were desecrating our faiths.

But the sheykh refused to be drawn into Rosen's righteous anger. Instead, he calmly and firmly repeated that God wanted the children of Abraham to live in harmony and that his own sheykh loved the Jews and considered them his children—all the simple, even banal truths that had impelled this man to risk his life by boarding a plane from Cairo to Jerusalem and challenging the whole Muslim fundamentalist world.

An Orthodox Jewish scholar, known for his dovish politics, asked the sheykh: "If idolatry makes God subservient to man's creation, isn't using religion for political aims a modern expression of idolatry?"

Like Rosen, he was trying to entice the sheykh into a substantive dialogue. But the sheykh merely offered variations of his earlier statements. I, too, was beginning to feel restless: Now that we were finally talking, why couldn't we go deeper?

A man with an American accent asked the sheykh about a reference he'd made in his talk to the pharaoh who had enslaved the Israelites: "You seemed to indicate that Islam considers Pharaoh a prophet. But I always thought that Islam saw him as evil."

In fact, the sheykh had said no such thing. But before he could reply, Rabbi Rosen intruded. "What difference does it make what Islam thinks of the Pharaoh!" he shouted. "For God's sake, you have a man sitting here who has come from Cairo to speak about the most pressing issue facing religious people today, and that's all you can think of asking him?" In his outburst, I sensed Rosen's frustration not only with the pedantic questioner but with the sheykh himself.

Sheykh Ishak, trying to ease the questioner's embarrassment, said quietly, "If I gave the mistaken impression that Islam considers Pharaoh a saint, I apologize."

Someone asked the sheykh to sing a Sufi song, and he happily complied. "When Muhammad came to Mecca," he sang, "the moon rose in fullness." His song had the same deep and steady quality as his speech, as if the two were interchangeable.

He blessed us all that our "truest prayers" should be fulfilled, and our encounter with the Islam of peace was over.

As audience members gathered around the sheykh, a friend introduced me to Dr. Abed Khalili, who taught Islamic studies at a local Palestinian college and was one of the few Muslims in the room. Khalili was tall and lean and prematurely bald, with a trim graying beard and thick black eyebrows, imposing an unnatural brooding on his soft, round face. I asked him what he thought of the sheykh.

"You Jews see a turban, and you think he must be a very holy man," Khalili said. "But in Sudan every kiosk owner wears a turban. When he spoke, he made a mistake in quoting from the *hadith* [the collected stories of the Prophet Muhammad]. Among the Palestinian Muslim hierarchy, no one has even heard of him. I doubt if he's a real sheykh at all."

"I'm no expert in the *hadith*," I said, "but I'm moved by his courage in coming here."

"No serious Muslim would meet Israelis in Jerusalem, especially at this time. The Israelis are building settlements and destroying houses of Palestinians at a faster rate than ever."

"But you're here," I said.

He smiled, as if caught. "I come to these gatherings because I'm curious. When there's peace and justice, then we'll have our religious dialogue."

"But don't religious people have an obligation to help bring peace closer?"

Khalili shrugged. For all his easy contempt of the sheykh's courage and his Palestinian self-pity, which placed the entire blame for the conflict on Israel, I liked him. He was ironic but soft-spoken, an upholder of orthodoxy who seemed more reluctant than zealous. And most of all he was here.

I joined the line of Jews and Christians waiting to speak to Sheykh Ishak. Even if Khalili was right about the sheykh's knowledge of the *hadith*, it didn't matter. The Islamic colleges were filled with experts on the *hadith*, but here was a man who seemed to offer the spiritual qualities I was searching for in Islam. I hoped I could get to know him in the few days he'd be among us. The sheykh took my hand and gently pumped it, as if taking the measure of my being. I asked, through his translator, if we could meet. He touched his heart and opened his palms, as if to say: What I have is yours.

3

The next evening I met Sheykh Ishak in the lobby of his hotel. The fact that he was staying in a "Jewish" hotel in West Jerusalem, rather than an "Arab" hotel in East Jerusalem, subtly reinforced his message of outreach to Israelis. Tonight he'd been invited to break the fast with an Arab family, and I was tagging along. The sheykh's translator wasn't joining us, so we sat in the lobby in silence, waiting for the arrival of a staff person from Yakar to drive us to dinner. The sheykh seemed oblivious to the stares of American tourists. A woman in a wheelchair rolled herself over to him, to get as close as possible. "He's beautiful!" she exclaimed.

We drove in silence to Abu Ghosh, an Arab Israeli village about fifteen minutes from Jerusalem just off the highway toward Tel Aviv. The sheykh pressed the joints along the fingers of his hands, as if they were prayer beads, silently repeating the names of God. His movements were spare and fluid and forceful. I felt his self-containment as an implicit rebuke to my restlessness.

As we drove through Jerusalem, he watched the streets with a still alertness, observing a young woman driving a van and Hasidic young men hurrying by like a cluster of ravens, our modernity and our religiosity equally perplexing to a visitor from Mecca. I felt grateful that Jerusalem's billboards, unlike Tel Aviv's, avoided sexually suggestive advertising, in deference to the city's large traditionalist population. Keeping the streets of Jerusalem innocent made it possible for a sheykh from Mecca to come to Israel and not feel violated. There needed to be a part of Israel, I thought, that was protected from the crassness of the West and where the Muslim sensibility wouldn't feel assaulted by a hostile culture. How else would we make peace with Islam if not through religious Jerusalem?

Yet this purity had been won at a terrible cost. In the 1980s, ultra-Orthodox hoodlums had waged an arson campaign against bus shelters that posted suggestive advertising. Sometimes the mere photograph of a fully clothed woman was enough to draw an arson attack, as though this were Afghanistan. The reason Jerusalem's billboards weren't like Tel Aviv's wasn't that secular advertisers respected the city's spiritual integrity but that they'd surrendered to fundamentalist violence. In recent years I'd lost my post-Holocaust sentimentality toward the ultra-Orthodox and saw their growing strength as a threat to democratic Israel. Nothing better symbolized that threat than the arson attacks against the city's bus shelters. Yet here I was, implicitly grateful to those arsonists for protecting the sanctity of Jerusalem. And that paradox defined my "Israeliness": I lived at the point where the modern state of Israel met the Holy Land. The secular-religious divide wasn't happening only in Israeli society but within me.

Abu Ghosh was what Israeli Jews called a "friendly" Arab village, which meant that you could drive in without worrying about getting a rock through your windshield. The village had refused to join the Arab attack on Israel during the 1948 war and had maintained peaceful relations with its Jewish neighbors ever since. And it had prospered. Its handsome white stone houses and olive groves spread through the hills. The village's main industry seemed to be the "authentic Middle Eastern" restaurants located along "Shalom Street," which catered to Jews who wanted to eat good *humus* and *kanafe* but who were afraid to travel to the West Bank or even East Jerusalem. If I'd planned it, I couldn't have arranged a gentler passage into Islam.

Lena and Nabhan Jabar lived in one of the village's more modest houses, with a patch of cement in place of a garden. Lena was a young woman who taught Islamic art at an Israeli teachers college and helped coordinate Yakar's Muslim-Jewish dialogue efforts. She and Nabhan had invited the sheykh for dinner after hearing him speak at Yakar. Nearly everyone in the village of Abu Ghosh was related. Nabhan and Lena were first cousins.

Brothers and uncles and neighbors crammed into the little house to greet the sheykh from Mecca. Yet they also seemed pleased to find me, a religious Jew coming to honor Ramadan. Lena's brothers—one a truck driver, another a hospital orderly—assured me that they had "many Jewish friends." Lena, an academic and interfaith activist, was the family success story. In my ignorance of the Arabs who lived among us, I was surprised that a Muslim woman would be permitted to outshine the men.

We were led to a long table offering a Palestinian feast of lamb, fried pastries, stuffed grape leaves, and spiced spinach. The sheykh took a random seat, but our hosts pointed him to the head of the table. Laughing, he took the place of honor. To deny honor meant flaunting your modesty. Anonymity, recognition—it all seemed the same to him.

The sheykh broke his fast sparingly—a date, an olive, a slow sip of water—reluctant to anchor the soul. In the corner of the dining room, a TV played blurred scenes from Mecca, where the great square was filled with pilgrims gathered to celebrate the chief event of Ramadan: the revelation of the Koran to the Prophet Muhammad. I felt a Jewish unease viewing that scene of Muslim power, imagining its combined force of quantity and intensity turned against Israel. The sheykh said, "When I complete my journey in Jerusalem, I will go on pilgrimage to Mecca." Suddenly the menacing mass had a benign face.

After dinner, we moved to the salon. Plush red couches and armchairs lined the walls, and plastic flowers in porcelain vases crowded the coffee tables. The sheykh sat in a corner, and the armchair beside him was left empty, to be filled by a succession of people seeking his advice or simply his company. I was moved by the ease with which he was absorbed into the family. He was treated with love more than reverence—entirely approachable. And he responded with equal ease, as though he'd always known these people. He stroked cheeks and held hands and laughed and interpreted dreams. He playfully confiscated the cigarettes of a teenage boy and insisted he promise to quit smoking. To each person he showed a different face, corresponding to need. Sometimes the chair remained empty for long minutes while people chatted among themselves, until someone recalled the sheykh's presence and approached him. Sheykh Ishak used those intervals to press the joints of his fingers and silently invoke God's names, turning his body into an instrument of prayer. Generous but self-contained, he was happy to speak, happy not to speak.

Lena's grandmother—tiny, toothless, kerchief tied beneath her chin—sat across from the sheykh, just watching him. She had nothing to discuss; she only wanted to be in his presence. Lena told me that her grandmother had been on hajj to Mecca three years ago, with the first group of Arab Israelis allowed in by Saudi Arabia. I asked the old woman to tell me about the pilgrimage. "When we reached Mecca," she said, in a high and distant voice, "everyone wept. There were so many people; it felt like the Day of Judgment. In Mecca you don't eat or shop. I fasted and prayed. My home seemed like a dream. I was sure God was going to take me, and I made myself ready."

The thought of dying in Mecca had given her peace. And now a sheykh had come from that place of transition between this world and the next, and she was happy to sit quietly before him, drawn by that Meccan quality of fearlessness before death. "Since my grandmother returned from Mecca," Lena said, "a part of her is already in the next world."

Lena's husband, Nabhan, added, "The prophet speaks about a person going on a journey. He stops to rest under a tree and then continues on his way. The short time he spent sitting under the tree is the time we spend in this world."

I had so many questions to ask the sheykh. I wanted to discuss spiritual practices, the recollection of God, how faith can overcome fear. I waited for a pause in the procession and, with Lena translating, asked him what he'd thought as we were driving through the streets of Jerusalem.

"I was thinking about how Jerusalem returns the love of all those who come to her," he said. "I was thinking about how much Jerusalem loves me."

"The sheykh is a romantic," said Lena.

"Yes," he said, laughing, "the romantic sheykh!"

A family member approached, and our conversation ended.

Lena, plump and pretty, was the only woman in the room not wearing a kerchief. She had the exhausted look that came from constantly mediating between opposing expectations that others held of her and that she herself shared. Raised by her Muslim family to be deferent and educated by secular Israel to be brash, she responded with the sadness of someone who knew she would never be whole. She was a modern woman and a dutiful wife and daughter, and every · encounter tested anew the limits between those warring selves.

Being an Arab Israeli, an identity that often seemed an oxymoron, only deepened the strain. Anger vied with goodwill. She was so committed to dialogue between Arabs and Jews that she'd turned that goal into her profession; yet the Palestinian tragedy threatened her family's cohesion. The same Israel that made Lena among the freest Arab women of the Middle East had turned her husband into an illegal alien. She'd met Nabhan, a Palestinian refugee living in Amman, on a visit there in 1994, and they'd married shortly afterward. Nabhan had returned with Lena to Abu Ghosh, but the Israeli authorities, fearing an influx of refugees, hadn't yet given him citizenship or even residency papers, though Lena was, of course, an Israeli citizen.

Nabhan had black wavy hair, black eyes, a long curving nose

mounted on a thick mustache. It could easily have been a brooding, angry face, but Nabhan was determined to be an optimist. I asked him how he was holding up, and he said, in his formal English, "Very fine, sir, the finest." Only gradually did he reveal, in asides during conversation, that he risked deportation at any moment and that he subsisted on menial jobs though he was a lab technician by training and that just recently he'd been cheated out of four thousand dollars of back pay by a building contractor who knew that Nabhan, an illegal alien, wouldn't dare complain to police.

I asked Nabhan about his life, and he told me that he was born in the village of Emwas in the West Bank, bordering Israel. During the 1967 Six-Day War, the Israeli army entered Emwas and two neighboring villages and forced everyone out. I knew the reason why: Those three villages, overlooking the Jerusalem–Tel Aviv road, had been guerrilla bases and had kept Jerusalem under siege during the 1948 war, and the army wanted to prevent any threat to the capital. Nabhan, age six, trekked with his family to Ramallah. "It didn't take us too long," he said, laughing. "We walked fast."

He had a sixteen-year-old handicapped cousin, Nabhan continued. The boy's mother, fearing he'd slow the family's flight, abandoned him at home. "She said she'd be back in a few minutes, but he was smart and knew she was lying," Nabhan said, laughing. "So he hitched up a donkey and got to Ramallah before anyone."

"How could a mother do such a thing!" demanded Lena. But she seemed more offended by Nabhan's matter-of-fact tone.

Nabhan said, without apology, "Crazy things happened in those days."

He continued his story, in the same deliberately detached voice. His father joined the Jordanian army and resettled the family in a decent neighborhood in Amman. Then came Black September, the 1970 war between Jordan and the PLO. Nabhan's father refused to fight fellow Palestinians and went AWOL. Meanwhile, Nabhan hid in a basement with his grandfather and aunt; in an adjacent room, his mother was giving birth. Nabhan was sitting on his aunt's lap when a mortar shell exploded; her skull shattered against the wall. Nabhan escaped with shrapnel in his leg, which his grandfather later removed with a knife. A pregnant cousin was killed in the blast. A few hours later, Nabhan's mother gave birth to a girl; the baby was stillborn. "There was a lot of death then," he said, without emotion.

I don't know what astonished me more: the story itself or Nabhan's laconic manner. "But how did you cope?" I asked, inadequately. "You must have had nightmares."

"Only later. At first you're glad to be alive. You just go on. That's all."

"I ask him that same question all the time, and he laughs," Lena said. "I don't understand him."

"When you have faith in God, then everything is possible," he said. "My aunt was holding the Koran when she was killed. There was one verse I heard the older people reading in the cellar before the explosion, and I thought about it a lot afterward: 'Say: He is God the One the most unique, He has begotten no one and is begotten by none.'"

It seemed a logical verse to inspire a boy who had sat on the lap of his aunt while her head exploded and who had seen the death of a pregnant cousin and a baby sister emerge stillborn: God's greatness was manifest by rising above the terrible cycle of birth and death.

"But I tell you this, sir: Many people suffered a crisis of faith. They looked at all our disasters—1948, 1967, 1970—and thought, 'Why do these terrible things keep happening to us? Maybe God has abandoned us.' But my faith only got stronger. My mother always said to me, 'Everything that happens is from God, and everything from God is good, even if we can't understand it.' Now I look at my life, and I realize she was right."

Just as his people were struggling with apparent rejection by God, my people were experiencing the return of God's grace. Mere weeks after the Six-Day War ended, I traveled, together with my father, to

Israel for the first time. I was fourteen, and it was a summer of reunions. My father reunited with his two brothers whom he hadn't seen in twenty years; the Jewish people reunited with its biblical landscape. We traveled the hilly roads of the West Bank, seeking ancestral graves. Abraham and Sarah in Hebron, Rachel in Bethlehem, Samuel in Ramah: cool, dark, cavelike houses with humped stone tombs and blackened marble ledges on which hundreds of candles burned. At each holy site we wrapped the black leather straps of tefillin around our arms. My father touched the stones with reverence, as though discovering the graves of his parents, the absent graves of Europe's unburied Jews.

Like many survivors, my father had rejected God after the Holocaust, and though he'd raised me formally Orthodox ("just so you should know"), I grew up without belief. But Israel's biblical-like victory, and the leap from Auschwitz to Jerusalem, tested our faithlessness. If Jews could turn from God because of the Holocaust, then it was only reasonable to embrace Him now. God had done *teshuvah*, repented; with the magnanimity of victors, we forgave him. Our God in the summer of 1967 wasn't the God of vengeance or even glory but of reprieve, the benevolent God of Israel who protected His people from destruction. Israel's victory over the Arab world's intended genocide meant that the Nazis no longer had the last word on Jewish history. Israel allowed my family to return to normal life, to trust the empowerment of the good. Without Israel, we would have been left defenseless against the Holocaust.

Yet here was Nabhan, intruding on my myth. Had he offered the usual Palestinian recriminations, I would have known how to respond: Your side repeatedly tried to destroy us and then complained about the injustice of defeat. Israeli policy could be summed up in the difference between the fate of Nabhan's village, Emwas, and that of Abu Ghosh: destruction for those who tried to destroy us, prosperity for those who offered us peace.

But Nabhan didn't make it easy for me. He wasn't accusing; he was still the refugee boy observing his world without the mediation of ideology. Nabhan's threat to me went far deeper than politics. He challenged my myth of Jewish redemption, my defense against Auschwitz. That moment of spiritual epiphany in the summer of 1967 had to accommodate a six-year-old refugee boy walking toward Ramallah and a handicapped teenager abandoned by his mother. More than guilt, I felt sullied by smallness.

Nabhan said, "I am very interested in Judaism, sir. I have read the Koran one hundred times, and also the New Testament and the Torah each five times." A precise man.

"What is the essence of Islam for you?" I asked.

"Not to harm anyone with your tongue or your hand; that is a *hadith*. Except those who harm you, for your dignity. But I'm not the most religious person, sir. I'm only a little Muslim."

"For me, Nabhan, you're a big Muslim."

"Thank you, sir."

At first I'd thought his use of the word *sir* was obsequious, but now I realized that he was simply giving the respect he expected to receive in return.

"Nabhan, I'm not just being polite, I mean it. For me you are a big Muslim because you don't hate. Another person who went through what you did would hate the Jews."

"Why hate the Jews? It's the politics, not the people. Muhammad was very friendly with his Jewish neighbors. He spoke in the Koran of coexistence with the Jews. This helped me to understand the situation correctly."

"But he also expelled the Jewish tribes of Arabia," I said.

"That was politics, not religion." Expulsion, as he well knew, was the way of the Middle East, beginning perhaps with our venerated forefather, Abraham, who expelled Ishmael from his tent.

"I never heard any Muslim teacher say you must kill Jews," he added.

"Come on," I said.

"Not without a reason," he conceded. "But you must be careful not to hate. Hatred can't be controlled. You start with hating the Jews, and you will end up hating your own family. Whatever bad or good happens to us is God's will. *Kulu min Allah*—everything comes from God."

In a lesser person that theology could induce passivity. But for Nabhan, as for Sheykh Ishak, the awareness that everything not only came from God but ultimately reverted back to Him had freed him from anxiety and produced an astonishing courage. Perhaps that was what I needed to learn from Islam: how to face life and death with the equanimity of a believer.

Nabhan went to speak to the sheykh, perhaps asking his blessing for a resolution to his problems. The sheykh listened gravely, then vigorously massaged Nabhan's chest, as if to stimulate his heart, summoning love to protect him from anger.

Nabhan returned to my side. "Do you know the teachings of the Sufis?" he asked.

"Only in the most basic way," I replied. "I have a long list of questions for the sheykh. I was hoping to learn from him about prayer and developing an awareness of God's presence. But there doesn't seem to be any time. And now he's about to leave, and I feel like I'm wasting the opportunity."

"If you want to understand him," Nabhan said, "you must look into his eyes."

Instead, I looked into Nabhan's eyes, and I found a sadness so complete it left no room for bitterness or hate.

4

On the last morning of the sheykh's stay in Israel, I returned to his hotel to join him on a pilgrimage to Hebron's Tomb of the Patriarchs, burial place of Abraham and Sarah, Isaac and Rebecca, Jacob and Leah.

Hebron was home to the West Bank's most extreme Muslims and Jews, who validated each other's worst fears with mutual massacres and who saw in the other's humiliation a glorification of their own faith. Hebron transformed a national conflict into a holy war over Abraham's patrimony. The worst atrocities of the Arab-Israeli conflict had happened in Hebron: In 1929, a Muslim pogrom destroyed its ancient and defenseless Jewish community, murdering sixty-seven people and mutilating dozens more. In 1994, Dr. Baruch Goldstein massacred twenty-nine Muslims as they bent in prayer in the Tomb of the Patriarchs.

Yet until the Goldstein massacre, the Tomb of the Patriarchs—which Muslims called the El-Haram el-Ibrahimi, in honor of Abraham, and Jews called the Machpelah, a Hebrew word implying "doubling," for the biblical couples buried there—had been the only holy place in the world where Muslims and Jews mingled. Under centuries of Islamic control, Jews had been humiliatingly restricted to the seventh step leading into the building and forbidden to pray inside. Yet when the Israeli army entered Hebron in the 1967 War, it allowed the Muslim *Wakf,* or religious trust, to retain control over the building, rejecting the demands of right-wing Jews to impose Israeli sovereignty. Hebron's outraged Jewish settlers saw the government's refusal to claim the Machpelah exclusively for Judaism a sign of Jewish weakness, an affront against God.

It was precisely the Machpelah's ambiguous status between Judaism and Islam that had drawn me. The very name *Machpelah* hinted at another doubling besides the couples buried there: It was fated to contain two rival faiths. Though Muslims and Jews held services in different rooms, sometimes their prayers would unwillingly coincide, and the urgent call of the muezzin would merge with the rapid melodic chant of Hebrew prayer. It wasn't unusual to see a Jewish woman with a kerchief tied behind her head and a Muslim woman with a kerchief tied beneath her chin standing together in prayer before the cenotaph of Mother Sarah.

Of course the Machpelah wasn't immune from the hatred of Hebron. Sometimes Muslims tore Hebrew prayer books, while Jews deliberately stepped on prayer rugs, trying to block each other's channels to God. Yet daily life had its own insistence. Improbably, Hebron produced a working model, however reluctant, of religious coexistence.

In those years before the Goldstein massacre, the Machpelah had been my favorite place of pilgrimage, the Holy Land's farthest accessible root, more intimate than the Western Wall, with its grand plaza and crowds. I would sit on the stone floor, close my eyes, and feel my whole being exhale in relief; I was home, back in the collective soul of Israel, a pinprick of light in a vast field of illumined points, each one another soul. Then the collective soul of Israel itself became a mere point of light in the vast soul of humanity, which became a point of light in the vaster soul of planetary life, until the mind went numb with expanse.

Perhaps the Machpelah had managed to encompass two warring faiths because its roots predated religion. According to Jewish legend, the entry into the Garden of Eden was located in the Machpelah. While searching for a missing calf, Abraham came upon a river of light that led into the cave of Machpelah. There he met Adam and Eve. By linking Abraham with Adam and Eve, the legend reinforced the Jewish belief that Abraham's role was to heal the fragmentation caused by the first sin and lead humanity back to the Garden, or that state of consciousness in which human beings knew they were part of a greater whole. With the expulsion from Eden, we no longer experienced an integrated existence, and each soul entered the illusion of separateness. Abraham's task as monotheist, then, was to shatter the idols of fragmented consciousness and restore humanity's "spiritual sight," our ability to perceive oneness.

Since the Goldstein massacre I'd returned several times to the Machpelah, but my prayers had been lethargic and my meditations diffuse. I couldn't overcome Goldstein's presence; I kept imagining him firing, reloading, and firing again into rows of men arched in prayer. In the most decisive way possible, Goldstein had imposed the idolatry of separatism onto the sanctuary of wholeness. For me, the Machpelah was no longer an entrance back into the Garden, but only its exit.

I found Dr. Muhammad Sheweiki, the sheykh's translator, waiting alone in the lobby of the hotel. An Islamic scholar, he had a graying goatee, thin strands of hair stretched across his bald head, and a pensive look, as if some essential detail of his research had just eluded him. He was in a cranky mood, suffering from a cold or perhaps an upset stomach, some vague disturbance no doubt aggravated by the Ramadan fast and that was making him wonder whether a man of his delicate disposition should be fasting at all. He retrieved from his attaché case a plastic bag filled with pills, swallowed a handful, and grimaced.

The sheykh was now officially late, which only made Sheweiki more cranky. I asked him to tell me something of his life as we waited; unexpectedly, he revealed himself to be a man of extraordinary courage. As a high school student in an Arab village in the Galilee, Sheweiki discovered the history of Zionism and decided, like many young Arab Israelis, to emulate the Jews by becoming a Palestinian nationalist. But he also reached another, far less common conclusion: that Zionism was a legitimate movement of national return. And so the same process that turned him into a self-conscious Palestinian also helped him make peace with his Israeli identity.

At the Hebrew University in Jerusalem, he majored in Islamic studies. He began as a secular Arab nationalist, but inspired by a Jewish teacher who combined modernity with religious commitment, he gradually returned to Islam. Yet unlike most secular Muslims—and secular Jews—who turned to religion, Sheweiki didn't opt for an easy orthodoxy but as usual insisted on his own way, searching for the components of a liberal Islam. He had learned that rare skill of seeing your own culture with a loving detachment. Unabashedly, he looked toward Israel and the Jews for inspiration. He knew that Israeli culture was often vulgar and unformed, that Israelis acted like insecure refugees constantly trying to prove that they'd really come home. Yet Israeli culture had the courage of self-criticism, while Islam had become self-referential, smug. "I saw how Jews felt free to examine their own history and traditions and politics," he said to me, "and I wanted to be a free person too."

He was now writing a book about liberalizing Islam, especially its relations with women and non-Muslims, and was studying the classical sources for confirmation of his ideas. For example, the fact that medieval Islam hadn't insisted on conversion but allowed Jews and Christians to practice their faiths, albeit as inferiors to Muslims, could be a basis for a modern Islamic acceptance of religious pluralism. But he readily admitted that even in the absence of support from the sources, he would advocate innovation. "What possible justification can there be for jihad in an era of interfaith dialogue?" he demanded, his voice high and insistent. "Every Muslim will tell you about jihad of the heart: how you have to fight the evil inside yourself. But there is also a jihad of war. And that means you are prepared to wipe out the other. Physically annihilate them. And what is the meaning of dividing humanity between the House of Islam and the House of War? Maybe in medieval times it made sense, but in an era of globalization? How will Islam be part of the world if it clings to those ideas? It's time to examine everything, even the Koran itself. Yes, why not? We have to stop being afraid. Islam is strong enough to withstand scrutiny. If there was such a thing as a Reform Muslim, like your Reform Jews, that's what I'd be." A one-man Islamic denomination.

By Middle Eastern standards, Sheweiki's ideas were extremely dangerous, most of all to himself. He readily acknowledged that if he lived in an Arab country he would probably be a target for assassination. His irony was that, as an Arab Israeli, he was at once a second-class citizen in a Jewish state and the freest Muslim in the Middle East. So no matter how angry he'd get against Israel's occupation of the territories or its reluctance to admit Arabs fully into its national identity, he stubbornly persisted in calling himself an Israeli. He was constantly balancing identities: He was a Palestinian who would never live in Palestine, an Arab nationalist who wanted to be part of the Israeli nation, a practicing Muslim destined to be an outcast in Islam. It was no wonder he often felt exhausted and depleted: He needed several bodies to carry his contradictory identities. When he got discouraged, he said, he took heart from the Prophet Muhammad, who suffered and struggled till the day he died.

Sheykh Ishak appeared, and he too was cranky. He complained to Sheweiki that one of the rabbis who'd invited him to Jerusalem seemed to be ignoring him. The sheykh suspected a deliberate slight. I was glad for this small revelation of pique, this crack in his regal calm; somehow it brought me closer to his humanity.

We had some time before the taxi to Hebron was to arrive, and so we settled into a corner of the lobby. Sheykh Ishak looked like a prince on the silk maroon couch; wherever he was, he seemed to belong.

"Is inner peace a precondition for being a peacemaker?" I asked.

"Someone who lost something can't give it to others," he replied. "But it is God who decides who has inner peace."

"Isn't there anything we can do to reach inner peace?"

"Through repetition of God's names, and asking for God's mercy."

"Does the sheykh think often of his own death?"

"No, no. I'm not afraid of death and not from what comes after death. God has promised peace to believers, in this world and in the next."

He assumed I'd asked whether he was afraid of death, but what I meant to ask was whether the recollection of death could draw a person closer to God and deepen his inner peace.

"What are the stages in ascent toward God?"

"The first stage is that God deals with those close to Him as His slaves. Then, as His beloved ones."

"In Judaism we have a prayer asking God to relate to us the way a father loves his sons, and if we're not worthy of that, then like a master to his slave."

"As a Muslim, I can't ask God to deal with me as a son. God has no son."

"The prayer asks that God deal with us with the love that a father has toward his son," I explained.

"That's better," he said, with abrupt authority.

"What does the sheykh consider to be the greatest quality of God?"

I expected him to say mercy or justice, the two divine qualities emphasized by the Koran. But again he confused me. "God's greatest quality," he said enigmatically, "is His presence. His constant presence among us."

A delegation of interfaith activists arrived, interrupting our flawed attempt at conversation. They were three Jewish men and a German woman, a Lutheran theology student who said nothing, only smiled, trying to demonstrate her goodwill.

"What can we do to further the Muslim-Jewish dialogue?" asked one man.

"Rabbis and sheykhs must appear together in public as often as possible," the sheykh replied. "We have to get our people used to seeing us together."

They seemed disappointed by the vagueness of his answer. "Are there other sheykhs who think like you?"

"Yes, but it's easier for me to speak out. I have money and property. I am well known, I have courage. But if I were getting a salary, I'd be a slave. Some said to me in Mecca that I shouldn't come to

Jerusalem. I said, 'I'm not a clerk of King Fahd or King Hussein. I'm not Saudi or Palestinian. I'm a Muslim from among the Muslims, and I have the right to go on pilgrimage to Jerusalem.' I told them, 'I'm in Mecca for forty years. If you attack me, I'll open my mouth and tell the whole world everything that goes on here!'"

Assuming his visitors were all Jewish, the sheykh added, "Jews and Muslims are closer to each other than to Christians. We both have religious law; the Christians don't. We have fast days; they don't. We forbid the use of images; they pray to images. We believe in one God; they have three gods."

The Lutheran woman stopped smiling, but she didn't challenge the sheykh. She was used to being deferential around Jews and Muslims, as if personally responsible for the Holocaust and the Crusades. Nor did any of the other interfaith activists speak up. I thought I should defend Christianity to the sheykh; I was, after all, on an ecumenical journey. I wanted to tell him: "You've assumed a medieval Islamic and Jewish notion of Christianity, Sheykh Ishak. But Christians who speak of three aspects of God aren't any less monotheistic than kabbalists who invoke God's ten divine qualities. Sacred images that encourage devotion to the one God aren't like pagan idols that celebrated a pantheon of competing gods. In a secular age, all believers belong to the same camp. When a Muslim blows himself up on a bus in Jerusalem or a priest is arrested for child molestation or a rabbi proclaims that Jewish blood is more sacred than gentile blood, the good name of religion is disgraced. We are all implicated in each other's failures."

But I kept silent. This is their meeting, I told myself. It's not my place to intrude. But my silence, I knew, wasn't motivated only by tact. The sheykh's linkage of Judaism and Islam pleased me, even if it meant excluding Christianity. Was I really going to jeopardize a Muslim-Jewish alliance that could counter the threat of an Islamic jihad against Israel for the sake of abstract principles of religious oneness? I knew I was repeating the Middle East's pattern of exclusivist coalitions: Christian fundamentalists and Jews against satanic Muslims, Christian liberationists and Muslims against oppressor Zionists. Still, the temptation of a Muslim-Jewish alliance was too great, and the sheykh had flattered my Jewishness.

We drove to Hebron, about an hour's distance south of Jerusalem. The road wound through the West Bank's terraced hills. Soon we came to Gush Etzion, or "the Gush," as religious Israelis affectionately called it, a bloc of settlements midway between Jerusalem and Hebron. White stone houses with sloping red roofs filled the hills. This area had been settled before Israel's independence; in the 1948 war, it was conquered by the Jordanians, who expelled the Jews. For most Israelis, the Gush wasn't occupied territory but a part of Israel.

Just as I couldn't decisively choose sides in the secular-religious divide, I was ambivalent about Israel's bitter left-right debate. I knew the effect of the occupation on the Israeli soul. I would return home from reserve duty in the territories and yell at my wife and children, unable to make the transition from policeman in a refugee camp to middle-class citizen. But I also understood the settlers' attempt to reclaim the land that had been the center point of our longing through the exile. We were the generation entrusted with return to the biblical heartland, and we were that same generation now being forced to give it up.

The taxi driver, an Arab from East Jerusalem, pointed to a new road emerging from the hills and said to the sheykh, "That used to be an olive grove."

"Do you mean they tore down trees?" he asked, incredulous.

Sheweiki said to me in Hebrew, "The sheykh comes from far away; he doesn't understand our reality."

Sheykh Ishak said with quiet anger, "On my land, a tree is like a child."

He stared out the window with silent ferocity. "Allah, Allah,

Allah," he said, deep and slow, somewhere between prayer and despair.

All my political and historical arguments were irrelevant before the sheykh's mourning for the uprooted trees. Yes, we belonged to this landscape, but we'd returned with the clumsiness of exiles.

We came to Hebron. *"Salaam aleikum ilhamdul'allah,"* the sheykh said quietly, greeting the city's living and dead.

Hebron, in Arabic, was called El Khalil, "the friend." (The Hebrew name for the city, *Hevron,* was likewise a derivative of the word *haver,* "friend.") The name referred to Abraham, whom Muslims called the friend of God. A friend of God was beholden to no one; when God's name was desecrated, a friend felt the shame so keenly he was prepared to risk his life to undo it. Like Sheykh Ishak: defying Saudi princes and the Muslim hierarchy to redeem the name of Islam with his Ramadan pilgrimage with the Jews.

Most of Hebron was now under Palestinian control. Only a sliver remained under Israeli rule, but it contained Hebron's prize, the Machpelah. We entered the city from the Palestinian side. At a checkpoint protected by walls of iron barrels, Palestinian policemen crowded around a fire. Though it was Ramadan, the streets couldn't manage even the pretense of festivity. Strings of little plastic Palestinian flags sagged from lampposts, remnants of the long-forgotten celebration of Israel's withdrawal. Crowds of men in mismatched suits and women in white kerchiefs and gray housecoats and high-heeled slippers with glitter buttons mingled in the road with old Peugeots covered with dust from the biblical hills.

We crossed through back alleys to the Israeli side, without passing any border, and came to the Machpelah, a massive crenellated fortress of yellowed stone. Its foundations were Herodian, over which a Byzantine church had been built, and finally, over the church's ruins, stood a mosque, one faith displacing the other. Only on Israel's watch had that pattern of usurpation been broken. Soldiers patrolled the Machpelah's neglected plaza, where weeds grew through the massive cracked stones; jeeps and an ambulance waited for the next attack.

I asked the sheykh how he felt seeing Israeli soldiers at the entrance to the Machpelah. "In Mecca mosques are also guarded by soldiers," he replied. It was a startling answer. The sheykh was saying that he saw no difference between Muslim and Jewish soldiers. He was implicitly offering a new Islamic way of dealing with the Jewish people, not as inferior but equal, entitled to our own patch of sovereignty in the Middle East.

For Sheweiki, this was too much. "But these are Israeli soldiers!"

"The uniforms aren't important," the sheykh said curtly.

"They are symbols of the occupation. Maybe a civilian presence, but not soldiers."

"If they respect the holiness of the place and allow everyone who wants to pray to enter, they are doing their job," the sheykh replied, with a firmness that discouraged further argument.

I told him about conversations I'd had with Palestinian officials, including the Palestinian Authority's minister of religious affairs, who told me that when the Machpelah reverted to Islamic control, Jews would be barred from praying there, just like the past.

"This is a mosque, and it belongs to Islam," the sheykh said. "But Jews have the right to pray here. Our fathers didn't have the right approach. This is the place where our two faiths meet."

The sheykh and Sheweiki entered through the Muslim entrance, and I went around the corner to the worn stone plaza leading to the Jewish entrance. Baruch Goldstein had destroyed the Machpelah's dare against borders: Jews and Muslims no longer mingled easily within the Machpelah but were confined by the army for security reasons to separate areas, even to separate entrances. I passed through one row of metal detectors at the bottom of the stairs and then more metal detectors at the top. Mounted cameras followed me through the cavernous peeling halls.

The building contained three shrine rooms, each one dedicated to a biblical couple said to be buried in the cavern below. The Jews prayed in the two small rooms built over the graves of Abraham and Sarah and of Jacob and Leah; the Muslims prayed in the large hall that faced Mecca and was devoted to Isaac and Rebecca. It was as fair a division as the army could manage, but it left both sides feeling aggrieved and excluded from beloved parts of the building.

I came to the room of Abraham and Sarah. Two stone cenotaphs, guarded by bronze gates, faced each other on either side of the room. The large humped stones were covered with carpets embroidered with Koranic verses and so heavy with dust that I could barely discern their colors. Faded gold letters etched into the chipped marble walls proclaimed God's oneness. The room was too small for its grandiose vaulted ceiling, from which hung old brass lamps and crystal chandeliers missing bulbs.

The return of the Jews to the Machpelah had transformed this room into a makeshift synagogue, crammed with benches and wooden stands on which to lean while studying and piles of prayer books and a velvet-covered Torah ark. On the walls hung posters with prayers for special occasions, like blessing the new moon. The messiness expressed an inner turmoil: the anxiety of a people that had only tenuously returned home and still feared another uprooting. I longed for the simplicity of our biblical forefathers. I wanted to fall on my face before the God of Abraham, just as Abraham himself no doubt had prayed. I thought of the Muslims on their prayer rugs in the adjacent, inaccessible hall and envied their ease in this ancientness, their instinctive link with our common Bedouin roots. We had been away from this land for so long we'd forgotten its simple movements of surrender.

An iron padlocked door separated this room from the hall of Isaac and Rebecca, marking the spot, once an open passageway, from where Goldstein had fired. Settlers had hung a poster on the door protesting the exclusion of Jews from the adjacent hall, without mentioning that Muslims were similarly excluded from this room or that Goldstein had been the cause of the army's decision to partition the building. Nothing alienated me more from Hebron's settlers than their self-righteousness, especially at this spot. Indeed, their combination of self-pity and arrogance is what produced the Goldstein massacre.

There was a time when I appreciated Hebron's radical settlers. I admired their courage in clinging to this city; I could even understand their militancy, intended to ensure that the Muslims didn't again deny us the right to pray at our birthplace. I'd resented my colleagues in the media who portrayed the settlers as monstrous while ignoring Palestinian provocations and Hebron's tortured history. In my reporting, I'd tried to present Hebron as a struggle between two peoples with deep and legitimate claims to the city, which was its true tragedy.

But since the massacre I no longer wanted to "understand" Hebron's Jews, who so readily "understood" Baruch Goldstein. Even those among them who disagreed with his act refused to accept responsibility for the ideology that had produced him. Though sensitive to any slight against Jews, they couldn't acknowledge the enormity of Goldstein's massacre, blandly calling it "the event." Palestinians in Hebron whom I'd interviewed over the years were no less morally obtuse: Most claimed that the 1929 slaughter was a Zionist invention. Jews and Arabs agreed that Hebron could mourn only one massacre.

A group of settlers arrived, and afternoon prayers began. The young men wore large *kipot,* or skullcaps, whose tightly knit stitches seemed intended to thwart any alien influence from seeping in. If they knew I'd come to the Machpelah with a sheykh, they would probably see me as a traitor. Once I would have readily joined them in prayer, asking God for the strength and peace of Israel. But now Goldstein stood between us. I didn't want to pray with his admirers. Not here. Instead, I wanted to share in the sheykh's devotions. Goldstein had killed Muslims in prayer; I wanted to pray with them. But that of course was impossible.

I took a seat on a bench in the back, close to the iron door. Whatever aversion I felt for that spot was overcome by a desire to be as close as possible to the sheykh. Just being conscious of his presence on the other side of the door meant that in some sense I was praying with him. I imagined the sheykh kneeling toward Mecca and invoking, for its Ramadan pilgrims, the blessings of Abraham, whom Muslims believe built the Kaaba, the cubelike structure that is Islam's central shrine. I felt closer to the sheykh than to those swaying around me and whose language of prayer I shared.

I walked over to the bronze gate guarding the cenotaph of Abraham. I bowed my head against the bars curled like petals and prayed for the sheykh's protection.

I returned to my place on the bench near the iron door. Everyone stood for the *Amidah,* the silent prayer that is the core of the afternoon service. If the sheykh were in my place, what would he do? Boycott the settlers or join his prayers to theirs? A man who could forgive wounds inflicted between peoples, I assumed, would rise above differences within his own people; surely he loved his fundamentalists no less than the pluralists of other faiths. He prayed with any fellow Muslims among whom he found himself. He didn't examine the political or moral credentials of those Hebron Muslims with whom he was now bent in prayer. If he could pray with his problematic people, I concluded, I could pray with mine.

I joined the minyan, but with this change: Wherever a prayer asked God to intercede for the people of Israel, I silently appended the people of Ishmael. "Blessed are You Who heals the sick of Israel—and of Ishmael. Blessed are You Who blesses His people Israel—and His people Ishmael—with peace." Our prayers routinely asked for the health of Israel, the peace of Israel, the prosperity of Israel. The ghetto had penetrated Judaism so deeply that we'd forgotten how to pray for the world. The ultimate expression of that Jewish alienation from humanity was Baruch Goldstein.

Had they heard my prayers for Ishmael, my fellow worshipers would have considered me a blasphemer, a subverter of the tradition's intent. I took mischievous pleasure in the thought that, since participants in a minyan functioned as a single soul, everyone here was implicated through me in prayer for the Arabs. For the first time since Goldstein had violated the Machpelah, I felt at peace within it. Goldstein, then, had left me this legacy: My sense of home here was now conditional on an affirmation of the Muslim presence.

I found the sheykh outside the Machpelah. He was quietly repeating the name of Allah, watching the sullen street of shuttered restaurants and pottery shops that had thrived before the Intifada of the late 1980s had frightened away the tourists. A bent old man kissed the sheykh's hand; the sheykh held the man's face with both his hands and blessed him. A cross-eyed boy carrying a plastic pail filled with lentil soup told the sheykh he was distributing food to the poor for Ramadan; the sheykh laughed with pleasure and stroked the boy's cheek.

We walked toward our taxi. A crippled man sat by a fire to keep warm; the sheykh looked at him intently, as if his gaze could heal. A small crowd followed, keeping a respectful distance and watching his every move, treating the towering man in white like a caliph who had come to reawaken Islam's glory in Hebron's broken streets.

We drove toward Jerusalem. I intruded into the sheykh's silence and asked, "Did you experience a connection with our father, Isaac?" He had, after all, been praying in Isaac's hall, and his own first name was Ishak—Isaac.

"My meeting was with Abraham," he replied, sounding far away, distracted. "He is the stronger presence in the mosque."

"How did your experience here compare with your visit to Al Aksa?" He had gone the previous day to the Temple Mount.

"Al Aksa is a place where you fulfill your religious Muslim duties," he replied. "But this is a spiritual place. When you are here, there is no meaning to time or space. Just a direct connection to God." He paused, and only reluctantly resumed. "Today I made my preparations for the pilgrimage. Now I am on the road back to Mecca."

I should have left him alone. But this was my last opportunity to be with him, and so I persisted. "What is the spiritual relationship between Ishmael and Isaac?" I asked, not quite knowing what I was groping for.

"I wondered about that same question inside the mosque. Why is Isaac buried among the Jews and Ishmael in Mecca, among the Muslims? What does each represent? The revelation of Islam is the names of God; the revelation of Judaism is the qualities of God. A Muslim accepts a gift from God with simple faith. A Jew receives a gift from God and asks, 'What is its purpose? What is its nature? What color is it?' He must know the qualities. The Muslim is content with mystical faith."

The sheykh's words upset me. His analysis seemed like an implicit assertion of the superiority of Muslim over Jewish spirituality. The orthodox of all faiths were adept at that kind of clever formulation that proved that their religion was the most perfect revelation. Kabbalists liked to speak about the supposed difference among the three monotheistic faiths: Christianity was abstract love, Islam concrete judgment, and Judaism the perfected synthesis between the two.

"I have a Jewish question about quality," I said, and I laughed to hide my irritation. "Is the sheykh saying that the quality of Muslim devotion is higher than the quality of Jewish devotion?"

"Not higher, different. Each is a different expression of another beautiful aspect of God."

I stopped asking questions and considered his point. My relentless questioning, my inability to sit with him in silence and accept his presence as sufficient, came from precisely that restless Jewish need to analyze and understand. At its best, the Jewish quest for divine qualities resulted in genius: Kabbalah, after all, was the science of God's qualities. But that obsessiveness could also obscure spiritual insight, precisely what had happened to me with the sheykh.

Now I realized why Rabbi Mickey Rosen was so frustrated that night at Yakar, why so many Jews who heard the sheykh had hoped for "deeper" spiritual insights. The sheykh's message was his presence—his quiet speech and firm silence, his purposeful yet flowing gestures, his ability to adjust to any circumstance, whether eating dinner with a working-class family or meeting with journalists or the president of Israel. All week he'd been trying to explain to us the essential Muslim meaning of simple presence. He had told the interfaith activists in the hotel lobby that the most important step rabbis and sheykhs could take is simply to appear publicly together, but they'd been disappointed. He had tried to explain to me that God's most important quality was His presence, but I had mistaken his answer for elusiveness. For a Muslim, the presence transcended the qualities, dispelled the need for understanding God's attributes. The only quality of God worth knowing was His godliness, His very being. The sheykh's gift to Israel, I finally understood, was a gesture of divine mimicry: He was offering us his presence.

The sheykh said, "In the mosque I received a new way to bless Abraham: 'Father of the prophets.' That is not a Muslim title, but a title that belongs to everyone."

"Sheykh Ishak," I said, summoning my nerve, "I appreciate your emphasis on the connection between Judaism and Islam. But Christianity isn't a lesser form of monotheism."

"Your sense of the deeper spirituality is true," he said, without defensiveness. "Culturally, Judaism and Islam are similar, because we have religious law. But I see Christianity as an extension of Judaism."

"So on bottom there is no spiritual difference between Muslims, Christians, and Jews?"

"You have understood me," said the sheykh.

5

For weeks after his departure, the sheykh's presence lingered. I would suddenly notice my careless speech and movements; compared to him, I seemed barely in control. Somehow this man, whose life was still a mystery to me, had managed in a few encounters to become a role model. I wanted to speak with his essential spareness, move with his slow and steady gestures that recalled poured oil, and most of all relate to others as he did, with a goodwill as spontaneous as breath.

With the sheykh gone, I was back to where I'd begun, trying to find an entry into Palestinian Islam. Lena Jabar organized a series of Muslim-Jewish encounters at Yakar, and I attended several sessions. An Arab Israeli Islamic college, which encouraged dialogue with Jews, cosponsored the series. A lecture was followed by group study, and it was moving to see young Jews and Muslims sitting around long tables with Xeroxed sheets of sacred Jewish and Muslim texts, discussing charity, fasting, and prayer. Still, most of the participating Muslims, understandably nervous about being there at all, seemed intent on defending the faith rather than pursuing honest and mutually self-critical dialogue. One Islamic scholar, extolling Islam's "unsurpassed" record in respecting women, told the group, "There is no wife beating among Muslims, none at all!" When some Jews appeared dubious, he said, "Maybe an occasional slap for some outrageous behavior, but always well deserved!" At another session, an Islamic scholar revealed that he'd discovered in the sources an Islamic equivalent of the Jewish concept of *Shekinah,* the female aspect of God that parallels the Hindu notion of the Mother, Who creates and nurtures: The Muslim version, declared the scholar, was green and had horns.

Those experimental study sessions were brave and flawed and essential, but they weren't for me. I appreciated the attempts to discover similarities between *Shariyah* and *Halakhah,* the Muslim and Jewish legal systems, but I was looking for a different kind of encounter, based on meditation and prayer, the experience of shared intimacy with God.

In fact, there was historical precedent for such experiential dialogue. Scholars had recently discovered a Jewish Sufi movement in medieval Egypt, led by rabbinic descendants of Maimonides. Convinced that the Sufis had preserved the secret techniques of Israel's biblical prophets, they had adapted Sufi chant and dance in their own Jewish worship. Perhaps Sheykh Ishak, coming from Cairo, was a reminder from history that the time had come to renew those secret links between Judaism and Islam. Neither faith lacked scholars, and I would never be among them. So I might as well use my ignorance for good purpose, I thought, and pursue my search for Islam's heart.

But who would help me?

I phoned Muhammad Sheweiki, hoping he would introduce me to Palestinian mystics, but he was busy writing his book. Then I tried Abed Khalili, the contemptuous Muslim I'd met at Sheykh Ishak's talk at Yakar. Khalili was an active participant in interfaith dialogue, as well as a devout Muslim who spent all-night vigils in the mosque— precisely the combination of openness and rootedness I was searching for. He would be delighted, he said, to help me discover Islam.

At his suggestion, we met in the lobby of the American Colony Hotel, a few minutes' walk from the walls of the Old City and one of Jerusalem's few neutral meeting points for Arabs and Jews. We were an odd sight: a bearded religious Jew and a bearded religious Muslim among the foreign journalists and businessmen drinking coffee at adjoining tables.

Though Ramadan had ended, Khalili was fasting. Pious Muslims, he explained, fasted on Mondays and Thursdays throughout the year. That's also a Jewish custom, I said. We were both happy to discover the parallel: Muslims and Jews needed those reassurances of similarity.

I complimented Khalili on his excellent English, and he explained that he'd done a doctorate in Islamic studies in Boston. But those years in America, he added, had only confirmed for him the superiority of Islam over the West. "I am happy for the opportunity to explain to you why Islam is the best religion. Really. Westerners think Islam oppresses women. But you come to my house, and you'll see me washing dishes and changing diapers. Really! That is the true Islam. Respect for women as the nurturers of life. The suicide bombers who kill women and children are sinning against Islam. Islam forbids me to kill even women soldiers. If an Israeli woman soldier were to shoot at me, I would have to hide!"

He laughed and then abruptly turned serious. "The Palestinian national movement won't make place for Israel, no matter what agreements they sign. But Islam makes place for you as a Jew. How much longer can your society remain like a military camp against the Muslim world? Is that the life you want, always worrying about security? You need a paradigm shift. Accept your place under Islam—not 'under,' with Islam! In Europe they massacred you, but in Islam you thrived."

He wanted to know why we Israelis were obsessed with security. The reason was Khalili himself. "You know the history of Muslim-Jewish relations is more complicated," I said. "Islam treated Jews as inferiors."

"Not true! There is the caliph, and under him all are equal, Muslim and Jew. No one ever treated the Jews better than Islam."

"We don't want to be 'treated' by Islam, any more than you as a Palestinian want to be 'treated' by Israel. We want to preserve our own sovereign state."

"The nation-state emerged only after the Renaissance, and it has failed to provide for human happiness. The Middle East has to find a better model of cooperation."

By which he meant reviving the caliphate. Retreat into a perfect past, like the Jews who were dreaming of reviving the biblical kingdom.

I knew what was coming next. After a few sessions of Muslim-Jewish dialogue at Yakar, I had learned the litany of "proofs" of Islam's superiority: how Islam was the last revelation and therefore the most perfect, how it alone respected the prophets of all three monotheistic faiths, how biblical criticism proved that the Bible had been distorted by human intervention and that the Koran transcends mere story and offers the pure unmediated word of God. To which the Christian apologist would counter that Christianity alone offers salvation through divine incarnation. And the Jewish apologist would add that Judaism was the pure faith from which emerged those two simplistic versions intended for the pagan masses.

He said, "Abraham is the root, Judaism the trunk, Christianity the branches, and Islam the beautiful fruit." The fulfillment, as if he were parodying Christianity's old theology toward the Jews.

"Why do you bother attending interfaith gatherings?" I asked.

"To explain the true Islam. And perhaps to convince people to become Muslims. I tell you frankly, I hope that you will become a Muslim. Really! You see why I can never become a politician; I speak too honestly."

"And what happens to those who don't become Muslim?"

"If they were never exposed to Islam, they will be judged on Judgment Day by their merits alone. But if they know about Muhammad and the new revelation and still reject it . . ."

"Hell?" I asked.

He nodded sadly.

"If that's the situation," I said, "you're doing a terrible thing by going to interfaith gatherings and turning all of us blissfully ignorant heathens into heretics."

"I know," he said, guiltily. "I worried about it a lot. But if I'm invited, I have an obligation to represent Islam."

Then he said, holding out hope for my salvation, "Here's my e-mail address. Any question you have about Islam, write me and I'll be happy to reply."

And that said it all about Islam's accessibility in the Holy Land. We lived perhaps fifteen minutes away from each other, and I was supposed to communicate with Khalili by e-mail.

He was late for afternoon prayers, and so I drove him to the Old City. I watched him disappear into a crowd of Palestinians huddled in a light rain against the crenellated stone wall, and I felt again the Israeli fear of Islam. How many people in that crowd, I wondered, would even be willing to speak with Jews as Khalili was? And yet even he could speak only the language of medieval triumphalism.

More than ever, I missed Sheykh Ishak. In all his talks he hadn't offered any apologetics or boasted of Islam's singular greatness. He didn't have to prove Islam's nobility; he embodied it. Yet the very fact that my first real connection with Islam had been a visitor from abroad only emphasized my inability to find a Muslim spiritual connection in this land. For a few days, Muslim devotion had been tantalizingly within reach. Yet now Islam receded again, as vital and pervasive and elusive as air.

Id el-Adha

I

Eliyahu Charanamrit McLean was born into spiritual chaos. The breakdown of traditional religion was embedded in his name: His mother was Jewish, his father Christian, and they raised him in an obscure subsect of Sikhism in Hawaii that preached the universal truth of all faiths. (His Sanskrit middle name meant "the pool of nectar at the feet of the Lord.") Eliyahu's parents, former flower children, had met in California in the late sixties. His mother, an escapee from Brooklyn, was hitchhiking to a commune, and his father, son of a Baptist pastor, picked her up.

Even as a child, Eliyahu had searched for his own spiritual identity, a specific commitment from which to embrace universalism. He liked his parents' Sikh group but suspected he wasn't really a Sikh. At age twelve he convinced his parents to enroll him in a Japanese cultural school that a friend attended, wondering whether he could become Japanese. That lasted two days. He decided he was in the wrong place when the teacher said that students had to ask permission in Japanese to go to the bathroom.

Then he attended a friend's bar mitzvah at a Reform temple and discovered Judaism. Though he hadn't been raised with any Jewish identity and wasn't even circumcised, and though the temple was at once too modern and archaically formal, somehow he knew he had come home. He told his parents that he, too, wanted a bar mitzvah, and they were liberal enough to indulge his interest in mainstream faith. His mother's father flew in from New York and brought his grandson the gift of a Jewish name: Eliyahu, after Elijah, the prophet who prepares the way for messianic revelation. Until then he'd been known as Olan, the name his parents had given him because it sounded like the name of the Norse god, Olaf, and linked him to his father's Viking roots.

In high school he joined a Zionist youth movement and became a pro-Israel activist, distributing pamphlets about Israel's vulnerability, including a map of the Middle East with Israel so small its name couldn't be written within its borders. In late 1990, he left Hawaii to spend his junior year of college studying at the Hebrew University in Jerusalem. When the Gulf War began a few months later, most of the overseas students fled back home; Eliyahu stayed. Almost every night the air-raid sirens announced a new missile attack, and Eliyahu joined Israelis in putting on a gas mask. It felt like an ancient ritual, entering the death mask and merging his identity with the tribe. Eliyahu bound his fate to Israel and knew this was where he was meant to be.

Yet it was also a time for him of deep disappointment in Israel. The Intifada was in its fourth year, and Eliyahu learned of the terrible complexity of the conflict, that not all Palestinian arguments were propaganda after all. He befriended a Palestinian family whose son had been killed by Israeli soldiers during a riot and brought students from the Hebrew University to refugee camps. During spring break he traveled to Cairo, where he met a Sufi sheykh and converted to Islam. It happened suddenly, without premeditation. The sheykh taught him the *Shahadah*, the proclamation of Islamic faith, and Eliyahu found himself standing before three Muslim men and declaring, "There is no god but God, and Muhammad is His messenger." Perhaps the conversion was a way of expressing anger at Israel, or perhaps it was an attempt to make peace with the Middle East, an intimation of spiritual work to come. Whatever its motive, the conversion was sincere; Eliyahu joined the surrender of the Muslim prayer line and the ecstasy of the Sufi circle.

His conversion to Islam turned out to be only a prelude for a deeper commitment to Judaism. Returning to Israel, he met a group of former American hippies who'd become, in their way, Hasidic Jews. They wore side locks mingled with long hair and thick *kipot* knitted with bright patterns that covered their heads like bowls. They lived in their own village, where they had too many children and too little money and danced through Sabbath prayers, restoring a joy to Hasidism that the Holocaust had nearly destroyed.

Two years later, Eliyahu underwent a circumcision ceremony and became a practicing Jew. Somehow, through all the convulsions of his life, he had the wisdom, or the divine guidance, to fashion a stable spiritual identity, rooted in Judaism yet open to other faiths. He saw his religiously eclectic childhood as a useful preparation for what he hoped would be his life's work: to stand within Judaism and reach out to Islam.

He learned Hebrew and Arabic and moved to an Arab village in the Galilee. Working with local high schools, he brought together Jewish and Arab students for encounter sessions. But outraged fundamentalists forced him to leave the village. The pretext was that he had accepted an invitation from local Muslims and joined a parade celebrating Id el-Fitr, the end of Ramadan. Participation in a Muslim feast by an Orthodox Jew wasn't seen as respect but as subversion.

He moved to Jerusalem and joined the staff at Yakar, where he worked on Muslim-Jewish dialogue. His great insight was that the two faiths could best be reconciled through their mystical traditions. Together with Muslim friends, he traveled the villages of the West Bank and the refugee camps of Gaza, searching for Sufi sheykhs whose emphasis on the heart might open them to encounters with

Jews. Though Sufism was now peripheral here, it was once widespread in Palestinian villages, until nationalism displaced mystical passion in the early twentieth century. Even now, the remaining Sufi sheykhs were revered as healers and exorcists, and considered fully orthodox, if eccentric, by other Palestinian Muslims. Through the Sufi sheykhs, Eliyahu hoped to gain entrance into the mainstream of Palestinian Islam.

Though no longer a practicing Muslim, Eliyahu felt grateful for his Cairo conversion and still identified in some way with the simplicity and universalism of Islam. The message on his answering machine opened with greetings in Hebrew and Arabic, *Shalom aleichem, Salaam aleikum,* and his soothing voice reconciled those words to a common language of civility and prayer. Perhaps his work in religious dialogue was an attempt to make peace between the Jewish and Muslim parts of himself.

Only someone as improbable as Eliyahu Charanamrit McLean could get away with ignoring the basic ground rules of the Middle East conflict. He prayed with the most extreme ultra-Orthodox Jews in Jerusalem and met with Muslim fundamentalists in Gaza, neutralizing suspicion by honoring their intensity. In Hebron, he spent Friday night with friends in the settler compound and then crossed the barricades the next morning for lunch with Muslim friends. For Eliyahu, there was no contradiction. They all belonged to Hebron. He knew that a true peacemaker must overcome anger and judgment and learn the way of empathy. He subverted this world with a taste of the next, where paradoxes are reconciled in an embrace of the heart.

Eliyahu had recently turned thirty but seemed much younger, perhaps because of his guileless smile. He had a face meant to be admired in profile: strong nose, delicate lips, long and curly black beard. He wore an Asiatic Muslim skullcap, stiff and gold-embroidered, though a turban would not have been out of place. His long side locks were sometimes tucked behind his ears, sometimes left dangling like shredded rope; when he felt more hippie than Hasidic, he simply tied them behind his head into a ponytail.

Eliyahu tried to subsidize his minimalist bachelor's existence by organizing Muslim-Jewish encounters for interfaith groups, which sometimes paid him and sometimes didn't. He lived in a nearly bare one-room apartment whose only indulgence was stacks of books about Judaism and Islam. He was an instinctive hippie who struggled with time and lost. He was invariably late for appointments, relating to schedules as possibilities rather than commitments, subject to forces released by the universe. That, after all, was how it worked in Hawaii. Spending the day at the beach, he explained, was an acceptable pretext for missing appointments. Still, he realized that to make an impact in Israeli society, he had to learn to live differently. He tried: He'd buy a watch but then misplace it, as if to free himself of time. Lately, he'd managed to work his average lateness down to about half an hour; his goal, he said, was to reach fifteen minutes.

Confronting the seemingly impenetrable wall of Palestinian Islam, I realized I needed a guide. And Eliyahu offered to fill the role. All I needed to do was suspend my frustration at his flexibility with time and my despair about Muslim intransigence toward Israel and follow him wherever the path led, into the most frightening and inaccessible places, hoping that God appreciated Eliyahu as much as I did.

And so here we were, driving to the West Bank village of Karawa near Nablus, to meet a Sufi sheykh named Ibrahim, whom Eliyahu insisted loved Jews. According to Eliyahu, Sheykh Ibrahim had received a vision of Moses, who told him that his job was to welcome Jews into his home and help make peace between Judaism and Islam. "He's all heart," said Eliyahu.

It was a February afternoon, too bright for a thirsty land whose rainy season was about to end. As we penetrated into Samaria, the northern West Bank, the stone-mottled hills seemed to close up behind us. We passed a village where Palestinian flags were flying from the antennas of flat-roofed houses terraced into the hillsides and a settlement with red-roofed houses clustered on a hilltop where Israeli flags were flying on poles—like old-fashioned armies showing their colors before battle.

For all my love for Eliyahu, I was wondering if I'd made a disastrous mistake in trusting his judgment. An Israeli Jew didn't simply get into his car one afternoon and drive to a Palestinian village, unarmed and without protected glass on his windshield. I lived beside two Arab villages in Jerusalem, yet I'd never considered entering them, and the same was true for all my Jewish neighbors. Our world ended where those villages began; Jews who drove in by mistake were lucky to emerge with only broken windows. In an Arab village, my Mitsubishi would instantly mark me as a Jew. Even the cars were tribal here: Jews drove Mitsubishis and Subarus; Palestinians drove Peugeots.

We passed a village whose name I recalled from the Intifada. A Palestinian suspected of collaborating with Israel had been lynched there from a telephone pole. But Eliyahu said, "I heard there's a Sufi sheykh in the village. I'll have to check it out." Where I saw threat, he saw opportunity for ecstasy.

"Eliyahu," I confessed, "I can't believe we're doing this without any protection."

"There's nothing to worry about," he said, and he offered me his slow hippie smile, which only made me more anxious. "We're under the protection of the sheykh."

"That makes me feel a lot better."

Ignoring my sarcasm, he told me a story he'd heard from the sheykh. A car filled with Palestinian men stalled near the sheykh's village and would move again only in reverse. One passenger suggested that they search for a Sufi sheykh who could help exorcise whatever demon had possessed the car. The men began to repeat aloud the names of every village in the area, testing the car's response. When they called out, "Karawa," it abruptly changed gears and flew in the direction of Ibrahim's house. The sheykh, of course, was expecting them. "You had to come here for a blessing," he said, then sent them safely on their way.

The sheykh, added Eliyahu, was a well-known healer and exorcist. Great, I thought, a voodoo sheykh. I mistrusted miracle stories, and exorcisms even more. True spiritual work was incremental, a constant wearing down of the needs of the body and the imperfections of the personality until the soul peeked through. I was trying to live daily life with an awareness of God's watchfulness and intervention. But the protection of a village exorcist? That, it seemed to me, was where Eliyahu strayed from faith into gullibility.

We came to Karawa. I removed my *kipah* and asked Eliyahu to do the same. "It's a Sufi *kipah*," he said. "Don't be so nervous."

"At least tuck in your *payot*," I implored, referring to his side locks.

"This is a very sweet village," he replied. "There's nothing to worry about."

What could this young American possibly understand of our pathological geography? He smiled at me, perhaps in pity, and pulled his side locks back into a ponytail.

We drove onto a narrow, barely paved road that wound up a hill through olive groves. We passed clusters of young men. I tried to avoid eye contact; Eliyahu smiled and waved. At the top of the hill was a traffic circle, courtesy of the Palestinian Authority. It was an absurd creation; we were the only car on the road. Clearly, it had been built to mark the authority's presence. We were now in "Area B" of the West Bank, which meant Palestinian civil control and shared military rule with Israel. In practice, though, the Israeli army almost never entered Area B. We were essentially on our own now. Under the protection of the sheykh.

We parked in a muddy lot before a half-built mosque attached to a two-story house. A man in his mid-fifties, small and barefoot in a plain brown robe, greeted us at the door. He laughed when he saw us, kissed Eliyahu repeatedly on either cheek, and then hugged me.

"Who's that?" I whispered to Eliyahu.

"The sheykh," he said.

"That's the sheykh?" I exclaimed, indiscreet with disappointment. I don't know what I'd expected, but it certainly wasn't a balding little man with a paunch and no beard who looked more like a clerk than a holy man.

The sheykh led us through a hallway, where wires protruded from cinderblocks, into his receiving room. Foam mattresses were lined against the stained and peeling green walls, from which hung drums and cymbals for use in the Sufi ceremony called the *zikr,* or "recollection" of God. The sheykh sat down, cross-legged, on a mattress, flanked by two recharging cell phones. He held a string of brown beads, which he counted vigorously, as though afraid he wouldn't have time to complete the round. He looked at us, and his whole face contorted with delight. The eyebrows rose, the eyes widened, the dimples in his cheeks deepened like a happy sigh. His slightly protruding lips were pried open with laughter, and his sturdy white teeth glowed. "So you've come to the house of the Sufi sheykh!" he said in Hebrew and laughed.

He pointed to a framed drawing directly above his head and explained that it depicted the entry into Jerusalem of the seventh-century conqueror Caliph Omar. "I honor Omar because he allowed the Jews to come back into Jerusalem!" he said, nearly shouting, as if addressing a crowd. For other Muslims, Omar's entry into Jerusalem meant its conquest for Islam, but for Ibrahim, it meant sharing the holy city with the Jews. Instinctively, I removed my *kipah* from my pocket and placed it back on my head. I sensed that Ibrahim would be pleased.

Eliyahu told Ibrahim that I'd been afraid to wear the *kipah* in the village. To my surprise, the sheykh upheld my caution. "Not everyone in Karawa knows the Koran," he said. "What does the Koran say? 'Mankind! We made you into nations and tribes that you may know each other.' What does it say? To kill each other? No! To know each other. To know? Each other! What does my brother Yossi Halevi know? He is a religious person, what is his wisdom? Who is Ibrahim, and what does he have to teach Yossi Halevi? What did God create in you that He didn't create in me?"

I looked at him more carefully now. His nose seemed an extension of his sloping forehead, and even his protruding stomach seemed a natural projection from that gentle but unstoppable flow. His facial features were strong, but none dominated, as if solicitous of each other's place. The effect was a tenderness surprising in such an assertive face.

Eliyahu told Sheykh Ibrahim that we were interested in helping to make peace among the religions. "There already exists peace among the religions!" the sheykh exclaimed. "They are all the same before God. All the same? Before God! Only their followers fight among themselves. Moses, Jesus, and Muhammad are all the same. None is greater than the other. *None* is greater than the other!"

"You don't consider Muhammad the greatest prophet?" I asked, surprised. I had expected the usual Muslim apologetics, at once patronizing and defensive—how only Islam recognized all the prophets and was therefore the most perfect monotheistic faith.

"Prophets don't argue among themselves who is greater," he said emphatically.

I closed my eyes, pulled toward meditation. But the sheykh insisted on interaction. "Ask, Yossi Halevi! You have questions? Ask!"

"Sheykh Ibrahim, how do you open the heart?"

"Repeating the ninety-nine names of God purifies the heart," he said. "It makes the heart feel safe."

A sense of safety, then, was the precondition for love. Precisely what Palestinians and Israelis routinely denied each other.

Eliyahu said to me, "There is a hundredth name, but it's a secret."

"Do you know it?" I asked the sheykh.

"Secret!" he said, mimicking Eliyahu's English, and opened his mouth wide and laughed.

Eliyahu said, "Will the sheykh tell Yossi about the vision of Moses?"

"The Prophet Moses, peace be upon him!"

The sheykh told me the story. In spring 1990, "in the fourth month," he had gone to pray at Nebi Musa, the desert shrine near Jericho that Muslims revered as the burial place of Moses. Only afterward did he realize it was Passover, the festival of Moses. "Suddenly a great light came down. A great light! First I felt it in my heart, then I saw it with my eyes. A voice said to me, 'Ibrahim.' I was very afraid!" He laughed. "'Who are you?' I asked. 'I am the Prophet Moses. I know you, Ibrahim, I know you have only love in your heart for all people. Jews will come to your home, Ibrahim. You will welcome them, feed them, and give them a place to sleep and talk to them about love of God.' 'But how can Jews come?' I said. 'There is a war going on! A war of stones! Soldiers will come to take away my children to prison! They'll think I want to kill them, and they'll try to kill me!' That's what I thought. The only Jews I saw were soldiers. But the Prophet said to me, 'Don't be afraid, Ibrahim. Many Jews will come to you in peace. Many Jews will come to you? In peace. Also, soldiers will come to talk about God.' Also? Soldiers. 'But who am I that Jews should come to me? I'm not a Jewish rabbi. I'm a Sufi sheykh from the village of Karawa!' The Prophet Moses said, 'A time will come, and you will see with your eyes what I am saying to you.'"

The sheykh laughed. "And now look! Here is Eliyahu, here is Yossi! Many more Jews will come. Ibrahim's house will be filled with Jews, just like the prophet promised. The job of Sheykh Ibrahim is to open his home to all people who were expelled from the Garden of Eden onto this earth."

I said, "I was afraid to come to you."

"And I was afraid that Jews would come!"

We laughed.

"The prophet said to me, 'There is no war between Moses and Muhammad. No war! Only between their followers. God wants His children to love each other. He wants Yossi Halevi to love Ibrahim and Ibrahim to love Yossi Halevi. Not to hate, not to fight, not to be afraid—to love! The Sufi heart loves the Jews. The Sufi heart? Loves the Jews!'"

I realized now why the sheykh had greeted our arrival with such delight: We were the fulfillment of the prophet's prediction. Jews were beginning to come, even if so far there were only two of us. Listening to Ibrahim's story, I felt I'd entered a world whose rules I didn't know and over which I had no control; my free will was restricted to the way I chose to react to predetermined events. The only worthy response, it seemed to me, was to suspend my doubts and open myself to possibility. Clearly something had happened to transform a village sheykh into an apostle of love. And to whom, after all, should God speak in this land if not a Palestinian trying to reawaken the heart of Islam?

"Who is Sheykh Ibrahim?" he asked, rhetorically. "A man of war. A man of war! War against hatred. War against war!" He clapped his hands like cymbals and laughed, and we laughed with him, perhaps from relief, perhaps simply for being together. This was a face of Islam I had never imagined: exuberant with laughter, the Islam of love.

The call to prayer came from a nearby minaret. Sheykh Ibrahim said, "There are regular mosques and there are Sufi mosques. Go to a regular mosque and you find guests from the world. 'Hello, you are from Morocco. Hello, you are from Spain.' But go to a Sufi mosque and you have guests from heaven. From? Heaven!" He pointed, clapped, widened his eyes, and extended his hands with wonder, seeming to startle himself with his own intensity. "When your car needs gas, where do you go? To the supermarket? No, you go to the gas station. To? The gas station! When you want love for God, where do you go? To the love station! To the Sufi mosque of Ibrahim! The mosque of love and peace!"

He spoke the Hebrew word for love like an extended exhalation: *"Ah-ha-vaaah."* I felt absorbed into the rhythm of his breath. I recalled what Nabhan Jabar had said to me that night in Abu Ghosh: To know a Sufi sheykh, you must look into his eyes. And so I looked now into the eyes of Sheykh Ibrahim. I felt the space around us slowly expand. The wall behind him dissolved, and then Ibrahim receded, blurred. I entered meditation. Ibrahim was saying something, but it sounded far away. I felt a stirring in my chest, as if someone had pressed against my heart.

2

I was driving Sheykh Ibrahim through the Judean desert, to the shrine of Nebi Musa. I wanted to stand with him at the spot of his revelation, experience something of the power of that transformative moment. Less generously, perhaps I was also hoping to test the legitimacy of the vision, discover whether the sheykh was a fantasist or a genuine man of God.

The sheykh had been delighted by my offer to drive to Nebi Musa. He was always ready to travel, restless with activity. He took calls at all hours from desperate Palestinians whose family members were possessed by jinns, or evil spirits; even now he carried two cell phones, which rang incessantly.

Eliyahu, who was also in the car, told the sheykh that hundreds of Palestinians in Gaza were convinced they'd become possessed by Hebrew-speaking jinns. "The sheykhs are very busy trying to exorcise the Jewish jinns," said Eliyahu. The ultimate Israeli occupation.

"Most jinns are heretics," the sheykh said. "But once I met a jinn who wanted to study the Koran."

"So what did you do?" Eliyahu asked.

"I taught him the Koran!" the sheykh said, laughing. Usually, though, his encounters with jinns were less uplifting. Just the other night, he'd gotten a call from a man in Bethlehem: "Help me, Sheykh Ibrahim! The jinn wants to marry my wife!" Though it was close to midnight, Ibrahim left for Bethlehem. "I saw the jinn with my eyes. It was black with long fingernails. I fought for hours against him. For hours! It's hard work getting rid of a jinn!" He laughed again.

This was too much for me. "Why is it," I asked, "that only Muslims are possessed by jinns? Why don't we hear about Jews or Christians being possessed?"

"Not only Muslims!" exclaimed the sheykh. "The jinns hate all the people of God! Muslims, Christians, Jews! The jinns? Hate the people of God!" Even as an exorcist, he insisted on religious pluralism.

I was deeply drawn to Ibrahim, this sheykh whose joy was to receive Jews in his home, but talk of jinns depressed me. Ibrahim's real exorcism work, it seemed to me, was purifying Palestinian Islam from hatred. I tried to direct the conversation away from Eliyahu's fascination with jinns and asked Ibrahim to tell us something of his life and how he became a Sufi sheykh.

He came, he said, from a long line of sheykhs from the Rifa'i order, which originated in Iraq and specialized in healing as well as ecstatic worship, a practice that sometimes included piercing oneself with skewers and even swords. As a boy, he'd studied the Koran with his uncle, a Rifa'i sheykh, who taught him that love was the highest form of worship. When he was older, Ibrahim studied Middle Eastern history ("all the wars!") at Damascus University and became a high school principal in the West Bank town of Ramallah.

In 1986, when Ibrahim was forty-three years old, his uncle summoned him. "Soon I am going to die," he told his nephew. "None of my four sons are worthy of becoming the next sheykh. You will take my place." Ibrahim knew his own worth: He was a good man who loved his students and made no enemies, who gave to charity and said his prayers and fasted on Ramadan. But he wasn't a holy man. "Who will teach me how to be a sheykh?" he asked. "Angels and saints from heaven," the old man replied.

One night, not long after the sheykh died, Ibrahim was awakened by a great light. He fell to the floor. A voice spoke to him from the light. Ibrahim tried to get up and greet the visitor. When someone enters your home, you welcome him. But Ibrahim fell down again. The voice said, "God wants you to be a Sufi sheykh." Ibrahim said, "I'm ready." The voice continued, "You remember what your uncle said. Now is your time. Now? Is your time."

After that vision, the weeping began. Whenever he prayed the name "Allah," he wept uncontrollably. His wife had recently died of cancer, and he assumed that was the cause of his breakdown. But then it got worse. At night he would dance in circles, like a fan on the ceiling. And he began speaking in a language he alone understood. Neighbors were convinced he was possessed.

Finally, he went to see Sheykh Abdul-Rahim, head of the Rifa'i order in the Palestinian territories and a respected exorcist. Ibrahim appeared in Sheykh Abdul-Rahim's mosque in Gaza late one night, babbling in his private language. Sheykh Abdul-Rahim sat Ibrahim beside him and began speaking in the same incomprehensible language. "You are experiencing too much light," Sheykh Abdul-Rahim told Ibrahim. "I'm going to lessen the intensity, until you're ready to take it in. You have seven children, you have to be a father for them. Go home. When the time comes, you will become a sheykh."

Ibrahim returned to normal life, more or less. He stopped weeping for no apparent reason and resumed his job as high school principal. At night, though, he would dream that beings of light flew him to Mecca and taught him the names of God. Though he'd never been to the holy city, he became intimate with its mosques and streets. In the morning when he'd say his prayers, he would feel the night's sensation of flight. Finally, Ibrahim returned to Sheykh Abdul-Rahim, ready to take on the light.

"Did Sheykh Abdul-Rahim formally train you?" I asked. I had read of the Sufis' forty-day seclusion and of a series of gradual mystical steps known as "stations," and I wondered whether Sheykh Abdul-Rahim had instructed him in those practices.

"Sheykh Abdul-Rahim asked me, 'Do you want to drink of the waters of Eden?' I said, 'Sheykh Abdul-Rahim, I am ready to drink.' He put his hand on my heart and I drank."

"But what was the experience of drinking?" I persisted.

"It was tasting the waters of Eden," he said.

"But . . ."

"Yossi Halevi! If Sheykh Abdul-Rahim asked you to drink from the waters of Eden, what would you say? You would say, 'Sheykh Abdul-Rahim, I am ready to drink.'"

Was Ibrahim being vague because he didn't have much to say? Were his experiences delusions? Or perhaps I was asking the wrong questions. Sheykh Ishak Idriss Sakouta had warned me of the potential for misunderstanding between Jews and Muslims: Jews needed to know the qualities of God, Muslims simply to experience His presence. Was I blocking my ability to enter Ibrahim's experience by trying to dissect it?

We turned off the highway onto a narrow road leading into pale hills, smooth and peaked like tents. Though not visible from here, the Dead Sea was close. On a clear day, I probably saw these hills from my porch.

The road came to a fortresslike mosque. The solitary building, the color of sand, seemed to rise from the desolation. Its corners were marked with minarets, and its walls were embedded with arched windows missing glass. Atop the walls were mounted at least two dozen domes, mimicking the ripple of hills. The building was surrounded on three sides by hundreds of thin, upright stones, marking the graves of pilgrims who had died here over the centuries or requested that their bodies be brought to this place.

Nebi Musa had been built by Saladin, who defeated the Crusaders and conquered Jerusalem. For that reason, it became a place of pilgrimage in the early twentieth century for Palestinians who compared their own war against Jewish immigration to Saladin's war against the Crusaders. Yet in Sheykh Ibrahim's encounter with Moses, the message of Nebi Musa was reversed: not to resist the return of the Jews but to welcome them home.

According to the Bible, Moses never crossed the Jordan and was buried in a hidden grave. But Muslim tradition placed his grave here, and I asked the sheykh about the contradiction. He didn't respond; he was silently praying, connecting with Moses. That, I realized, was the proper answer. It didn't matter whether Moses' bones were buried here or not; a holy place was energized by the prayers of pilgrims, which drew the soul of the saint.

"No talking now," Ibrahim said when he finished praying. He spoke in a near-whisper, his ebullience gone. "No eating or drinking. We go to the Prophet empty. The Prophet Moses, peace be upon him, knows Ibrahim, he knows Yossi Halevi, he knows Eliyahu. He is waiting for us to ask him for help." He added, "Inside, we will speak in English, not Hebrew. Not all Muslims understand the Koran." This time, I didn't have to ask Eliyahu to remove his *kipah* and tuck in his side locks.

On the arched wood door leading into the courtyard was a poster listing the prophets venerated by Muslims, including Moses and Jesus. Each name appeared in its own circle surrounded by flower petals. Inside the largest circle was the name Muhammad. I recalled what Ibrahim had said to me at our first meeting: The prophets didn't argue among themselves which of them was greatest.

The large courtyard, flanked by rooms in which pilgrims once slept, was nearly deserted. The walls were peeling and badly in need of paint. Bizarrely, stalls sold not only soda and homemade toffee but children's toys and fake leopard-skin pocketbooks. "Look, but don't buy," the sheykh admonished, upset with the commercialism at this place of revelation. "Look? But don't buy."

Off the courtyard, a verandah led to a small mosque. A few old men were sitting on the floor reading the Koran. Ibrahim joined them inside. Eliyahu wandered off to explore the empty rooms along the courtyard, while I stood at the entrance to the mosque and watched the sheykh prostrate himself. His heavy body assumed the grace of prayer; he was bowing and kneeling and touching his head to the floor, smoothly and repeatedly until he seemed to be performing a single movement. This was as close as I'd ever gotten to Muslim prayer. One step across the threshold and I could join him in his devotions. But that was forbidden.

When he emerged, I asked him, using the Arabic term of respect I'd learned from Eliyahu, "Ya sheykh, where did the Prophet appear to you?"

Wordlessly he led me by the hand to a barred window looking into a room adjacent to the mosque. He pointed through the bars at a stone cenotaph covered with dusty rugs: the reputed grave of Moses.

We stood together in silence. The late-afternoon sun softened the stone walls.

"Now we pray," he said. "The Prophet is waiting for you, Yossi Halevi."

Silently, I asked Moses to open my heart to Muslims as he had opened Ibrahim's heart to Jews. The sheykh prayed silently, too. He could have stood by the cenotaph, but he chose to remain outside with me. Perhaps it was important for him to pray here with a Jew. He cupped his hands through the bars, and I did the same. As we prayed, I felt a physical pressing against my heart.

"Now pray for your wife and children," he instructed, and I did.

I had never thought of Moses in personal terms, as an intercessor; he belonged to the Jewish people, not to me as a simple Jew. But

Ibrahim was telling me: You have a connection with a great soul, so why not seek his help? I felt grateful to the sheykh for restoring to me a relationship with Moses, who had set in motion the process of Jewish migration to this land, which, centuries later, was still dynamic enough to uproot me from my place of birth and bring me to the Middle East. And I felt grateful to Islam for anchoring Moses to the Holy Land, creating a place of pilgrimage where he could be invoked. Moses had brought the Jews here, but Islam had brought back Moses. Now Nebi Musa would be part of my spiritual geography, a holy place where Moses had appeared to a Palestinian sheykh and demanded reconciliation between Muslims and Jews.

"What is it that you love about the Prophet Moses?" I asked.

"That he suffered so much in his life but never lost his love for God and for his people," he said without hesitation.

"When Moses appeared to you, ya sheykh, what did you say?"

" 'How will the Jews come? There's a war going on! Who is Ibrahim that they should come to his house?' "

The urgency of his voice revealed that a part of him was still arguing with Moses, still perplexed at the turn of events that had brought us together to this place. Yet who would understand Ibrahim's reluctance and confusion better than Moses himself, who argued with God for choosing him as His emissary?

"Did you know any Jews before Moses appeared to you?" I asked.

"No one! Not a single Jew! But I never had hatred in my heart for the Jews."

"Not even during the Intifada when soldiers came into the village?"

"Not even then. I always kept my sons away from trouble. None of them went to prison even for one day."

"What did the light look like, ya sheykh?"

He drew his hand quickly before his face, like a veil. "A light from the sky. Like a beam. So strong I couldn't move my hands or legs. The light filled my heart and came up to my eyes. Then the light showed me the shape of the Prophet Moses."

"What did the Prophet Moses look like?"

The words emerged with difficulty. "Long white beard. Very strong, very big. Light coming from every part of his body."

He seemed to forget my presence. "Why did he come to me?" he asked himself. "Who am I? A holy man? No! An ordinary person. An ordinary person. It is a blessing from God."

He leaned against a pillar and wept. Inside the mosque, men were chanting. A bird sang from a withered vine.

3

Sheykh Ibrahim became an essential part of my life. We spoke constantly. I looked forward to the phone ringing, hoping it would be his invigorating voice: "Yossi Halevi, *akh sheli,* my brother! You know someone in Tel Aviv? You know someone in New York? This is the Sufi sheykh, calling from heaven!" He didn't merely greet you but announced you to the cosmos: "Yossi Halevi!" he would say, laughing partly with the pleasure of repeating your name, partly in recognition of the put-on. He was playing the role of the merry sheykh, and he didn't care if you knew he was acting because that only deepened the delight. He would shout and widen his eyes and point with mock urgency, then dispel the tension with laughter.

I heard his laughter in the call of the muezzin. Once I awoke in the middle of the night, convinced I'd heard him laughing. He laughed the way less exuberant people depended on smiles, to express friendliness and benign intent. Sometimes he laughed after a statement, for emphasis; sometimes he spoke and laughed at the same time, accenting his words with joy.

We invariably spoke about the same things: how much we loved each other and how God wanted peace in the land of the prophets, as he called the Holy Land. Perhaps his constant proclamations of goodwill were intended to convince himself that he really did love the Jews, to purge himself of whatever Palestinian rage remained in him. When I tried to discuss politics, he said, "Yossi Halevi, there are enough politicians in the land of the prophets. But where are the prophets in the land of the prophets? Where are the prophets!"

Arabic words began to possess my speech, as if a Palestinian jinn were speaking through me. I found myself saying *aywah,* instead of "yes," even using the sheykh's vehemently affirmative intonation, *"Ay!-wah."* When I wanted to say "with God's help," *inshallah* involuntarily emerged.

Islam even penetrated my meditations. The meditation method I used was kabbalistic: imagining the four Hebrew letters of the Tetragrammaton on my forehead and observing their shape, color, permutations. Now, when I sat down to meditate, those letters rose like minarets and were capped by domes.

One night, my ten-year-old son, Gavriel, fell on his head and was hospitalized with a concussion. I called Ibrahim and asked for his prayers. The next day I phoned to tell him that Gavriel had been released. "I was fighting for him all night!" he said, laughing.

I drove to Karawa, this time without Eliyahu. As I crossed the last Israeli checkpoint and entered Palestinian-controlled territory, my anxiety returned. I tried to calm myself; I was, after all, under the protection of the sheykh.

Though he had no organized community, he did have followers, or Hasidim, as he liked to call them in Hebrew, mostly people whom he'd exorcised or healed. One of his Hasidim, Haj Muhammad, was lying on a mattress in the sheykh's little receiving room when I arrived. He was a fat man brooding into a thick mustache; though it was a cool day, he sweated and breathed with effort. In one hand he held a pack of cigarettes, in the other a cell phone.

"Haj Muhammad comes from a holy family of Sufi sheykhs," Ibrahim explained. "He is a very rich businessman! He has a palace with four stories in Nablus. Four stories! Haj Muhammad, tell Yossi Halevi why you leave your four-story palace in Nablus to sleep on a mattress in Ibrahim's house in the village of Karawa!"

Like a child reciting the correct answer, Haj Muhammad replied, "When a battery runs out of energy, you throw it away. But when a person's energy runs out, he can't throw himself away. So I get into the car and drive to Sheykh Ibrahim. After a few hours I feel like a human being again. And then I'm ready to go back into the world."

"He calls me every night," the sheykh said affectionately. "One hour, two hours, sometimes we speak the whole night! I give him light. From the heart. Light? From the heart. When a cell phone runs out of energy, you plug in a transformer. Ibrahim is the transformer of love!"

Now the time had come for the ritual of praising the sheykh. "Tell him the story of the mosque," Ibrahim prodded Muhammad, smiling with anticipation.

Muhammad dutifully complied. A Sufi community in Nablus, he began, had decided to build a mosque at the tomb of a holy sheykh. But every time they tried to build, the structure would collapse. "The sheykh didn't allow a mosque over his tomb," said Muhammad. "He had high-voltage power."

"So they called in Ibrahim to convince the sheykh to let them build the mosque," interrupted Ibrahim, unable to restrain himself. "I said to the sheykh, 'These people want to build a mosque. To build? A mosque! Why don't you let them?'" He shouted with exasperation, eyes wide and arms spread. "The sheykh answered me in my heart: 'A mosque is good,' he said. 'But only if the family of Haj Muhammad builds it! I don't want anyone else to give even a shekel!' Haj Muhammad immediately agreed to pay for everything. The mosque was built, and this time it didn't fall!"

Muhammad nodded, confirming the details.

The story seemed to me both boastful and absurd. Still, I tried to suspend judgment. I was, after all, in a world whose codes I didn't know. Nor could I dismiss Ibrahim's capacity for the miraculous. The very fact that I was sitting in the home of a West Bank sheykh—and feeling relaxed while wearing a *kipah*—was a kind of miracle. In the midst of hopeless conflict, the sheykh had created a place of safety. I needed to keep open and see where our relationship would lead.

A young couple escorting an old, dazed woman came to the door. "More work!" the sheykh said, laughing. "Work for the saints in heaven!" The old woman, he explained, had come for a healing. I asked if I could observe him work, my journalist's impulse overcoming my sense of spiritual tact; to his credit, he said no. "Talk to Haj Muhammad about God!" he urged as he left the room. "He is a Sufi sheykh!"

"You're a sheykh?" I said skeptically to Muhammad.

"I'm supposed to be," he replied. "I have these things." He pointed to the drums and cymbals hanging on the wall. "But I don't have time for it. I own a quarry. One hundred fifty people work for me."

And then he abruptly turned on his own pride. "What is any of it worth?" he demanded. "Only God is real."

This failed sheykh, caught in the material world and in his own massive body, came to Ibrahim to be reminded of who he was. Ibrahim's relationship with Muhammad was the opposite of his exorcism work: He was trying to implant in Muhammad the soul of a Sufi sheykh, possess him with a sense of the sacred.

When Ibrahim returned, I asked him if he wasn't concerned that his visitors had spotted a Jew in his home. The Palestinian Authority, after all, sometimes jailed coexistence activists who organized meetings between Arabs and Jews without permission of Arafat's regime. Our meeting was subversive. Peace was supposed to be left to the politicians, not the believers. It was a matter of technical arrangements, not alignments of the heart.

Ibrahim said, "I asked the angels the same question. The same question! 'What will my neighbors say? What will they think in the Authority?' The angels said to me, 'Ibrahim, don't be like the Prophet

Jonah. Don't be like the Prophet Jonah! Don't run away from your job! We are protecting your mosque. Don't be afraid!'"

"I'm still afraid to come here," I confessed.

"Yossi Halevi! If you love God and your heart is open, why be afraid?"

He looked at me and laughed, as though he were my exorcist, expelling the jinn of fear.

4

A Sufi sheykh named Abu Falestin was becoming popular in the Galilee, and I offered to drive Eliyahu up north to meet him. We invited Ibrahim, who was always ready for a trip. "Why not meet the Sufi sheykh?" he said.

A newspaper profile I'd read about Abu Falestin noted that until his transformation into a sheykh he'd been known in his town, Sakhnin, as *majnun,* the crazy one. He had been the worst goalie in the history of Sakhnin's soccer team, once allowing eighteen goals in a single game. He was said to have such a temper that he sometimes beat his followers. Yet Arabs from all over the Galilee were going on pilgrimage to Abu Falestin, who was believed to be a miracle worker. Despite his name, which meant "father of Palestine," he opened his mosque to Jewish visitors.

Eliyahu phoned Abu Falestin and asked permission to visit. The sheykh mocked his immigrant's Hebrew but invited him to come. Eliyahu in turn invited his friend Gabriel (Gabi) Meyer to meet us at Abu Falestin's mosque. Gabi lived in a vegetarian village not far from Sakhnin. Like Eliyahu, he was a combination of hippie and Hasid who loved Islam. Gabi was from Argentina, where his father, a prominent rabbi, had helped opponents of the junta escape the country; finally, Gabi's family, too, had to flee. Gabi hung out with a group of Israeli musicians who fused Hebrew and Arabic and Indian motifs, trying to create a new Israeli spirituality that would restore Judaism to the East. Recently he'd traveled with the group to the Sahara to study Islamic trance music. Gabi invited the musicians to join us in Abu Falestin's mosque. I was, as usual, edgy about a new Muslim encounter and didn't want to tamper with our welcome by bringing uninvited guests. But Eliyahu assured me there was no need to worry. Abu Falestin could handle a few more Islamic Hasidic hippies.

We arrived in Sakhnin in the early evening. A grandiose minaret, easily twice the size of others in the Arab town and visible for kilometers, dominated a little side street. Colored lights were strung on the facade of Abu Falestin's newly built mosque, as though announcing a festival. We removed our shoes and entered a large, brightly lit room. Except for framed quotes from the Koran and photographs of impassive, white-bearded sheykhs, no aesthetic touches eased the mosque's functionalism. Even the floor was covered with a bland wall-to-wall carpet rather than Oriental rugs.

Several dozen men were sitting on mattresses, smoking and drinking coffee. They stared at us; no one offered greetings. We quickly found some empty space near Gabi and his two friends, all of whom wore white robes, kaffiyehs around their heads and necks, and knitted white *kipot* that could have passed for Muslim or Jewish. The Arabs wore Western clothing.

Sheykh Abu Falestin sat alone on a cushion in front of the room, smoking a cigarette with the passion and self-loathing of a man aware that each inhalation was bringing him closer to his death. His face was lean and sharp; a meager beard outlined his jaw. His nostrils flared and he squinted beneath menacing eyebrows. Before him was a brazier filled with coals and sand and holding a copper coffeepot. He put out his cigarette in the sand, took a little shovel, and played with the burning coals. He was perhaps in his early fifties, though it was hard to tell. Anguish had burrowed into his face like age. An immaculately pressed white robe hung on his long thin body, incongruously conveying purity and peace.

Men with averted eyes placed ashtrays before us and wordlessly offered cigarettes. The hospitality was formal, not welcoming. A man approached with a copper kettle, poured bitter coffee into a thimble cup, and handed it to me. When I finished drinking, he handed the cup to Eliyahu and refilled it. The fellowship of the mosque: Everyone drank from the same cup.

Platters of food were laid for us on the rug: large pitas made of cracked wheat, pastries filled with spinach, humus with newly pressed olive oil that burned the throat. Each time Ibrahim dipped pita into humus he said, *"Bismillah,"* in the name of God, loudly, perhaps trying to impress our hosts. No one spoke; only our chewing broke the silence.

When we finished our meal, hastily eaten under the stares of our hosts, Ibrahim asked Abu Falestin which Sufi order he belonged to. Ibrahim's own order, he offered, was the Rifa'i, led by Sheykh Abdul-Rahim of Gaza.

"Never heard of him," said Abu Falestin curtly.

Ibrahim tried the names of other sheykhs but got no response. He became flustered: When sheykhs met they invariably inquired into each other's spiritual lineage, evoking the protective presence of their masters. But this sheykh seemed oblivious to courtesy and custom.

Abu Falestin turned to Eliyahu. "Tell Ibrahim," he said, switching from Arabic to Hebrew, "that I'm not interested in his sheykhs. What use are sheykhs to me? I don't need people to tell me about God; I only need God." He pointed to heaven. Ibrahim sat quietly and didn't respond. His mouth dropped slightly open and he stared into the distance.

Eliyahu, upset, whispered to me, "He's humiliating the sheykh." For Eliyahu and me, Ibrahim was "the sheykh," our link with Islam's heart.

"Let's go," I whispered back impatiently. "This guy's a clown."

"You never know what Allah has planned," Eliyahu said, trying to calm me. "We've come all this way, we might as well see what happens next."

Abu Falestin retrieved several newspaper articles, which he kept beside his cushion. He held up a clipping from an Israeli newspaper. "They say I am the most popular sheykh in the Galilee!" Then he showed us a clipping from a Jordanian newspaper. "Here they write that I am ignorant of the Koran." He sneered. Finally he displayed a letter signed by professors from Hebrew University: "They thank the sheykh for sharing his wisdom with them!" He tried to smile but grimaced instead.

A disciple entered the mosque, approached Abu Falestin, and kissed his hand. The sheykh in turn grabbed the disciple's hand and furiously kissed it, with demonstrative humility.

None of Abu Falestin's disciples dared ask any questions; this was the sheykh's solo performance. So everyone turned in surprise when one of Gabi's friends, with a shaved head and a Vandyke, suddenly spoke. "Ya sheykh," he said, "I was thinking of Joseph, who was thrown into the pit by his brothers and then became a king. Each of us has a part of himself that is a king and a part of himself that is lost in the pit. Could the sheykh give a blessing for the Joseph that is imprisoned in us?"

He was trying to link Jews and Muslims through a figure portrayed lovingly in both the Torah and the Koran. But Abu Falestin wasn't impressed.

"I see you have a beard like a sheykh," he said mockingly. "Do you know who Joseph was? Even in the pit he was a king! He was never a slave! Joseph is beauty, Joseph is purity, Joseph is untouchable!"

It was a classic clash between Muslim and Jewish sensibilities. Islam insisted on the perfection of its spiritual heroes, while Judaism stressed their humanity and their struggles.

Now Gabi tried his luck. Since Abu Falestin was renowned as a dancer of the *zikr*—the Sufi ceremony of active meditation, coordinating dancing, chanting, and breathing—Gabi confided to the sheykh his own *zikr* difficulties. "Ya sheykh, in the Sahara they say that God dances. But I find that after a *zikr*, I collapse and feel strangely depressed. I can't explain it. Can the sheykh give me advice on how to cope with this?"

Gabi was asking for help in handling the transition from ecstasy back to ordinary consciousness; instead he received orthodox dogma.

"You think God has a body?" shouted the sheykh. "That He dances?! You are confusing God with form. God doesn't dance, God is the dance. The wind that moves the branches of the tree."

Eliyahu tried his luck. "How does one deal with imperfections?" he asked.

"By recalling your own death," the sheykh replied, suddenly mild. "Every minute, every second, with every breath. Who is Sheykh Abu Falestin? A name. An empty shirt. A corpse! I walk on the heads of great men, doctors and professors. They are buried beneath my feet. Donkeys, even pigs, walk on them. And soon others will walk on me."

He spoke compellingly. If our encounter with Abu Falestin had begun at this point, I would have been enticed. Yet this same man had waved newspaper articles attesting to his renown and humiliated Sheykh Ibrahim to aggrandize himself. Was he so totally unaware of his own contradictions? Or was he simply mad: one of those infused with an excess of light, as Sheykh Abdul-Rahim had put it to Ibrahim?

On one level, of course, it was farce. If I hadn't been so nervous about sitting in a mosque, I would have been tempted to laugh out loud. And yet it was moving to watch Sheykh Abu Falestin in all his contradictory modes, exposing the struggles the rest of us learned to conceal.

By suspending consistency, he created an atmosphere of expectation. What would the sheykh say next? Perhaps what I'd dismissed as hypocrisy was instead the tantrums of a soul seeking a perfection it couldn't achieve. Or perhaps his constant awareness of death disoriented him, so that he veered between self-aggrandizement, grasping for recognition above the mass of doomed men, and self-negation, despising the false immortality of fame. Like Joseph, at once slave and king.

"When you get angry," Abu Falestin calmly explained, forgetting his own rage, "think of death. Always keep your own death before you. Someone may owe you money; maybe your wife didn't prepare the food you like; maybe your boss has held up your check. But if you remember that you could die tomorrow, you will stop being angry. We stand between two breaths: inhalation, which is life, and exhalation, which is death. At any moment you can exhale your last breath."

Eliyahu was right: You never knew what Allah intended. This crazy man was capable of moving insights. The notion of a human being suspended between two breaths seemed to me the basis for a powerful meditation. I resolved that when I felt anger coming on, I would try to imagine each exhalation as my final breath.

Abu Falestin finished a cigarette and immediately lit another. "I'm a strange sheykh. I say strange things. Have you ever met a sheykh like me? I came into this world from the dirtiest place; when I die I will be reborn in the Garden of Eden, the cleanest place. Make your mind and heart a fit place for God to live. Your hands and legs are the soldiers, your mind is the general, your heart is the king. Hold it up like a mirror, and you can see the stars."

Back in the car, I asked Ibrahim what he thought of Abu Falestin. Ibrahim's restraint had been impressive. After his initial attempt to befriend Abu Falestin as a fellow sheykh, he had wisely accepted the anonymity our host had assigned him. I never loved him more than in that humble silence.

"There are many paths," Ibrahim said now, without grievance. "We heard tonight a particular path, emphasizing death. Death is not the path of Sheykh Ibrahim. The path of Ibrahim is love. Both are valid approaches. If a sheykh gets light from the Beautiful Name of God, his light is love, he's always happy, laughing, welcoming people. If a sheykh gets light from the Awesome Name of God, his light is severe. Did you see Sheykh Abu Falestin laugh even once?"

"What about the way he insulted people?" I pressed, suspecting that Ibrahim had deeper feelings about Abu Falestin than he was letting on.

Ibrahim smiled. "Some sheykhs speak from the mouth, some speak from the heart. What is the best blessing to ask from God? The best blessing? To make peace between people. Better than asking for God's blessing is to ask for His love."

5

Rabbi Menachem Froman was an unlikely hero of Muslim-Jewish reconciliation. A founder of the Gush Emunim messianic settler movement and spiritual leader of the West Bank settlement of Tekoa, he had the spare face of an ascetic and the contented smile of an ideologue. His intense blue eyes, deeply receded as though to keep them from leaping from their sockets, invited you to glimpse the heavens. His gray beard hung stiffly like a pillar down his chest. A *kipah* rimmed with a motif of menorahs covered his head like a helmet; side locks dangled like straps. He wore a black suit and open-collared white shirt, but the somber effect of his rabbinic clothes was negated by his sandals, which he wore even in winter.

Yet appearance and place of residence and even ideology were misleading. No one was less deserving of the stereotype of the fanatic settler than Menachem Froman. For years he had been Israel's leading and virtually lone proponent of dialogue with Islam. Secular peace activists feared religious Muslims and tried instead to make peace with Westernized Arabs, while Orthodox Jews mistrusted dialogue as a threat to their self-contained world. Froman searched for elusive partners in any Muslim country that would admit him. He met with clerics in Egypt and Jordan and Kazakhstan and tried to convince them of the legitimacy of Israel's existence on religious grounds, precisely the basis for their rejection of the Jewish state. He'd even intended to fly to Iran, but the Israeli government had stopped him.

He was best known to the Israeli public for his bizarre, courageous, and ultimately futile outreach to Sheykh Yassin, head of
Hamas, the fundamentalist terrorist group. Froman had spent hours
with the sheykh in his Israeli prison, trying to convince him to suspend Hamas's suicide bombings. "Because of your followers, millions of people around the world think of Islam as a murderous
faith," Froman told the sheykh. "You are an old man. When you die,
God will play for you the TV scenes of the bombed buses. What will
you say then?"

When Yassin was released from prison, Froman traveled to the
sheykh's home in Gaza and was photographed greeting him while
wearing tefillin, extending a hand of peace bound in the straps of
Jewish devotion. Yassin invited him onto the stage of his welcome-
home rally, and the settler rabbi, embodiment of the Zionist enemy,
calmly faced thousands of Hamas supporters chanting death slogans
aimed at his people. Froman's neighbors in Tekoa mocked him as the
media rabbi, chasing after murderers and exploiting Jewish ritual for
the cameras. Some tried to expel him from his rabbinic post and
stopped talking to him altogether. Even many Israelis who weren't
on the right saw his courtship of Hamas as naive and irresponsible.
But Froman persisted. He was ready to talk to any Muslim, under
any circumstances, to help transform religion from a pretext for
hatred into an instrument for healing.

For Froman, promoting Muslim-Jewish dialogue was part of the
same messianic commitment that had led him to settle the West
Bank. This was, after all, the age of miracles. If the Jews had been
replanted in the biblical land, just as the prophets had predicted, then
surely the prophets' vision of peace between Israel and the nations
was also within reach. And the most urgent place to begin was healing the ancient feud between Isaac and Ishmael.

Nor was West Bank settlement, he argued, inherently inimical to
peace with Islam—only the settlers' attempt to impose Israeli sovereignty on the territories. Froman was willing to concede sovereignty,

even over his own settlement. What mattered to him was simply the right of Jews to live in the land of Israel, just as Arabs had the right to live in the Galilee. When the messiah came, every nation would in any case forfeit something of its independence. Froman even advocated internationalizing Jerusalem: Why shouldn't Israel anticipate the messianic era and turn the holy city into the capital of God's kingdom?

Froman's peace-making efforts weren't merely pragmatic. He loved Islam. Like the descendants of Maimonides who had created a kind of Jewish Sufism, Froman believed that the Muslims had preserved mystical secrets of ancient Israel that the Jews had lost when they went into exile. In the Muslim immersion of the body in prayer he saw the movement of the high priest on Yom Kippur; in the Sufi dance, he saw the ecstatic inducements of the prophets.

Froman spent much of the day studying mystical texts while wearing tefillin. He dreamed of combining his mystical passion with his outreach to Islam, and he searched for Muslims with whom he could study kabbalistic and Sufi texts and perhaps even dance and pray. He'd found Islamic clerics willing to join him in denouncing violence and affirming peace, but a Muslim soul partner eluded him.

And then he met Sheykh Ibrahim. Eliyahu had brought Ibrahim to an interfaith conference that Froman was also attending; the sheykh and the rabbi talked through the night, holding hands. They were very different personalities: Froman was ironic and Talmudically long-winded, Ibrahim spontaneous and direct. Froman was a religious scholar immersed in texts, while Ibrahim seemed to know only enough of Islam's sacred works to offer a requisite quote. Yet they shared a longing for ecstasy, a love of laughter, an inclination to showmanship, and, most of all, a willingness to enter dangerous territory for the sake of religious peace and a courageous indifference to the judgment of their own communities, which paradoxically respected them as religious figures but dismissed their passion for peace with the enemy.

They began visiting each other's homes, casually dropping in until they forgot how unusual it was for a Palestinian sheykh and a settler rabbi to fraternize. Ibrahim had no political qualms about coming to Tekoa. The land of the prophets was intended for both Muslims and Jews. Since neither Ibrahim nor Froman owned a car or knew how to drive, they relied on students and followers to chauffeur them. That is how they lived generally, buoyed by the largesse of the cosmos. They showed up in each other's homes late at night, when both men felt most alive. They were residents of the same sleepless territory, the nocturnal Holy Land, where the messiah pressed against the darkness and angels appeared in beams of light, and decent men confronted their failure to become embodiments of their best desires.

A phone call from Sheykh Ibrahim: "Yossi Halevi! My brother from the world of souls, where are you! I'm in Rabbi Froman's house. We're waiting for you! Come quickly. It's a *piguah ahavah!*"

I laughed at his invented Hebrew phrase. A *piguah* is a terrorist attack; *ahavah* means love. A *piguah ahavah,* then, is a "love attack." What made the phrase so mischievous was that Ibrahim had provocatively chosen the one word, *piguah,* that best defined Jewish fear and rage toward Muslims to convey his own harmlessness.

The sheykh had been in Hebron exorcising a jinn and had decided to drop in to Tekoa. He was in the neighborhood, as he put it. Technically, he was right. The distance between Tekoa and Hebron was perhaps a half-hour drive. Yet only Ibrahim and Froman would consider the mutually negating geographies of Arab Hebron and Jewish Tekoa to be the same neighborhood. In the love between rabbi and sheykh, even distances on the West Bank contracted to their natural dimensions.

Though I tried to avoid the West Bank's back roads at night, I couldn't resist an invitation to a *piguah ahavah,* and I headed out for

Tekoa. The narrow road was unlit; I took comfort from the minarets rising in the desert hills, their tips illumined like lighthouses.

Tekoa was built as a dare on the edge of a vast desert wadi. About two hundred families lived there, and—unusual for an ideological West Bank community—they were a mix of religious and secular. Residents raised goats, grew mushrooms, and experimented with alternative energy. From the road Tekoa appeared forbidding, its red-roofed houses clustered together and imposed on the landscape. But from within, the settlement relaxed into gardens and stone-marked paths.

In the hallway near the entrance of the Froman house, a part of the wall had been deliberately broken, in mourning for the destroyed Temple. But the words of Isaiah, chiseled onto a stone plaque, countered with a vision of the Jewish return to Jerusalem: "And when you see this, your heart shall rejoice, and your bones shall flourish like grass." Those emotional poles of intensity and relief defined the Froman home. In one sense, this was an ideological bastion, where the Fromans' ten children were being raised to serve the Jewish people and the land of Israel. Yet this cramped house with inadequate rooms and damp walls was a happy clutter of books and toys and children's art. The walls were covered with watercolors of the nearby desert, painted by Froman's wife, Hadassah. The living room was a cross between a children's playroom and a yeshiva, including a wooden bench where Froman spent his long nights bent over religious books.

Despite its strict Orthodox Judaism and ideological commitments, this was a house of freedom. When one son flirted with the far-right Kach movement, Menachem and Hadassah didn't try to dissuade him, even though Kach, spiritual home of Baruch Goldstein, represented the antithesis of their Judaism. Nor did they intervene when a daughter joined the meditation group of a Hindu guru in Tel Aviv. The Fromans' front door was always open, and children of all ages constantly dropped by. Even if some of Tekoa's adults kept their distance from the eccentric rabbi, their children loved to hang out in the Froman home, the only place where they were likely to meet left-wing politicians and New Age hippies and even a Muslim sheykh, all considered alien or hostile in the settlement's constricted world.

Sheykh Ibrahim was laughing in the living room with Menachem and Hadassah and their daughter Shuvayah ("God returns"), who had recently completed her army duty and was studying to become a teacher. Hadassah and Shuvayah were barefoot and wore floor-length Indian-style skirts that were a happy compromise between bohemianism and religious modesty. A young man named Muhammad, who was the sheykh's driver for the evening, was silently smoking cigarettes.

"Yossi Halevi!" the sheykh proclaimed, like a sportscaster announcing a remarkable play. He fell on me and repeatedly kissed me on either cheek. I felt he could have continued kissing me indefinitely. He led me by the hand and sat me beside him on the couch. We held hands for long minutes; the sheykh wouldn't release his grip. Menachem and Hadassah beamed at us, delighted to see affection between a Muslim and a Jew.

The sheykh recounted a dream of one of his followers: "The sheykh's mosque was filled with Jews. Filled with Jews! In one room, Jews praying. In another room, Jews eating. In another room, Jews sleeping. My Hasid couldn't understand what was happening! 'Sheykh Ibrahim, why is your mosque full of Jews?'"

We laughed with the sheykh.

"Tell Yossi Halevi how Sheykh Ibrahim healed you," the sheykh urged Hadassah.

Obediently, she told me that she'd long suffered from kidney problems; getting up in the morning had been especially painful. Then the sheykh performed his healing, reciting a verse from the Koran over a glass of water and instructing Hadassah to drink it. The next morning, for the first time in years, she awoke without pain.

"Thanks to the God in heaven!" Ibrahim said. "This story makes

Sheykh Ibrahim very happy. Why? Because God has heard my prayers. God? Has heard? My prayers! I am not a prophet, I am not an angel, I am not a saint. But God has heard my prayers!" He clapped and spread his arms.

Froman raised his eyes and turned his palms upward, thanking God for the sheykh.

"How did you do it?" Shuvayah asked.

"I didn't do anything. I prayed to God to send a saint to examine Hadassah Froman. The saint whispered to me a verse from the Koran, through the heart, not the ear!"

Until now, I had regarded the sheykh as healer and exorcist in the same way: symbolically, exorcising our hatreds and healing our wounds. That seemed to me his true spiritual power. Yet perhaps I'd underestimated Ibrahim.

"What was Hadassah's verse?" I asked.

He quoted: "'And say: Truth has arrived and falsehood perished. For falsehood is bound to perish.'"

It seemed a particularly apt verse for Hadassah Froman. Her gaze was frankly penetrating, probing for truth, while her stubborn mouth was set to proclaim and defend the truths she discovered. Her life was a series of hard commitments. She had moved to Tekoa when it was still a desert hill and raised a family in a mobile home until permanent houses were built, then endured a decade of Intifada when simply traveling the roads turned her children into frontline soldiers; and now she had followed her husband into another kind of desolation, the lonely path of dialogue with Islam.

Hadassah said to the sheykh, "When you prayed before, I felt the power in the whole house."

"Right, my mother is the most spiritual person here?" asked Shuvayah.

"One of the spiritual people," the sheykh replied, smiling.

Hadassah said, "Muslim prayer makes so much sense to me. The combination of body movements and repetition of a single phrase focuses the devotion. Our prayers can be so heavy; we have so many words."

But then, fearing she'd gone too far in her criticism of Judaism, she quickly added, "We all have our particular path. In the end of days, we'll be one, that's for sure. But now we're still in the time of separation. The sheykh lives beyond separation. Of all the Muslims we've met, he is the most able to get to that place of oneness." She spoke with admiration and perhaps a little envy. The sheykh seemed an emissary from the messianic time whose pull had brought her to Tekoa and determined her life. Yet she herself remained caught in that time of transition when the messianic oneness could be glimpsed but the world of distinctions still imposed its commitments.

Menachem said, "Sheykh Ibrahim, I know many Muslims, but you are the first who was willing to come to my home even though I live in a settlement."

"When I told people that I was going to visit Rabbi Froman, they said to me, 'Sufi Sheykh, don't go to the settlers! They hate Arabs. They'll kill you!' I was afraid! Maybe they'll kill me! But the angel said to me, 'Don't be like Jonah the Prophet! Don't run away from your job!' So I went to Rabbi Froman's house. Do they hate the Sufi Sheykh in Rabbi Froman's house? Or do they love him? Is there hatred in this house or is there love?"

Froman sat down on the couch beside the sheykh and rested his head on Ibrahim's shoulder.

The absence of awkwardness was perhaps the real miracle of this encounter. No protracted silences, no careful formulations to avoid offending sensitivities, only the happy random talk of friends. When the conversation quieted, the sheykh intoned, "Thanks to the God in Heaven Who has brought us together." Menachem raised his palms in a silent amen.

"The sheykh was telling us about your visit to Abu Falestin," Hadassah said to me. "Menachem and I also went to see him. He showed no respect to Menachem. He feels threatened by anyone of stature."

"It's sad that there is only one Sheykh Ibrahim and only one Rabbi Froman," I said.

"Rabbi Yossi," Menachem said, teasing me, "I must strongly disagree. When the Prophet Elisha was being chased by the soldiers of Aram, he was protected by invisible soldiers of fire. God has to open your eyes. You need to see all the invisible rabbis and sheykhs trying to make peace. We're protected all the time by beings of fire. What is there to be afraid of, Yossi Halevi?" He adopted the sheykh's habit of calling me by both my names.

Shuvayah said, "I bet the sheykh can see many more people than us sitting in this room right now."

Ibrahim raised his eyebrows, pointed at Shuvayah, and laughed, as if to say: You caught me.

Ibrahim was charmed by the rabbi's lovely daughter, who had long blond hair and her mother's bluntness and resolve. "My Hasid," he called her. He had obviously never met a young woman like her: traditional but restless, respectful of her elders yet unafraid to challenge them. She was filled with questions, which she blurted randomly. What does Islam say about the soul? Do you believe in reincarnation? Are there different kinds of jinns? "Ask, Shuvayah, ask!" the sheykh encouraged, while Menachem rolled his eyes in feigned exasperation, then smiled with pride.

"What about dreams?" demanded Shuvayah. "Do you have interpretation of dreams in Islam like we have in the Talmud?"

The sheykh assured her that Islam had a fine tradition of dream interpretation.

I told the sheykh about a dream I'd recently had. I was in Hebron with my wife, Sarah. Suddenly, without provocation, Palestinian police opened fire on us. We instinctively understood that this wasn't just a random incident but the start of the next war. As Israeli soldiers escorted us into a truck, Sarah said to me, "I want a divorce." "A divorce?" I said, stunned. "But we've never even fought!" When I awoke, I sensed that the dream wasn't personal but symbolic. My Sarah was obviously symbolic of Mother Sarah, who was buried in Hebron. But what did it mean?

For the first time, there was awkward silence. No one appreciated the dream's reminder of the real world outside the Fromans' living room. Simply by invoking the possibility of war, I had violated the suspension of reality necessary to maintain our Muslim-Jewish gathering, our *piguah ahavah*.

"This is the time of peace, not war," the sheykh finally pronounced. "There are dreams and visions. Dreams? And visions. Yossi Halevi had a dream, not a vision."

The sheykh retrieved a scrap of paper from inside his robe and made a note. "Tonight, Yossi Halevi, I will say two prayers. One for you and Sarah. The other for Hebron." The first prayer in case my dream was personal; the second prayer in case it wasn't.

The conversation quickly resumed its happy freneticism, impelled by Shuvayah's enthusiasm.

"Can a Jew go to a Muslim teacher?" she asked the sheykh.

"When a teacher goes to God," he asked in turn, "where does the student go? To Tel Aviv?" Laughter. "Where the teacher goes, there the student goes."

"So what was wrong with this woman in Hebron whom you exorcised?" asked Shuvayah, as if we'd just been discussing her case.

"The doctors said she had a psychiatric problem," answered the sheykh. "I checked her—not me, the saint whom God sent checked her. She had a jinn in her body."

"Who is possessed more, women or men?"

The sheykh replied diplomatically, "Both."

Shuvayah insisted, "But who more?"

Menachem said, "Women."

The sheykh nodded. Shuvayah made a face.

"Women are more spiritually open," Menachem offered.

He retrieved a kabbalistic work from his chaotic bookshelves and asked Shuvayah to read aloud its description of an exorcism of a young girl. Ten scholars, read Shuvayah, circled the girl and chanted, *"Shalom aleichem,* out, out, out." The demon staggered, lifted the girl's left leg, and was expelled from her smallest toe.

The sheykh nodded vigorously with recognition. "No rest in the war against the jinns! If I sleep, the jinns will kill me or my family! If I sleep a little bit, they'll kill me a little bit! A sheykh called me at two in the morning and said, 'Sheykh Ibrahim, I am protecting you from the jinns! A hundred jinns are coming against you!'"

"A hundred jinns!" repeated Shuvayah, laughing with amazement.

"A thousand jinns!" shouted the sheykh.

He was right. He was surrounded by jinns, human jinns. So was Menachem Froman. At any moment the jinns could strike, maddened by the love between rabbi and sheykh.

Two young women, friends of Shuvayah, dropped by. They wore long skirts and T-shirts and sandals, at once informal and chaste. They whispered among themselves and moved close together, shy in the company of such strange strangers. Shuvayah spoke for them: "We'd like a blessing from the sheykh." Menachem, laughing, said to one of the young women, "What will your father say? He'll think I'm trying to convert you to Islam." One by one they approached the sheykh, who placed his hands on their heads and offered a silent blessing. "Amen!" said Menachem, almost shouting with delight.

It was time to go. Froman embraced the sheykh's driver, Muhammad, and said to him, "Drive safely, and call us when you get home." That is what settlers, veterans of the Intifada gauntlet, said to their own children when they went on the road. Froman felt such intimacy toward his guests that he apparently forgot that Muhammad's car had Palestinian license plates and so was hardly at risk of getting stoned.

The sheykh rode with me back to his village. As we slowly pulled out of Tekoa's parking lot, Menachem ran over to the car and extended his head through the sheykh's open window. They kissed each other on the cheeks, then kissed each other's hands, as if only an exaggeration of love could dispel the hatred between Palestinians and Jews.

We drove out the electronic gate, past the soldier in the guardhouse protecting the settlement as though it were an army base. "The Sufi heart is like a fountain," Ibrahim said. "Whoever is thirsty, let him drink."

Then, suddenly subdued, he said almost to himself, "To go from being a high school principal to a Sufi sheykh is very hard. Why did God choose me for this job?"

"Because you have an open heart," I replied dutifully.

"And it flows outward," he said.

6

I was driving through a cold and foggy night with Sheykh Ibrahim and Eliyahu. The hills and the road were hidden by mist. I didn't feel in control of the car, which seemed to be impelling itself through the white darkness. I tried to relax. Moving through fog and relinquishing control were key elements of the Ibrahim experience.

We were heading toward the Sufi mosque of Sheykh Saud Abu-Laben for its weekly Thursday night ceremony of *zikr*. For Sufis, *zikr*, which focused the mind on God through a controlled combination of chant and dance and rapid breath, was the ultimate moment of devotion. Whenever I'd asked Ibrahim for techniques of prayer, he invariably cited *zikr*. The problem was that the *zikr* circle was usually off-limits to outsiders, especially in this land. Eliyahu, who had participated in *zikr* after his conversion in Cairo, had been searching for a Palestinian Sufi community that would admit him into the sacred circle. But most Sufi groups were reluctant even to host Jews as spectators.

Perhaps tonight would be different. Sheykh Ibrahim, after all, often participated in the *zikr* of Sheykh Saud, who belonged to the Qadiri Sufi sect, which was closely affiliated to Ibrahim's own Rifa'i. And the mosque was located in the mixed Arab-Jewish town of Ramle, near Tel Aviv. Perhaps Ramle's Muslims, who were Israeli citizens and lived with Jewish neighbors, wouldn't be unnerved by Jews entering their mosque, even for *zikr*. Ibrahim assured me that he'd phoned Sheykh Saud, and there was no problem. "Tonight," he proclaimed, "Yossi Halevi and Eliyahu will do *zikr*!"

Eliyahu had brought Sufi-style *kipot* for both of us: large knitted skullcaps with large spaces between the stitches, forming patterns of emptiness. To wear a Sufi *kipah* wasn't only a sign of respect to our hosts; we were intentionally avoiding the standard Israeli knitted *kipah,* which Arabs identified with West Bank settlers. In the Middle East, what you wore or didn't wear, especially on your head, defined who you were.

We had chosen this night to visit Sheykh Saud's mosque because of the imminent Muslim festival of Id el-Adha, commemorating Abraham's sacrifice of Ishmael. Since it fell this year on a Saturday, when Eliyahu and I didn't travel, this *zikr* before the *Id* was as close to the festival as we'd get.

Id el-Adha embodied the Jewish problem with Islam. By placing Ishmael instead of Isaac on Abraham's altar, Islam had rewritten one of our most basic myths. Christianity had tried to expropriate the Jewish story by turning itself into the new Israel, but at least it hadn't distorted our founding myths; when the church finally made its peace with the Jews, it could readily respect its Judaic roots. With Islam, though, we argued over the root itself. Islam regarded the Torah (and the New Testament) as approximations of truth, alternately respecting the Jews for possessing a revelatory text and despising them for distorting it. That theological dispute was subtly replayed in the Palestinian-Israeli conflict. The Palestinians resented us as usurpers of their land, their homes, even their cuisine. But we resented them as usurpers of our narrative, inventing a national consciousness only in response to Zionism and with the sole purpose of displacing it; mimicking our millennial longing for Zion with a crude young nationalism whose motive often seemed hatred of the Jews more than love of the land. They even attempted to usurp our martyrdom, daring to call their partly self-inflicted suffering a holocaust. They were still trying to displace Isaac from the altar.

"Sheykh Ibrahim," I said, "we believe that Isaac was on the altar and you believe it was Ishmael. What do we do with our conflicting versions of the truth?"

The sheykh dismissed my concern. "There is no problem. No problem! What was Ishmael's greatness? What was Isaac's greatness? That they accepted whatever God wanted. That they accepted? Whatever God wanted! I wish for Yossi Halevi's children, for Ibrahim's children, to be like Ishmael and Isaac." The sheykh was admonishing me: Don't focus on the conflicting details but on the unifying message of the two narratives. Let it be Isaac, let it be Ishmael, or better yet, let it be both. There was enough room on the altar for all those Muslims and Jews whose love of God was stronger than their fear of death.

"How can we make peace between Sarah and Hagar?" Eliyahu asked the sheykh.

Eliyahu's point provided a necessary balance to my Jewish resentment of Islam: Palestinians had politicized Ishmael's usurpation of the altar, but we Israelis had continued Sarah's expulsion of Hagar from Abraham's tent.

"There is peace between Sarah and Hagar!" insisted the sheykh. "Why did Sarah expel Hagar? Because she was jealous of her? No! I know Sarah. She is good, she is holy! Sarah would never do such a thing out of anger. Sarah had to send her away! When Hagar was in the desert, what did she do? Cry out to God. Cry out? To God! Then the Bedouin saw her pray and they also started to pray! Hagar went to the desert to teach the Bedouin how to pray! How? To pray. That's why Sarah had to send her away!"

Ramle was a working-class town of graceless apartment blocs and old stone houses more ruinous than quaint. In honor of Id el-Adha, the streets were illumined with Christmas decorations, five-pointed stars, and strings of red and green bulbs. Perhaps the well-intentioned Jewish authorities assumed that non-Jewish holidays were interchangeable. The mosque of Sheykh Saud Abu-Laben was located on a side street, behind an empty lot. It was a sad-looking structure, without dome or minaret, little more than a shack with a corrugated roof—the Islamic equivalent of a Hasidic *shtiebl*, a poor, one-room synagogue.

The sheykh came out to greet us. He wore a high, triangular-peaked white hat, incongruously regal in such shabby surroundings. He was perhaps in his early thirties, with a sharp black beard and narrow eyes, a wary, watchful face. He embraced Ibrahim but held out a limp hand to Eliyahu and me. An old man in a gray beard and stiff white cap asked us bluntly in Hebrew, "Are you Jews?" We nodded with foreboding. He spoke in a harsh Arabic to Ibrahim; whatever he said, it wasn't welcoming.

We removed our shoes and stepped inside. Though only a dozen men and boys were sitting on mattresses against the walls, the long and narrow room felt crowded. The walls pulsated with cymbals and drums and drawings of the Kaaba and the Dome of the Rock. Each of the ninety-nine names of God was contained in its own little diamond, and there were quotes from the Koran in green and blue and yellow letters bound by still-visible pencil lines. There were framed photographs of the same stern, white-bearded man: Abdul-Rahim of Gaza, Ibrahim's sheykh and also Saud's.

We sat down in a corner. The old men and teenagers pretended we weren't there, while the young boys frankly stared. Ibrahim had obviously neglected to mention to Sheykh Saud that the visitors he was bringing were Jews. We had come to a place where we didn't belong. Maybe the very premise of my journey was flawed. What was the point of imposing myself on a faith that wanted to be left alone?

Fortunately, it was time for evening prayers, deflecting the awkwardness of our presence. The men arranged themselves in a straight line, the Islamic assembly of equality before God. To my surprise, Eliyahu simply stepped in. No one stopped him. He waved me over, and before I quite realized what was happening, I too joined the Muslim prayer line.

Ibrahim led the prayers. He shifted me forward and adjusted my shoulders so that I was fully aligned with the line. *"Allahu akbar,"* he called out, God is great, his voice deep and commanding. *"Allaaa-hu,"* he repeated, like a long exhalation, then quickly expelled *"akbar,"* as if any human description of His grandeur was superfluous. Israelis dreaded that call to prayer as incitement to murder: the terrorist's cry before pressing the detonator on a crowded bus. But Ibrahim restored to those words their benign intensity.

I entered the flow of Muslim surrender, so caught in the rapid hypnotic movement that I forgot my self-consciousness, even forgot to feel elated for having broken the barrier of Islamic prayer. *Allahu akbar:* bow and stand. *Allahu akbar:* kneel and prostrate and kneel. *Allahu akbar:* prostrate and kneel. *Allahu akbar:* stand. And again, over and over, disorienting and reorienting, aligning the self with the prayer line and offering the body to God. *Allahu akbar:* prostrate and kneel. I wanted to remain prostrate, embraced by surrender, but the will of the line pulled me up to my knees. My body lost solidity, as if its bones had been extracted; turning to water, a particle in a wave of prayer.

Two teenagers removed drums from the wall, while older men

took cymbals. This was the warm-up to the *zikr* dance. The drums and cymbals overwhelmed the little space; I felt claustrophobic with noise. I closed my eyes and tried to resist by meditating. The result was an instant headache. Meditation and *zikr* both aspired to the same goal, absorption of the separated self into oneness. But they used opposite means: physical stillness and vigorous movement, silence and cacophony. The forms didn't mix.

The dance began. Once again Eliyahu simply entered and waved me in. The tight circle opened and absorbed me. The two young men with drums stood outside the circle and beat the rhythm, only gradually accelerating. *La illaha ill'Allah,* there is no god but God. *La illaha ill'Allah!* Faster. *Allah-hu!* Exhale. *Allah-hu!* Exhale. Twist left, inhale, twist right, exhale.

Sheykh Saud stood in the center of the circle and moved from person to person, measuring the breathing and chanting and movement with his downturned palm, slowing down those going too fast and speeding up laggards. When I missed a step, he gently moved me back in sync. He knew how to quiet and to rouse, how much intensity each body could bear.

Saud stopped the dance and everyone stood in place. Exhale and bow: *Allah hai!* God is alive. Inhale and back upright: *Allah hai!* Faster: *Allah hai Allah hai Allah hai Allah hai.* The center of the circle seemed like a pool into which we repeatedly dipped.

Saud shifted us to slower breath and a more relaxed chant. But a bearded young man in a black robe kept bowing and shouting "Allah!" jerking up and down without rhythm, possessed by *zikr.* "*Allahhaiallahhaiallahhai . . .*" Saud grabbed his arm, but his momentum was too furious. Finally, he tackled him to the ground and restored him to our pace.

The circle moved again. *Allah-hu, Allah-hu!* Spinning. Rapid exhalation: *Hu-Hu-Hu-Hu.* God's name merging into breath.

Saud motioned to Ibrahim to enter the circle in his place. Ibrahim strode into the center with determined steps. Unlike Saud, he didn't only direct the dance but joined in. "A-llah!" he proclaimed. "A-llaw," a deep, joyous growl. He stepped and twisted and chanted and exhaled with elegant swiftness, like a man half his age. It was a remarkable performance, at one with the circle even as he led it. I felt I was seeing him for the first time. Only now, watching him as a controlled ecstatic, did I finally glimpse the context for his frenetic joy.

Ibrahim held up a forefinger. *"Wa-had,"* one. Then: *"Eh-had,"* one, in Hebrew. It was a generous and daring nod to Eliyahu and me. The dancers were so focused that they followed Ibrahim's linguistic shift without hesitation, back and forth between Arabic and Hebrew.

The circle stopped—rapid exhalation and repeated bowing. I began to sway. I lost my breath; I wanted to retch. Ibrahim noticed immediately. He held me by the shoulders and breathed slowly and demonstratively, until I felt my breath return in rhythm with his, as if he had resuscitated me.

The *zikr* lasted perhaps an hour. I felt charged, cleansed, as if I'd been submerged underwater and had learned to breathe in a new way. To my surprise, I felt purged of my unease in this place, at home among its lovers of God. They obviously felt the same way toward me. For the first time, we made eye contact and exchanged smiles. We were at once too exhausted, too energized, and too exposed to hide behind wariness. Even though we didn't know each other's names, we had together inhaled the name of God, joined in the brotherhood of the *zikr*.

We drank intensely sugared tea, ate baklava, and talked of the sweetness of God. The young man who'd convulsed during *zikr* paraphrased an old Sufi idea: "If you pray for the Garden of Eden, you'll go to hell. You pray only to receive God's love, not paradise." Sheykh Saud smiled and smoked a narghile.

This mosque was a family project: Everyone here belonged to the Abu-Laben clan. They were working-class people; the sheykh himself was a car mechanic.

"What do the other Muslims think of you?" Eliyahu asked.

"That we're crazy," replied Saud's father. "They think we chant the name 'Abdallah' instead of 'Allah.'" Laughter.

I asked Saud what he'd experienced during the *zikr*. "That our hearts kept getting closer and closer to God," he said, with the Sufi vagueness I'd so often encountered from Ibrahim. Yet that was as precise a definition of the experience as I needed.

Ibrahim, not to be poetically outdone, added, "Our souls went up to heaven like clouds."

"When I first entered," I said, "I felt like a stranger. But now I feel we are brothers."

"When you pray together," said the sheykh's father, "you form one heart."

I felt sad for this forlorn Sufi *shtiebl*. Here was an Islam with which we could make peace, yet it was almost absurdly peripheral. Still, maybe the fact that even a handful of Muslims and Jews had danced together was enough for God to work with; perhaps He would magnify our prayers, widen the circle of ecstasy.

Saud's uncle, Mahmoud, the old man who had initially demanded to know if we were Jews, eyed us warily through narghile smoke. Finally, unable to control himself, he demanded, "Why do you come from America to this land? You weren't born here. And my relatives who were expelled from Ramle in 1948 can't come back. Where is the justice?"

In another context I would have reminded him that his side had begun the 1948 war, that Arabs and Jews amply shared justice and injustice. But I was a guest, and it wasn't my place to quarrel. And maybe, too, the *zikr* was responsible; for now at least, I'd lost my interest in the argument.

Instead, I said only, "I didn't come to Israel as an individual but as a member of the Jewish people returning to its land. And now I've met my Muslim brothers who are also part of this land."

The answer seemed to please him, but he wasn't quite finished. He had one more test for Eliyahu and me. "If I prepare a sheep and bake it with rice and invite you to my table, would you come?" He was probing whether we, as religious Jews, would eat his nonkosher food, whether we would place ritual purity before the fellowship of the *zikr*. I'd said we were brothers; was that just a line?

Eliyahu and I explained that we were both vegetarians, but if he prepared a vegetarian meal, we would be honored to eat at his table.

Mahmoud relaxed. "There is a synagogue across the street, but we've never been to their services, and they've never been to ours," he said, with regret now instead of anger. In Ramle, Jews and Arabs visited each other's homes and celebrated and mourned together. But religion, potentially the deepest meeting point, remained untouchable.

The little clan escorted us to our car. We all embraced. "Come back soon," Mahmoud urged. "And bring more Jews like you."

As we drive back toward Karawa, Ibrahim said, "When we came in, they said to me, 'Ibrahim, why are you bringing Jews here? It's not enough we live with Jews all around us; we have to have them in the mosque, too?' Now they want you to move in with them. 'Come back! Bring your friends!' Now there is love between Eliyahu and Yossi and Sheykh Saud. The *zikr* cleans the heart."

He laughed. "It was better at Saud's than at Abu Falestin's. Love is better than death."

PART II

three

Lent

I

At first I'd taken Sister Johanna for a simple person, and only gradually did I realize how wrong I was and how pleased she would be by my mistake. While her fellow sisters were cloistered in silence, secluded even from one another, Johanna's job was to mediate between the convent and the outside world. Johanna tended to guests who came on retreat and addressed groups of noisy, friendly, secular Israelis who came for a quick look around and invariably asked the same practical Jewish questions about how the nuns earned a living and why they didn't marry, and then loudly berated each other for disturbing the silence as they walked through the halls. I wondered whether Johanna had been appointed to those duties because she was unsuited for more profound spiritual work. She was thin and slightly hunched in her hooded white robe, which didn't convey mystery but anonymity, precisely its purpose. She avoided overt piety, and her apparently untroubled personality seemed to me too cheerful, unspiritual. Yet years of struggle had gone into whittling away a brooding self-preoccupation. And as she chatted with visitors about the weather and the flowers, and laughed at the mistakes in her adequate Hebrew, another part of her was silently invoking God's presence and praying for alleviation of the problems that visitors, Jews and Muslims as well as Christians, brought to Johanna for the sisters' intercession.

Johanna was in her mid-forties when we met, and I didn't know then that she had lived almost half her life in silence. During that time, she had spoken with her fellow nuns only once a week, on Sunday afternoons, when they left the walled enclosure and strolled through the olive groves around the convent. Sometimes she would awaken in the predawn with a prayer, as though continuing a prayer she'd been reciting all night. Throughout the day she repeated an exercise she'd learned from Maria Teresa, the mother superior, silently chanting the words of the "Jesus Prayer," borrowed by the Catholic sisters from the Orthodox tradition. Using a breathing technique, she would inhale the words "Lord Jesus, son of God," then exhale the words "have mercy on me." After a while the chant became automatic, like breath itself. Inhaling Jesus, exhaling mercy.

The sisters made pottery to help support the convent. But to encourage detachment, no cup or vase was entirely done by any sister; instead, one woman shaped the clay, another drew the outline of a pattern, a third painted, and a fourth fired the final result. Johanna, who had been an artist before entering the convent, learned to renounce not just the artistic product but the artistic process itself. Like singing in the chapel: Twice a day they assembled there, each sister in her cubicle, invisible to each other and joining only their voices in ethereal harmony. It didn't matter if the gallery was empty or filled with guests; they immortalized their song by offering it to no one but God.

When Maria Teresa asked Johanna to exchange seclusion for work in reception, Johanna tried to accept without regret. Silence and speech were really no different: You could be garrulous in silence and silent in speech; it depended only on stilling the mind's outward groping. Even the repetitive talks she gave to Israeli groups, which she'd resented at first as rote, became another form of prayer, conveying something of the harmony of this house to the anxious people of Israel, for whose peace and safety Johanna and the sisters constantly prayed.

She grew up in Brussels. Her father had suffered severe head injuries in an army-related accident, yet the family never discussed his condition. The most important matters, Johanna realized early on, belonged to silence. One day, at age eight, she told her sisters that when she grew up she would be a nun. They reacted with incomprehension; the family was secular and never went to church. From then on, Johanna kept the decision to herself, another vital matter consigned to silence. Even as a teenager, when she briefly decided that she no longer believed in God ("God was so important to me that I had to vehemently reject Him") and the notion of becoming a nun horrified her ("Those pale old women in black; ehh!"), she knew she was fated to enter a convent.

In her early twenties she joined a Catholic-sponsored communal house whose residents included both "normal" and retarded people. They lived together in the same rooms and worked together in a pottery shop. The idea was to integrate the retarded into ordinary life. Instead, Johanna found herself wanting to be integrated into their world. She wanted to be like them: simple, transparent, without ego and self-consciousness. What defines a human being? she asked herself. Is it the body and the intelligence or the soul? These people didn't have fine bodies or minds, but they were beautiful souls, grateful for the least kindness. They seemed to achieve what Johanna had tried to do as an artist, to penetrate the surface of things to their essence. When the messiah came, she believed, those who would be revealed as his closest friends were precisely those who'd mattered least in our material world.

Yet a part of her resisted the humiliation of total identification with the retarded. She couldn't overcome the sense of "us" and "them"; losing that final distinction was as terrifying as death. And she couldn't allow herself to forget what a good person she was for sacrificing a normal life to live with "them."

One day, a wealthy woman, a potential donor, visited the house. Johanna was tinkering in the community's workshop. The woman, mistaking her for one of the retarded residents, said in the exaggerated way the normal speak to the mentally handicapped, "Aren't you a darling! And look how nicely you're working!" Johanna's first instinct was to correct the woman; instead, she bowed her head and said nothing. At that moment, she surrendered to silence.

The community housed a chapel, where the Host was on permanent display. Johanna began spending increasing time alone there. Her mind kept returning to the title of a book written by the community's founder, *Your Silence Is Calling Me*. The title referred to the silence of the retarded, but for Johanna that phrase now took on a different meaning: Jesus' silent suffering for humanity.

Johanna joined Sister Maria Teresa's order, entered silence, and moved to the convent in Israel. She emerged twenty years later with a merciless clarity about herself. But without morbidity; she lost the novice seeker's grim determination, which is merely a more subtle form of self-infatuation. She didn't make peace with her imperfections but no longer raged against them, accepting herself as a hopelessly flawed being. She was still capable of being judgmental and caught herself in unkind thoughts. But only by admitting your own imperfections could you appreciate God's perfection, become the imperfect child, safe in the Father's perfect love. She thought often of John the Baptist, who spoke of being a child in the desert. Uncomplicated, guileless, pared to essence. Just like the retarded, unbound by convention and with nothing to lose. Through silence, Johanna had in effect become one of them: useless to society, a broken vessel for God's perfection.

"Johanna, how do you give your life to God?"

We were sitting in the convent's reception room, adorned only with an icon of Mary, whose round black eyes seemed to take in the world's darkness.

Johanna said, "You don't give your life to God once. You do it every minute, in the choices you make."

"How do you work on yourself all the time?"

"You try to work on yourself," she replied, laughing. "Wearing yourself down a little more each time." She rubbed her hand against the wood table, smoothing it.

"How many times have I said to myself as a nun, 'Enough! I can't do this anymore.' Those moments help make you small. And if you overcome those moments, your smallness opens a new way."

"What does it mean to make yourself small?"

"The way to God is the way of smallness. To be a child. Even Jesus had to start as a child. Whoever asks God for humility will for sure get his request. And then watch out." She laughed. "Our effort is to cut the ground from under our feet. And even a little of the feet too. It's frightening. But you get such a feeling of inner freedom that you're ready to go through it again. You can get rebuked in every possible way. In community, there's always someone to say, 'Who do you think you are?' Even if not in words. We have so many corners of pride; it's the innermost sin. David said it in Psalms; don't you know it?"

"I'm very small in Judaism," I said.

She leaned forward and seemed to laugh with her whole body.

"The secret of God isn't just for the spiritual greats. It's for all of us. Even for the retarded. To be little gives an opening to God."

"What has been your hardest spiritual struggle, Johanna?"

"Overcoming sentimental love. The difficulty is to love truly, without discrimination. To love like Him. Totally and unequivocally, beyond the likes and dislikes of the personality. Jesus' message was love without borders. Telling the person next to him on the cross that he would be first to heaven. If you close your heart to even one person, it's not yet divine love. In the world, you are always making a border in the heart. You don't even see it. In the convent, you must see the border. It's easy to confuse sentimentality for true love. There is too much sentimentalism in the church. I heard a cassette from another order about Christmas; it was so emotional."

She slapped herself on the mouth. "I need another twenty years of silence," she said and laughed.

"It happens little by little," she continued. "God isn't in the clouds. How you prepare food, how you pray, how ready you are to ask for forgiveness. How do I sweep? Do I round the corners or am I thorough? That's love. I know that I don't yet love that way. For many years I thought I did. But my sins helped me see that I was fooling myself. If we see ourselves honestly, we begin to see God."

She spoke so vigorously, and her eyes widened with such delight, that I didn't realize she was actually speaking softly.

I was going to ask her if we could meditate together when she said, "Maybe we'll have silence now."

I closed my eyes. The four Hebrew letters of the divine Name swelled across my forehead and swallowed the space before me. A clock was ticking; the silence thickened and I stopped hearing any sound. My throat constricted, squeezing the desire for voice. The Name condensed to a point of light, pulling me in.

I opened my eyes. Johanna's head had fallen forward, impelled by the force of silence. She opened her eyes and looked in my direction but didn't see me. Perfectly still. Emptied. Then she focused, noticed me, and smiled. We sat a little longer in silence.

When she finally spoke, her voice startled me. It was so thin, so inadequate to the powerful presence that had overtaken her in meditation. I would have been less surprised had she roared. It was, I realized, merely a borrowed voice with which to interact with the world; her real voice was silence.

"That's what I wanted to say," she said, and I thought she meant: The silence is what I wanted to say.

"It's the silence of this place that pulls," I said, finding speech painful.

" 'Your silence is calling me.' The more you search for God, the more He drifts away, the more delicate He becomes. He doesn't want us to catch Him in our hand and say, 'This is God.' I don't know if you can see God in this world and live. But this sense of His delicateness is already a kind of dying. To live in the desert, to be worn down all the time, become more and more refined. The prayer of monks and nuns is so simple. It's one word: Father, Father."

The highest form of prayer, she seemed to be saying, wasn't to petition or even to praise but simply to acknowledge God's presence.

"Johanna, are you sure God is present?"

She spread her arms wide and smiled.

2

I will call it simply "the convent." No name, no locale. The sisters request anonymity, absent to all but God.

Thirty sisters lived here in absolute silence. Of all the monastic communities I'd begun to visit, this was the most relentless, the least forgiving of imperfection. Life revolved around prayer, self-examination, and the constant invoking of God's presence, without distraction. The convent was a laboratory of the soul, a halfway house between this world and the next. The sisters seemed to live in the body only formally. Physical needs were reduced to the minimum, so that when death came it would be in some sense redundant.

Yet to describe the convent as "otherworldly" was to distort its purpose. The withdrawal into silence was tactical, and its goal was ultimately fuller engagement with the world by creating a cadre of loving protectors for humanity. The sisters didn't hide from the world's misfortunes but embraced them. Maria Teresa, the mother superior, monitored the news like an intelligence service of a great power for which events in the most remote corners had strategic implications. Every Sunday, when they came together for their weekly communal meal, the secluded nuns would be briefed by Maria Teresa about the latest human disasters—earthquake in Turkey, famine in Ethiopia, suicide bombings in Jerusalem—to be incorporated into their prayers, and also the personal requests of visitors to the convent, like the Israeli child who wrote in the guest book, "Please pray for me to do well in school and that there won't be any terrorist attacks."

The atmosphere of the convent wasn't gloomy but charged with focused purpose. I would see the sisters fleetingly, usually in the chapel of white stone and pale wood, each nun in her own cubicle, hooded and visible only in profile, like birds. At those moments, hearing them sing as a single exalted voice, I wanted nothing more than to stay as close as possible to this eruption of divinity. In their presence I felt the tragedy of gravity, the possibility of flight.

Maria Teresa, who by necessity no longer lived in silence, was firm and loving in equal measure, severity protecting tenderness. Her spiritual mission was to toughen the good, empower love with the same vigor that human beings ordinarily reserved for selfish pursuits. Years of silence seeped into her speech, slowing and sharpening her words. Yet she laughed easily, imbued with a spontaneous vivacity, an almost unbearable alertness. She carried God seemingly without effort, invoking Him as naturally as breath.

She treated her nuns with a fierce maternalism, alternately berating, inspiring, cajoling. Everyone saw a different face of her, depending on what each required for growth. A nun who took pride in her renunciation needed to be humbled, taught to see the cleverness of the ego, which could thrive even from its seeming negation. Yet Maria Teresa wasn't raising meek nuns but fighters for God. A nun with low self-esteem needed to see the good in herself, so that her will could be a strong sacrifice for God. When one of her nuns was feeling unworthy, Maria Teresa instructed her to keep a journal recording her positive deeds and thoughts. Sometimes even vanity could be tolerated: A nun's desire to outshine her sisters wasn't motivated only by ego but by desire to serve. Jesus, Maria Teresa reminded herself, warned against uprooting weeds before the wheat seeds had taken root. In most people, including her nuns, noble and selfish motives mingled, and a wise mother knew how to undermine the bad gradually, without damaging the good.

I looked forward to my meetings with Maria Teresa, but she invariably insisted that Johanna join us. Then, after a few minutes of conversation, Maria Teresa would leave us alone. She was, of course, busy directing the convent and tending to her nuns. But as my relationship with Johanna deepened, I began to realize that Maria Teresa was deliberately encouraging our meetings, as if she intuited some struggle that Johanna and I were meant to experience together.

3

Johanna was upset. She'd just read a commentary by a French rabbi about the biblical concept of the place of "strangers" in the land of Israel. For non-Jews to be worthy of living in the Holy Land, wrote the rabbi, they must observe the seven Noahide laws, the basic biblical moral code. Muslims, he continued, fully adhere to the Noahide laws because, he pointedly noted, they don't place statues—idols—in their houses of worship. Clearly, he was excluding Christians from the category of Noahide observers. "We defile the land," Johanna said, bitterly.

I explained that the rabbi had based his commentary on an outdated Jewish approach devised at a time when Christians had persecuted Jews. I mentioned the names of prominent rabbis through the centuries who had disagreed with that distorted view of Christianity as nonmonotheistic, including a nineteenth-century scion of the famous Soloveichik rabbinic dynasty, who wrote a sympathetic Hebrew commentary on the Book of Matthew. But those rabbinic voices, I admitted, were a minority.

Maria Teresa, who had joined us, said, "Judaism and Christianity both sinned by seeing each other as a lie. But we feel that the church has changed while Judaism is still against, against. Judaism always has to say that Christianity is false. That isn't the way to spiritual growth."

For centuries, I explained, we'd lived under pressure of conversion, and while the Catholic Church no longer missionized Jews, Evangelical Christians still organized campaigns aimed at converting us. "Christianity left us no choice but to define ourselves in opposition to it," I said.

"Otherwise, the Jewish people wouldn't have survived," acknowledged Maria Teresa.

"But we're not living a hundred years ago," Johanna protested. "Now it is the Jewish side, not the Christian side, that speaks with contempt."

"Johanna," I said, "we've barely begun to emerge from the Holocaust. Now that we've returned to the land of Israel, a process of healing can begin. But it will take time."

Maria Teresa said, "In God's wisdom it is obvious that the people of Israel had to return to its land. But the purpose wasn't political or material but spiritual. The Jewish people doesn't understand this. Its goal is to be like the other nations. It's absurd. After one of the terrorist bus bombings, a good friend of ours, a religious Jew, told me, 'We have to avenge it.' I was very surprised by his attitude. But he said, 'We're not Christians, Maria Teresa, we don't turn the other cheek.' As if to say that Christians are silly in their love. Tell me, Yossi, where is the greater strength, to hit back or restrain yourself?"

I felt myself reddening with anger. "Let me ask you a question," I said. "Can Israel survive in the Middle East without being strong?"

"First turn to God," said Johanna.

"Our means are different than yours," added Maria Teresa.

"How can you compare a convent to a state?"

Johanna said, "That is precisely the difference between Christianity and Judaism. Christianity isn't about political rule; Judaism is."

I was trying to keep my voice from rising. "When Jews hear Christians say that your way is love and our way is power, it reminds us of Christian contempt for Judaism as legalistic. Now that we can finally protect ourselves, Christians lecture us about power. But when Christianity ruled half the world, power was moral."

Maria Teresa said only, "It's not exactly that way."

Johanna: "We had a Hebrew teacher who was very close to us. She told us how her young son hates Saddam. 'I hate him, I hate him.' She said it with such enthusiasm. She was so proud of her son. I realized that hatred is in the Jewish religion."

"You can find all kinds of voices in Judaism," I countered. "There are those who say it is a mitzvah to hate Amalek. But there's also the rabbinic legend about God silencing the angels who sang when the Egyptians drowned in the Red Sea."

Maria Teresa said, "You're right. But the problem, as Johanna says, is that there is hatred in Judaism, in the religion itself."

"And not in Christianity?"

"In the hearts of people, yes. But not in the religion."

"When I read those terrible verses in the New Testament about 'the Jews,' I see hatred."

Johanna: "When I read those verses, I tell myself, it's also me. It's not 'the Jews' who killed Jesus, it's all of us."

"You understand it that way, Johanna, and now the church does too. But for two thousand years those verses were an excuse for murder."

When I began my journey into Christianity, I'd vowed never to argue with Christians about the past. But that's exactly what I now proceeded to do. I dredged up all the Jewish grudges against the church: the whole history of contempt, from the statues in medieval churches depicting the synagogue as a bent and blindfolded woman to the conversion sermons Jews were forced to hear before Christian holidays. "It isn't a coincidence that the Holocaust happened in Christian Europe," I said.

Maria Teresa, her voice turning softer to mute any trace of indignation, said only, "Nazism was a pagan revolt against Christianity too. It isn't fair to link it with Christianity."

Instead of discussing silence and prayer and the presence of God, we had fallen into the Jewish-Christian disputation. In the Middle Ages, Jews and Christians had argued theology; now we argued history. I was angry at myself for so easily losing my calm, and angry at Maria Teresa and Johanna for their distorted view of Judaism. The premise of this convent, as Johanna had explained to me, was to make yourself small. But where was their theological humility?

I got up to leave.

"Friends?" Johanna said, extending her hand.

Of course friends, which is precisely why I felt so depressed.

I returned the following week. I didn't want too much time to pass before we met again, afraid I might withdraw in anger and hurt. I sensed Maria Teresa's appreciation. This time, rather than leave Johanna and me alone, she lingered.

Maria Teresa was full of questions about the latest troubles of the right-wing government of Benjamin Netanyahu, which was disintegrating from within. "The situation is *al hapanim*," she said, using a colloquial Hebrew expression that literally translates as "on the face" and means "lousy." I was taken aback, especially after our last conversation, by her emotional involvement in our complex affairs. She seemed anxious and depressed like any Israeli by the spectacle of our self-devouring.

"So?" Maria Teresa looked at me, friendly, frank.

"It was difficult for me last week," I said.

She nodded and waited for me to continue.

"You had some harsh things to say about Judaism and the Jewish people. But listening to you now, I'm surprised by how connected you feel to Israel."

"What did you think?" said Johanna, incredulous.

Maria Teresa said, "There's so much to say about the beauty of the Jewish people. Israel stands like a tree. Strong. In today's world there's so much wavering." She swayed, as though stirred by the wind. "Here there is uprightness." Now she sat rigid, resolute like a soldier.

Johanna: "In Europe, simple people don't think about spiritual questions. Here, okay, there is the problem of materialism, but even simple people are very spiritual."

Maria Teresa: "Simple people, average people, intellectuals. Faith in God is very strong. I'm often surprised by it. Many Israelis say, 'I don't believe in God.' But it's not true."

Johanna: "A Jewish atheist is a very specific concept." She laughed.

Maria Teresa: "I watch the families who visit here on weekends. How the parents behave toward their children, speaking to them with patience and encouraging them to ask intelligent questions. It's an example for the whole world. The strength of this people is the love of parents for their children. Not just the mothers but also the fathers. A Jewish child has two mothers."

Johanna: "In Israel, children ask like grown-ups and parents listen like children."

Maria Teresa: "When I see the devotion of Jewish parents, I understand something of Mary's love for Jesus. The grace God gave His people is the family. Each family is like a little sanctuary, and the father is like the priest."

The appreciation of these childless women for the Jewish family moved me. Maria Teresa sensed in Israelis the two spiritual qualities whose combination she valued most: strength and love. Remarkably, she saw in even the noisy Israeli families who intruded into the convent's silence a source of spiritual inspiration.

I said, "When Jews invoke God the Father, it's not the father of judgment but of mercy. The father who loves and protects his people. A father who is really a mother."

Maria Teresa said, "There are many beautiful holidays and customs in Judaism. But I don't understand what holds them all together. In Christianity the connecting idea is Christ. What is it in Judaism?"

"The love between God and the Jewish people," I replied. "The Jewish holidays commemorate moments in the divine experiment of intimacy with a whole people, as a kind of prelude for divine intimacy with humanity."

Maria Teresa went into silence. She smiled. Something elusive had fallen into place.

An Israeli couple appeared outside the convent. The man knocked repeatedly and called out, annoyed, for someone to open the gate. "Here comes the priestly father of a holy Jewish family," I said.

Johanna slapped the air in my direction and went to let them in.

4

Johanna had a present for me: a booklet in Hebrew about Edith Stein, the Jewish-born Carmelite nun who was killed in the Holocaust and canonized by Pope John Paul II.

Jews had been outraged by the Edith Stein affair. The canonization of Stein, who after all hadn't been martyred for being a nun but a Jew, seemed to many Jews an attempt to "Christianize" the Holocaust. Worse, Jews feared the canonization contained an implicit proselytizing message: that the most admirable Jews were those who'd become Christian.

I didn't share the outrage. Jewish protests over the canonization seemed to me misplaced. Whom the church declared as its saints, after all, was its own affair. And if we continued to treat the church like a criminal on probation and to examine its every pronouncement for traces of hostility or flawed contrition, we would squander this precious historical moment of reconciliation. Finally, it seemed to me that, in clinging to Edith Stein, the church wasn't trying to "Christianize" the Holocaust but to refute the attempt by many Jews to link it, even indirectly, with Nazism. In my difficult conversation with Maria Teresa, I too had made that connection, and she'd been right to rebuke me.

Still, I wondered now about Johanna's intention. Was she trying to build a bridge between us through a spiritual figure whom we could potentially share? Or was I being proselytized?

Johanna left me in the reception room while she did errands. The glossy booklet, titled *A Jewish Daughter, A Sacrifice for Our Time,* told the story of a German Jew, born on Yom Kippur into a loving middle-class family, who became a brilliant philosopher and found spiritual fulfillment in the church. According to the booklet, Stein embraced her martyrdom as the ultimate confirmation of her monastic vow to follow the path of Jesus. Awaiting deportation to Auschwitz in a Dutch detention camp, she took charge of cleaning and comforting the children whose mothers were too stunned to cope.

I looked through the booklet for hints of missionizing but found none. A triumphalist tone occasionally intruded: "The truth that [Stein] had sought was revealed to her . . . Jesus the messiah!" Yet the booklet was hardly an apology for the church's record in the Holocaust. Stein had written to the pope just after Hitler's rise to power, pleading with him to protest Nazi anti-Semitism publicly; the pope's reply, dryly noted the booklet, was to send blessings to her and her family. The booklet also contained these pointed words by Stein's niece at a 1987 papal ceremony: "Millions saw the pope today declare Edith Stein blessed. But in 1933, she didn't get any reply from the pope when she tried to turn his attention to the fate of the Jews. Nevertheless, I see the decree of my aunt as blessed as a sign of remorse for things that perhaps could have been done and weren't."

I didn't want to engage Johanna in a pointless disputation over Edith Stein, but I did want her to understand why, unlike Stein, I didn't need Jesus in my religious life. And so, when Johanna returned, I tried to explain something of the spiritual adventure of living as a

Jew in Israel, participating in the fulfillment of the Jewish fantasy of return to the land. For me to exchange Judaism for another faith, I said, would be an act of ingratitude not only toward those Jews whose prayers had helped create this time but toward God Himself, Who had placed me in the ultimate moment of the Jewish story. I came to the convent, I continued, to learn from its devotion. Yet my journey into Christianity was perhaps the end of Paul's hope of provoking the Jews to jealousy, as he put it, that is, trying to win us over by presenting the beauty of Christianity. For here I was, exposed to Christianity at its most glorious, yet feeling no longing for Jesus. I wanted to learn from Christian monastics, not become them.

"So you feel you can't accept Jesus," said Johanna, "because you would be betraying your past."

"Not that I can't accept Jesus; that it isn't necessary. You don't need Jewish observance. I don't need Jesus. And we can both reach God."

Johanna drew a circle in the air. All the religions, she said, are points along the circumference; all converge in the center. But the only way to move up from the center, toward ultimate intimacy with God, was through Jesus. Johanna's approach was one way for Christians to resolve the tension between religious pluralism and the New Testament's insistence that the way to the Father went through the Son: Everyone could approach God, but only Jesus offered what mystics called union. Johanna's approach was understandable. She had, after all, lived sequestered with God through Jesus, and she couldn't imagine that such holy intimacy was possible any other way.

"Maybe it's dangerous for you to open yourself to Jesus," she said.

"It is dangerous," I acknowledged.

"The problem is that you feel that if you give Jesus respect, you can't be a Jew anymore."

"No, Johanna, I feel a great deal of respect for Jesus. But there is no need for me to accept him in your way."

"Not in my way," she said. "In your way."

"I've already made peace with him in my way. I consider Jesus an emissary of God, just like the founders of all the great religions. I'm sure that Jesus is a very good address for prayers. But I have my own address."

"Why do you come here?" she asked.

"To be in a place where God is all that matters. And to learn from your silence."

"You don't have silence in Judaism?"

"Not now. We're still in the phase of resuming our physicality after two thousand years of disembodiment."

"And in the past you had silence?"

Her tone wasn't challenging but questioning; she genuinely wanted to know. I continually underestimated Johanna, forgetting that the years of silence had made her a wise and humble listener who wasn't afraid to examine her own assumptions.

"There were times when we knew silence," I replied. "The prophets were meditators. So were the kabbalists. Some of us are now trying to renew the Jewish meditation tradition." Maybe that was why I came to the convent: to relearn the silence buried in the Jewish cacophony of history and politics and peoplehood. The return of the Jews had reawakened this land with a restless vitality; I was searching for its hidden silence.

"Why was the silence lost?" she asked.

"In Jewish history there's a constant struggle between spirituality and . . ."

"Halakhah."

"No. Halakhah is the foundation of Jewish spirituality. At its best it brings an awareness of God into the small details of daily life. The struggle of Judaism is to constantly renew Halakhah and keep it from confusing the details for the spiritual goal."

She listened quietly and nodded. I had to remind myself again that she wasn't interested in scoring points, that a conversation here was different than in "the world."

"And if we don't accept Jesus as the messiah, Johanna?"

"It means that the people of Israel isn't accepting what God wants to give it," she replied.

Then she laughed, moving her fingers to simulate talking lips, as if her mouth were out of control.

She tried to soften the effect of her words. "Because the Jews are so open to hearing the word of God, we're confused about why they didn't accept Jesus. The first 'no' is the puzzle. Afterward it became harder and harder because of all the blows the Jews received from Christians. The church isn't pure by any means. We're sinners. We tried to put our own spiritual limitations on the Jews."

"Was that first 'no' a sin?"

"Who am I to say? I can't understand what happened. And I certainly can't say it was a sin."

She said something else that I didn't understand, and I asked her to repeat her words.

"You see?" she said. "We have no problem understanding each other about spiritual matters. But when we come to history, we find ourselves speaking two languages."

As if our misunderstandings would be resolved only when Jews and Christians learned to share silence.

5

It was Ash Wednesday, the beginning of Lent, the period of introspection leading to Easter. I had arranged an appointment with Maria Teresa, but when I arrived at the gate, a surprised Johanna told me that Maria Teresa was in Rome and that she herself had had no idea I was coming. "But just this morning I was thinking, Where is Yossi?"

We sat in the spare reception room and talked about Lent. It was a time, said Johanna, to stop looking at the sins of others and take responsibility for your own sins. "But it's important to keep a part of your mind on the fact that it's not really about me and my sins, it's about Him. Are you looking for yourself or for God? As Lent progresses, the emphasis slowly shifts away from our sins to God's presence. That's what protects us from getting too morbid about our failures."

"For Jews," I said, "the whole Easter period seems morbid. Jews see Christianity as death-obsessed. Or let's say that we have a hard time understanding it."

"Say it the first way," Johanna insisted. "We need to be honest with each other."

"Even though I know it's a distortion, it's ingrained in me, too."

"Christians see that Jewish attitude as an inability to deal with suffering and death as a part of life. I know a Jewish woman who lost her son. What could be worse than that? She went to rabbis, looking for comfort. But she was told terrible things. One rabbi suggested that she and her husband had sinned in some way. So now she comes here to talk. We aren't obsessed with death and suffering. But our relationship to the cross gives us a way of accepting pain."

I thought of the Holocaust survivors I'd known and whom Judaism had helped restore to sanity. I suppressed my anger and said, "You can always find foolish rabbis. But they don't represent Judaism."

She offered what she thought was evidence of Judaism's inability to face life's difficulties. "We have a tradition in the church of taking in the crippled, the retarded, all those no one else wants. But they're not supposed to be included in the synagogue."

"Where did you get that crazy idea, Johanna?"

"I was reading a book about Judaism, and it explained how the maimed were forbidden to enter the Temple."

"What does that have to do with synagogues? Go to any synagogue in Israel and you'll see handicapped people. It's total nonsense."

"You see the picture we have of each other?" Johanna said, delighted to be corrected. "We judge each other by our worst traits instead of our best."

Outside a wind shook the pine trees. In the cold dark room, Johanna seemed to recede. Only her eyes were visible beneath her hood, wide and alert with self-examination.

"Johanna, can you love the Jews for who we are, without expectations?"

"I want to. But it's very hard. Not because I need you to be like me. But because if I have something that brings me such happiness, I want to share it."

"It's like being a parent," I said. "You have all kinds of ideas about who your children should be, but in the end you love them no matter what. Maybe God doesn't want us to accept Jesus. Maybe we're a test for Christian love, to see whether you are capable of loving unconditionally."

"Not maybe," she said emphatically, "definitely. It's no coincidence that this conversation is happening today. You've given me my penance work."

I returned to the guest room that Johanna had provided for the day. The white room was fashioned from wood and stone; an arched window opened to pine forest. There was a cot with a hard mattress, a table for writing, and beside it, for dining, a smaller table with a wooden stool, so that even when you ate you avoided comfort and remained alert in prayer. Though the room contained only bare necessities, a compelling aesthetic was created by the careful arrangement of every detail. Jars with tea and preserves and olive oil were lined symmetrically on a bookcase made of straw. Meals were brought to the door on a tray brightened with a hibiscus flower.

I entered the small shrine area, separated from the living area by a bamboo divide. I sat on the sheepskin rug. An icon of Jesus hung on the wall. It was a Semitic Jesus, with long nose and pursed lips and black beard. One eye looked at me tenderly, but the other eye drifted off, as if he were torn between suffering humanity and distant visions.

A simple prayer formed: Thank You, God, for my friendship with Johanna and Maria Teresa. Thank You for admitting me into this place of purity.

6

A winter morning in the convent. Intense silence filled the building, as if it had been suddenly evacuated, leaving a residue of tumult.

Maria Teresa looked at me with her expectant smile.

"What is silence?" I asked.

"Silence isn't emptiness," she replied, like a theologian trying to define God by what He is not. "And it is more than a means. It is something of God Himself. God is beyond everything; so is silence."

Silence, then, was the human ability to share in God's being.

I asked her how she maintained awareness of God's presence through her busy day. "By silently repeating God's name," she explained. "When you have to concentrate on something else, you stop. But then the name returns on its own."

The phrase she internally repeated was the Jesus Prayer of the Orthodox church: "Lord Jesus, son of God, have mercy on me." I told her that I'd been trying to fill the blank moments of my day with a prayer from the High Holidays: *"Adonai, Adonai, El rahum v'hanun,"* Lord, Lord, benevolent God, compassionate and gracious. Like the Jesus prayer, it invoked God's mercy as the bridge between human smallness and divine grandeur.

Maria Teresa suggested I adapt the breathing exercise that accompanied the Jesus prayer: inhaling the words *"Adonai, Adonai"* and exhaling *"El rahum v'hanun."*

"Hold the breath for as long as it's comfortable," she advised. "Let it cleanse."

"So we inhale God's purity and exhale our imperfections?"

"You can use it that way. The breath is the movement of God. Entering us, filling us, drawing us toward Him."

She entwined her fingers and closed her eyes. Her lips formed an unconscious smile, and I saw what I imagined would be her face at death.

I closed my eyes and inhaled. *"Adonai, Adonai."* Exhaled: *"El rahum v'hanun."* Again, slowly, until the words became instinctive.

A phone in the room rang. I started. Maria Teresa opened her eyes like a slow exhalation, retrieved the receiver, issued quiet instructions as if she'd been expecting the call, then slipped back into silence. A seamless meditation between movement and stillness. She could manage that abrupt transition so naturally because a part of her always remained in silence.

I resumed the exercise. Inhale: God's perfection. Exhale: the limitations of the little self.

I found myself inside the Church of the Holy Sepulcher, the Jerusalem shrine Christians revere as the site of Jesus' crucifixion, burial, and resurrection. In my few visits to the site, I'd had difficulty transcending my cultural barriers and appreciating its holiness. Like most Jews, I was put off by the accumulation of icons and statues, the gaudy new dome depicting the sun with thick gold rays, the competing denominations staking out rival claims over every inch of sacred space.

Now, in meditation, I imagined moving from alcove to alcove, weighted by clutter and contention. Then I looked up at the cupola. It was transformed from its representation of the sun into the sun itself.

And then, unexpectedly, the Holy Sepulcher penetrated me. Became me. The maze of alcoves entered my chest; the cupola fit the contours of my skull. Exhale: expelling darkness from the chest. Inhale: filling the head with light.

Maria Teresa opened her palms, face up in a gesture of offering.

We sat quietly, waiting for the intensity to ease. I told her about my encounter with the Holy Sepulcher. She said, "Silence gives us a new way of seeing. To penetrate the surface of things. God's light in my eyes."

I'd grown up recoiling from the idea of even entering a church, which I'd feared as a place of menace; now a church—the ultimate church—had entered me.

Afterward, I met Johanna in the hallway. She looked at me carefully and said, "You're changing, friend. This place is changing you."

"Yes," I replied, "but not in the way you hope for."

"How do you know what I hope for? What I hope for doesn't matter. Only what God wants."

I sensed an opening and said, "Johanna, that booklet you gave me: I don't need it. I appreciate Edith Stein as a wonderful servant of God. But I have a whole history of Edith Steins who lived and died as Jews. I have Rabbi Akiva laughing while the Romans peeled his skin with an iron comb; I have the rebbe of my father's town whom the Nazis set on fire and who danced in the flames. Each of those souls is a paving stone on the Jewish road to God."

Johanna didn't immediately respond. We stood together in the dim light of the white stone hall. Then she said quietly, reluctant to intrude on the silence, "Each time we meet, drop by drop, we get a little closer to what God wants of us."

"I understand that for you it's inconceivable to reach God without Jesus," I said. "But other people have other ways."

"Maybe the Trinity teaches Christians that you can have distinctions and still be one in God. Maybe there are many roads." She smiled. "You see? I'm changing too."

7

Immediately after Shabbat, the Jewish Sabbath, I drove to the convent for an overnight retreat. Though I wouldn't be arriving until after the final bell at 9 P.M. and the last "Hail Mary" of the day, Johanna said she'd wait up for me. Like a mother.

I drove on the narrow road through olive groves leading to the convent. The silence seemed to intensify, as if the convent were drawing me into its aura. I sensed something of the relief that the soul must feel when it leaves this world, and the torment of ignorance is dispelled by the self-evident reality of God.

Johanna opened the gate and lightly touched my cheek with hers.

I retrieved a small bag from the car. "Is that all you have?" she asked.

"I'm only staying for one night."

"It's good to travel light," she said. "Ready at any moment to leave for heaven."

Johanna showed me to my room. Over the desk hung an icon of a matronly Mary, with several chins, extending both arms in welcome. In the shrine area hung a young and beautiful Mary, head tilted as if listening for a baby's cry.

I'd brought along a book called *True Devotion to Mary*, an eighteenth-century work that focused prayer to God and Jesus through the intercession of Mary. The book had come to me in unusual circumstances. One day, while in the office of my editor at *The Jerusalem Report*, I noticed a carton of books all related to Christian mysticism. "I didn't know you were interested in Christianity," I said to the editor. He wasn't. Someone had anonymously sent him the books, and he didn't know what to do with them. I took them home, selected the classics that interested me, and put the rest on a high shelf and forgot about them. But then, just as I was getting ready to come to the convent, I vaguely recalled that one of those books had been about Mary, whose presence was imprinted on icons throughout the convent and was clearly central in some way to its devotions. Without quite knowing what the book was about, I retrieved it and stuck it in my bag.

I showed it now to Johanna. Her eyes widened in surprise. "Where did you get this?" she asked. I told her the story.

"I think God has something in mind for you here," she said.

"I believe that, Johanna."

I asked her if she knew the book, and she said, "There is no devotion to Mary beyond this. It is the most extreme, the most total." She spoke with reverence, but offered nothing more.

When she left, I sat on the sheepskin rug opposite the icon of the young Mary and began reading. The argument of the book was that a hierarchy of intercessors was necessary to reach God. "Have we not need of a mediator with the Mediator Himself?" wrote the author, referring to Jesus. The way to reach Jesus, he continued, was through Mary, whose essence was mercy and who "has nothing in her austere and forbidding."

The author's devotion, as Johanna had warned me, was certainly extreme: Among other austerities, he advocated wearing a chain to symbolize the devotee's commitment to Mary. What moved me more was the author's description of Mary's humility. Nearly invisible in the New Testament narrative, silently watching over her son's body after the crucifixion, she was the prototype of silence, "singularly hidden," the archetype of humility. I thought of Johanna and her invisible sisters. This book seemed to describe their lives of silence, as if they were consciously modeling themselves after Mary, offering themselves as wombs for God.

I went to the chapel to meditate. Though no one was there, the white room felt restless, as if filled with invisible presences. I sat cross-legged on the cold stone floor. Before I could prepare myself, I felt pulled into silence, as though entering that part of the sea that suddenly drops into the depths.

An altar made of rough stones appeared. I placed a stack of

papers on top. The papers contained everything I'd ever written. How much had I written to serve God, how much for my own glory? I lit the pile and watched the smoke rise in silence.

The early morning bell barely penetrated, reluctant to intrude. Waking up in the convent was the most precious moment of the day. Unlike most mornings, I instantly roused myself, inspired by the invisible devotion stirring around me. Without effort I found myself silently invoking God's name, "Father, Father," as if joining in an ongoing chant.

I went for morning prayers to the balcony overlooking the chapel. Birds flew through the arched windows. I was pleased to have the balcony to myself and was instantly pulled into meditation by the sisters' perfect song, delicately coaxed from the silence. Meditating during their prayer was a strange role reversal: Communal prayer was the only time during the day when they were in speech, and meditation was the one sustained time when I was in silence.

I couldn't help peeking at their faces, which seemed to merge into a single transparent face, delicate yet determined. In their hooded white robes, they resembled shrouds. Utterly still. The candles on the altar seemed to make more noise in their flickering.

Maria Teresa circled the chapel, resting her hand on the head of each nun. Then she came upstairs to greet me. "Shalom, Yossi," she said, gripping both my hands in firm welcome.

Back in my room, I continued reading *True Devotion to Mary*. I came across this passage: "Mary must shine forth more than ever . . . in might, against the enemies of God, idolaters, schismatics, Mahometans, Jews and souls hardened in impiety."

I put down the book. There was no escaping it. I tried to resist my anger. Obviously, Jews weren't perceived in the convent as enemies of

God. The sisters prayed for the peoples of this land, in Hebrew and Arabic. Besides, Jewish texts were hardly free of contempt for gentiles; one of the most beloved kabbalists had written that the level of the Jewish soul compared to that of the non-Jewish soul was like the difference between the soul of a human being and an animal. All of us were heirs to theologies of contempt. Like Maria Teresa with her nuns, we needed the wisdom to sort the negative traits from our traditions without destroying their beauty. Let it go, I said to myself. Offer your anger to silence.

Johanna came to see me in the late afternoon. She wanted to know if I'd made progress with the book.

"It's hard for me to identify with it," I said, with a tact that was rare for me, especially in matters of Jewish honor. "But during this morning's prayers I felt devotion toward the nuns, if not quite to Mary."

"It's the same thing," said Johanna.

"Could you say something about the nature of devotion to Mary here in the convent?"

She placed her finger against her lips and smiled. "It's a secret. Not everyone would understand. Even some Christians would think it's excessive."

"Who is Mary for you, Johanna?"

"The most hidden one. She is pure love; she seeks nothing for herself. We know almost nothing about her from the New Testament. God can come through her womb because she is so small."

"Do you live with a constant presence of Mary?"

"The relationship with Mary is very intimate. To be a child in her hand. She speaks. Not in words. She opens my eyes, gives me ideas. Today, after four hours of prayer, I was very tired. I was making a bed in one of the guest rooms when I realized I'd put the sheet on the wrong side. I told myself, so it's backwards; who cares? But then I thought: What do you want, Mary? How would you do it? I knew she would do it the proper way. So I fixed it. It means that through me she has prepared the bed for the next person who will come here. By letting Mary decide, you bring her in and she prepares the way."

"So the bed becomes sanctified?"

"With God's love."

"What is the connection between Mary and silence?"

"She is my silence. Otherwise? What a racket I make. The biggest noise is we ourselves. If I give everything to her, that's the real silence."

"So the secret of this place is the silence of Mary?"

She smiled.

"You know, Johanna, for months I've been coming here and feeling a wall, something basic that was eluding me."

"Now you have a hole in the wall," she said, pointing to the book. "For the mouse to enter."

"Maybe I was meant to have this book."

"Watch out, friend," she said. "She may want you for herself."

There she goes again, I thought. Don't get so excited, Johanna, I'm not about to convert. For you, Mary is the literal mother of God; for me, Mary is symbolic of the Mother aspect of God, the primal force that creates and nurtures form and that Judaism calls the *Shekhinah* and Hinduism calls *Shakti*.

But maybe I'd misunderstood her intent. In any case, I didn't want to argue with her. We'd worked hard to transcend the pitfalls of theology and history, and I wasn't about to ruin the moment.

And so I said nothing.

No more disputations, no more words. Johanna had won. She'd converted me to silence.

four

Easter

I

How does a Jew approach Holy Week?

Historically, it was a time of Jewish trauma. In my father's town in Transylvania, Jews would lock themselves in their homes before Easter, hiding from their Christian neighbors, who blamed them personally for the crucifixion. Even for me, growing up in 1960s America, the crucifix had been a threat and a taunt. I would cross the street rather than pass my neighborhood's only church just to avoid the crucifix hanging outside, which seemed to me a celebration of Jewish death.

But those memories shouldn't have impinged. I was, after all, a victor of history, a citizen of a sovereign Jewish state and part of the freest generation of Jews that ever existed. I lived in a time when the Catholic Church had excised the old Good Friday prayer invoking the "perfidious Jews" and when many Catholics now offered a substitute prayer blessing the Jews, "the first to hear the word of God." We were no longer implicated in the crucifixion. For the church, the Jews were now the people who fathered Jesus, not the people who killed him. The deicide charge had been uprooted from the textbooks and passion plays of most mainstream Christian denominations, at least in the West. My father had been taunted through childhood as a Christ-killer; my sabra children had no idea what the term meant.

Yet as Holy Week approached, I found myself suspiciously lethargic, unable to choose a Christian community with which to experience the progression from crucifixion to resurrection. One community wasn't sufficiently ecumenical; another wasn't "interesting enough," as if I were seeking spiritual thrills. Finally I had to admit: I was afraid of Holy Week.

At lunch with a friend, a Conservative rabbi, I told him about my journey into Christianity and Islam. "How will you handle all those crosses?" he asked. I ignored the implicit rebuke and replied as reasonably as I could that the cross, while obviously not my symbol of devotion, inspired love for God among people whom I loved and respected. "You mean this?" he said, and he took two knives on the table and formed them into a cross. He defined my problem with brutal precision: Intimacy with the cross meant betraying all those Jews who'd been killed in its name.

The Jewish fear of the cross embodied the tragedy of Jewish-Christian relations. Where Christians saw God's love and self-sacrifice, we saw Christianity's crucifixion of the Jews. Until I overcame any lingering fear of the cross and learned to regard it as a devotional rather than an historical symbol, my encounter with Christianity would remain blocked. There was no Christianity without crucifixion and resurrection. Yet Holy Week seemed an impenetrable border. Could a Jew really experience anything of Christianity's ultimate moment?

My fear of Holy Week wasn't entirely anachronistic. The Orthodox churches, the most numerous among Christian denominations in Jerusalem, had barely begun confronting the implications of the deicide charge; the Greek Orthodox Church, the Holy Land's largest denomination, still referred to the "perfidious Jews" in its Good Friday liturgy. When I'd called the Greek Orthodox patriarchate, seeking permission to spend time in one of its desert monasteries, the official became so flustered that he simply hung up on me.

Even among Christians whose denominations had repudiated deicide, its residue surely lingered. A charge that had been integral to Christianity almost since its inception could hardly be erased in a single generation. A Jew in a *kipah* showing up in church on Good Friday was pushing the limits of interfaith tolerance. To open myself to the spirit of Holy Week, I needed to be free of self-consciousness. Yet how could I relax in church if I'd be wondering whether worshipers were looking at me and seeing Judas Iscariot?

I confided my problem to my friend Rebecca, a New Age–style healer in Jerusalem. Rebecca had grown up in a home at once Orthodox and open to other faiths; Christian ministers were frequent guests. And she was an actively identifying Sephardi, descendant of Spanish Jewry, one of the most tolerant religious cultures the Diaspora had produced. She often meditated in Jerusalem's holy places, of whatever faith. If there was any Jew who could help me, I thought, it was Rebecca. But when I mentioned Holy Week, she whispered as if transformed into a Marrano hiding from the Inquisition: "Holy Week was when they burned the Spanish Jews."

2

Germa Admasu, a layman who worked for the Ethiopian church in Jerusalem, was sympathetic to my request, but skeptical. I had phoned him on the suggestion of a mutual friend and explained that I was looking to experience something of the religious heart of the Ethiopian church. "What do you mean by *religious*?" he asked. "Do you mean the practice of ritual? Or do you mean loving God and trying to do His will with every waking moment? In the Ethiopian church, we have much ritual, that is true. But love of God? True devotion? I think you'll be disappointed."

The idea of experiencing Holy Week with the Ethiopians had seemed promising. Perhaps an African version of Christianity would allow me to elude historical memory and see Easter with new eyes. The Ethiopian Orthodox Church was considered by scholars to be the most "Judaic" of the traditional churches, and that too, I thought, might help temper my wariness of Holy Week. Like Jews, Ethiopian infant boys were circumcised on their eighth day, and many Ethiopian Christians observed Shabbat as well as Sunday and refrained from eating pork. Ethiopians believe that Menelik, legendary son of King Solomon and the Queen of Sheba, brought the Ark of the Covenant from Jerusalem to Ethiopia, where it supposedly remains hidden to this day. Ethiopian churches commemorate its presence by placing a talbot, or wooden replica of the Ark, in a shrine behind a curtain, through which only the priest is allowed to pass. However fanciful, the legend of the Ark suggested that something of the biblical experience of God's presence had been evoked in remote Ethiopia.

I met Germa inside the Old City walls, in a café where Arab men smoked narghiles under dated Christmas decorations hanging from the vaulted ceiling. Though he was a hefty man in his late thirties, whose hair was already turning white, he was shy and hesitant.

"Outsiders romanticize the Ethiopian church," he said, with a softness that made him sound sad rather than cynical. "In Ethiopia, it is still possible to find the old monasticism. But something happens even to the best monks when they come here. They can't handle the encounter with modernity. Some become crazy, some lose their God. There are no saints in Jerusalem."

Germa spoke with depressing authority. He had grown up literally inside the church, in a monastic compound a few minutes' walk from where we were sitting. After Germa's father, an army colonel, had participated in a failed coup against the Ethiopian dictator, Emperor Haile Selassie, the family feared that the emperor's loyalists might try to kill Germa, the family's only son, in revenge. And so, at age six, he was sent to Jerusalem, where his uncle was the archbishop of the Ethiopian Orthodox Church. "I thought that Jerusalem was in heaven. When the plane took off, I understood why we had to travel off the ground." It was 1965, and the Old City was then under Jordanian control. The monastery had no heat or electricity or running water. Most monks and nuns, awkward around a child, ignored Germa; when he'd slip into their rooms, they would throw him out. His happiest memory was of a nun he'd visit in the kitchen who told him stories about the animals of Africa. "She was so beautiful," he said, with the longing of an orphan for his mother. In fact, Germa didn't see his mother again until he was twenty-three years old; only then, after the emperor had been deposed, was it considered safe for him to visit Ethiopia.

He didn't remain there for long. He had been imprinted with exile and no longer belonged to his birthplace. "Ethiopia is a wounded land," he said. "It was like visiting a hospital." But he didn't quite belong to Jerusalem either. He had dated Israeli women, been a communist activist at a Palestinian university; but for both Israeli and Palestinian society, he was superfluous. In the end, he usually found himself alone.

He'd never married and lived like a kind of monk, in a spare room in the apartment of Jewish friends. The strain of balancing worlds had made him insecure. Though he was fluent in English, Hebrew, and Arabic in addition to Amharic, he spoke hesitantly, as if unsure of the accuracy of his words. He did odd jobs for the Ethiopian church and helped the monks pay bills and deal with city hall—part handyman, part foreign minister. "When I enter the monks' world I feel dizzy, like a time traveler," he said to me. "I move from the late twentieth century to the middle ages. After an hour with them, I don't know where I am."

He despised the church for its pettiness and insularity, yet he remained bound to it, his only real home. Perhaps in some way he even loved the church, for keeping the memory of the miraculous. He knew that holiness was real, that the soul could be exposed through a body made transparent by austerity and humility and prayer. "As a boy, I lived next door to a monk who was walled into his room. No windows, no doors, no exit. No possibility of receiving food. He lived that way for an entire year. When an opening was made in the sealed room, he walked out. What can I say about that?"

He longed for the company of saints, but they were no longer accessible, and those remaining in the monasteries, he insisted, were either charlatans or fanatics or well-meaning but ordinary men. He carried the sadness of someone who had not only seen the end of an era but had himself participated in its destruction; the very nature of his job, after all, was to help the monks adapt to modernity. Yet the outside world, oblivious even to the possibility of holiness, couldn't be fully home for Germa either. More than his physical exile, this was the real source of his dislocation: He craved a holiness he feared he could never possess. "You know what hell is for Ethiopians? To be separated from God. Like a child separated from his mother. I feel so far from God." He had the spiritual sensitivity to place the blame on himself: God wasn't far from him; he was far from God.

I told Germa that I was reading *The Way of Perfection,* by Saint Teresa. I pulled the book from my bag and asked him if he knew it. "Please put it away," he said. "The title is too painful for me."

We walked to the monastery that had been his childhood home. It was in the Christian Quarter, on a street of steps. The stone walls were blackened with old Intifada slogans. On a sign above the narrow door were written these words in English: ETHIOPIA EXTENDS HER HANDS TO GOD.

The little building felt gloomy, as if the years of deprivation had seeped into its stones. Germa took me to the room where manuscripts were kept. The room was long and narrow and reminded me of a well, deep but constricted. It exuded venerability and mustiness in equal measure. Two monks in black robes and black rimless caps sat beneath photographs of old patriarchs and emperors, including Haile Selassie, regal with sword and sash. Germa perfunctorily kissed the monks' sleeves.

From a glass-covered bookcase Germa retrieved a tome so heavy he had to lay it on his forearms. Its boardlike pages, made of cowhide, were covered with calligraphic letters in Geez, Ethiopia's sacred language. The book, he explained, was an account of Mary's life; as a boy he had memorized much of it. He spoke with a mixture of admiration and contempt. Look at this beautiful culture, he seemed to be saying, a whole civilization built around devotional books. But he also meant: In a thousand years, all that Ethiopia had produced was confined to this windowless room.

"What did you learn growing up here?" I asked.

"That the monastery isn't the only way to heaven," he said.

We left the building and entered the Arab market, crossed a narrow street lined with stores selling icons and *kipot* and T-shirts imprinted with Arafat's face, and descended the stepped alley to the Church of the Holy Sepulcher, which Christians believe was the site of the crucifixion and resurrection. A side entrance in the rambling stone building led to the Ethiopians' domain, two small chapels and part of the roof, which they uneasily shared with the Copts. In the past, Ethiopian and Coptic monks had physically fought over control of the area; one Easter, they had actually beat each other with crosses.

An Ethiopian monk sat at the entrance to the ground-floor chapel. He stood as we entered and removed his cap. "That's all he does, sits and stands, stands and sits," said Germa. "In Ethiopia they say he was a serious monk. But he came here and lost his mind." I looked at him again; he was staring into space.

The walls of the narrow chapel were stained with dampness and blackened with smoke. A vaulted roof compensated with height for the cramped space. A bright modern painting depicted the Queen of Sheba's encounter with King Solomon. Her attendants bore gifts of a gold chalice and ivory tusks. Solomon's attendants wore the black fedoras and side locks of Hasidic Jews. Unlike other Christian denominations, the Ethiopian church hadn't tried to erase the connection between ancient Israelites and postbiblical Jews.

I asked Germa about the Judaic practices of the church, and he said, "We don't study the New Testament until we're in our teens. First we are steeped in the Torah. Those are the stories of our childhood. Only then do we move to the Gospels. It is just as God did with His people. First He gave the people of Israel the sweet milk of the law in their spiritual infancy. Then, when they got older, they didn't need that good mother's milk anymore, and they graduated to the law of love. But it's hard to leave Judaism, which is the mother, the father, the milk."

That was the loveliest form of Christian contempt for Judaism I'd ever heard.

He continued, "The biblical God is anthropomorphic. He cares about His children, the Jews. He gets angry, jealous, pleased. Judaism's greatness is to bring God from the heavens into human spirit. Christianity carried that idea the next step, and brings God into flesh. In Christianity there are no laws. You want to fast or not, it's okay. You want to be a priest or not, it's okay. God says to us, 'I'm your Father. Anytime you want anything, knock on My door. You were a sinner? You're still my son. I have only two conditions. Don't forget that I'm your Father. And don't forget that I have other children, and you must see your brothers and sisters the way that I see you.'"

Up on the roof, we entered the little wooden gate leading into the maze of concrete huts where Ethiopian monks and nuns lived. The huts were covered with corrugated tin and fronted by green-painted wooden doors, so low only a child could enter upright. At the entrance to the common and very basic bathroom, twigs were burning to freshen the air.

This miniature monastic village had long seemed to me the most mysterious of Jerusalem's Christian communities. But Germa was determined to disabuse me of any lingering romanticism. "The monks here have all been ruined," he said.

We knocked on several doors; no one was home.

"Where do they go?" I asked.

"They visit their friends in the other monasteries. Or they walk around Jerusalem. I remember a time when you would look into these little houses and see a monk praying in every one."

A few monks were sitting on stools, warming themselves in the sun. A middle-aged monk with Oriental eyes was delighted to learn from Germa that I was a journalist. He startled me with his knowledge of Israeli politics, discussing the latest intrigues. "Israel is too divided," he said in Hebrew. "If Israel is weak, it will be bad for all of us." He spoke as a Christian in a Muslim Middle East, seeking the protection of the Jews.

I asked about his life in Ethiopia, and he told me that he'd lived in one of the strictest monasteries, where monks ate only root vegetables and spent long retreats in caves. According to monastic tradition, he said, if you managed to remain alone in a cave for forty days, the same length of time that Moses had stood on Sinai, you would emerge fearless, imbued with God. Yes, he had lived in a cave, but only for a week, he added, laughing. A snake had entered the cave; he made the sign of the cross, and it left. But at night the howling of wild animals had kept him awake with fear, and he fled.

"And how is it to be a monk in Jerusalem?" I asked.

"One moment I pray, the next moment I'm thinking about other things. It's not like the monastery in Ethiopia. There I had dreams of the saints; some actually saw them with their eyes. But here we are surrounded by people. We have to move to the desert. That's the only way for us."

But surely, I offered, it must be an uplifting experience to pray in this place.

"We have trouble with the Egyptians," he said, meaning the Copts. "They try to take everything from us. We have to be on guard all the time. God isn't in this building anymore."

Nearby, two monks were posing for a photograph with a Japanese tourist.

"Germa, is there really no one?"

"There is one," he admitted. "A true monk. But he won't talk to you."

"Let's try," I implored.

I arranged to meet Germa at the Ethiopian monastery in West Jerusalem, not far from the Old City, on a street barely wider than an alley with old stone houses covered in bougainvillea. High walls surrounded the monastery, which consisted of stucco shacks and a large round church in the center of the courtyard. The sense of enclosure was misleading; the gates were open and visitors entered freely. Even here, Ethiopian monks weren't secluded.

Haile Geiorgis, the "true monk" Germa had spoken of, was sitting on the steps of the church. A wooly gray beard barely filled the hollows of his face; high cheekbones pressed against his eyes. His robe was faded, somewhere between brown and gray, and hung shapeless over his haggard body. Other monks here wore velvet caps, purple scarves, and good shoes; he wore a cap made of plain black cloth and sandals, which exposed his deeply cracked heels.

Germa said to me, "He is the caretaker of the church. His health isn't good and he should have retired, but the other monks don't let him, and he's too humble to insist. They take advantage of his good nature. He suffers very much, sometimes happily." Germa added, "He doesn't like to talk. But he said you may ask him a few questions."

"Why are you certain that God is real?" I asked.

He laughed. "In my experience, I've witnessed God in many ways," he said, still bemused. "I have seen miracles. In our country, monks have cured the sick and risen the dead. It happens when you are alone, away from troubling surroundings. The way to revelation is by praying, meditating, and being sincere with people."

"What do you focus on in your meditation?" I asked.

Germa said to me, "He's too modest. He won't speak about himself."

Indeed, Haile Geiorgis avoided my question; he wasn't interested in discussing technique but attitude. "Two steps are important in meditation. First, you have to decide which side are you on. There is a war going on; light and darkness meet inside you. Are you with the light or the darkness? Your will has to be very strong to decide. But even once the decision is made, human beings don't have the discipline to reach the goal. The only way forward is to pray very sincerely to God. That is the second step. The first step is harder because it depends on you. The second step is easier because God has already come close. It doesn't take a lot of energy, just sincerity." He seemed to peer into me. "You are not the hero. God is the hero. After the Israelites built the Temple, they all knelt and placed their foreheads on the ground, in submission. When you can submit to God, you will feel a flow pulling you in a very strong and lovely way."

Germa, who'd been translating, said to me, "Ask him about his eating and sleeping habits." So I did.

"I eat once a day," he replied, "a vegetarian meal. In the evening I go for a walk and then go to sleep early. At midnight I wake up to pray. You don't know what a happy person I am."

He sat still, with folded hands, barely breathing. Then he seemed to notice me again, and said, "The effects of being in a place like this don't come through the ears and eyes. The message you need will be revealed to you just by being around us, even if we don't talk."

He stood up and walked away. Germa said, "That's all he's willing to say."

Disappointed, I entered the church. I left my shoes at the door, as the sign requested. The floors were covered with faded Oriental rugs; angels circled the cupola. A round stone structure like a hut stood in the middle of the church, housing the talbot, the symbolic ark. The walls were covered with bright paintings of Ethiopian saints in profile. One rode a lion, symbol of conquest of his animal nature; man and beast shared the same distended brown eyes. A typed inscription on a strip of paper read in fractured English: "Abba Samuel of Waldeba, founder of the famous monastery of Waldeba. This is the only hardest monastery where food is not allowed and monks who have choosed that life of abstinence feed themselves only by a kind of bitter root called kuarf. There, life is short for their greatest enemy the yellow fever shorten their beautiful life of prayers and sacrifices."

I sat on a rug, near a red cloth imprinted with crosses that protected the entrance into the area of the ark. I tried to meditate but was distracted by my perplexing conversation with Haile Geiorgis. What had he been trying to tell me? And was there something I could have said to win his trust, some question that would have shown him I was "serious"?

After a while I opened my eyes. I turned around and was startled to see Haile Geiorgis sitting on a bench against the wall just behind me. He was reading from a prayer book. He sat motionless and seemed impervious to me even now as I watched him. Though my meditation had hardly been deep, I hadn't heard him enter or even turn the pages of his prayer book. I had no idea how long he'd been sitting there. I wondered if he'd chosen that spot deliberately, to invigorate my meditation with his silence. He seemed to be saying to me now: If you want to know God, leave your questions behind and enter stillness.

3

Haile Geiorgis discouraged further meetings, and even Germa seemed to be avoiding me. Perhaps he felt he'd revealed too much, that no outsider could possibly understand the complexities of his life.

Holy Week for the Western churches came and went, and I hadn't found an appropriate community with which to challenge my fear of the cross; now Orthodox Holy Week had begun. But just as I was wondering whether my journey into Christianity had reached an impasse, I ran into a neighbor to whom I'd mentioned my project months earlier and who now, without prompting, offered a solution to my Easter problem. "Are you still interested in meeting Christians?" he asked me one night in our parking lot. "Because I'm studying English in a class with a very fine Armenian monk, and I'd be happy to introduce you."

When I'd first conceived of this journey, I had considered but immediately rejected contacting the Armenian church. I'd once written an article about the Armenian Quarter in Jerusalem's Old City, and what I knew of the Armenians suggested a lack of spiritual vitality. Communal life for the quarter's two thousand residents was consecrated to the memory of the 1915 genocide, when a million and a half Armenians, over a third of all Armenians then alive, were deported into the desert and massacred by the Turks. Posters on the quarter's stone walls showed blurred photographs of dead children and Turkish soldiers posing with a row of severed heads, accompanied by maps of emptied towns and of the key sites of the genocide. In the local school hung drawings of ancient Armenian warriors, the compensatory fantasies of a slaughtered people.

There was good reason for their obsession. Unlike the Holocaust, whose memory seemed to grow with the years, time and other atrocities had obscured the twentieth century's first foray into state-sponsored genocide. But the real source of the community's anguish was Turkey's refusal to admit that the genocide had even happened, let alone apologize and offer reparations. The Turkish government was even funding a "denial" campaign that had penetrated Western academia and transformed the genocide, once accepted as a given, into an issue of historical debate. And so nearly a century later, Armenian consciousness had distilled to rage—quiet, because Jerusalem's Armenians were expert at being an inoffensive minority between warring majorities, but self-destructive, especially to Armenian spirituality. Young people whose great-grandparents had experienced the genocide spoke with the bitterness of survivors. When I had asked a bishop, an old man with a tight mouth and pointed little beard, whether as a Christian he could forgive the Turks, he replied fiercely, "You forgive human beings, not animals."

The very rationale for the community's existence had become a sort of exalted spite: to survive the genocide, like the "eleventh commandment" to survive Hitler, which had inspired many post-Holocaust Jews. Indeed, the Armenian quarter evoked for me my old Brooklyn neighborhood: the same wounded suspicion of outsiders, the same loyalty to rituals whose true purpose wasn't to connect you to God but to the martyrs who had practiced them. Even the maps on the wall were familiar: a geography of grief made more desolate by its obscurity.

Among the competing claimants over Jerusalem, the Armenians were secluded in silence. The rest of the city knew them only by their monks, who quickly passed through the streets in their peaked black hats, and by their pottery, imprinted with blue swirls like vines in which birds nested. Though the Old City was enclosed by a massive stone wall, much of the Armenian Quarter was surrounded by an additional wall, the only one of Jerusalem's four quarters to insist on extra enclosure. The original purpose had been to protect the Armenian monastery, which still remained the heart of the community; but the wall had come to symbolize a wounded isolationism. Every night at exactly ten o'clock, the massive iron door that led into the compound was shut, as if to say to the outside world: We reciprocate your disinterest in our fate.

Yet it was precisely their trauma, I now realized, that might provide the solution to my Easter dilemma. What better way to outwit a Jew's fears of Christianity than to experience Holy Week with a Christian community that itself had suffered genocide? Its Easter symbolism might even resonate for me: Both the Armenians and the Jews, after all, possessed a national saga of destruction and rebirth, which Armenians naturally interpreted through the language of crucifixion and resurrection. If history was my problem, perhaps history would provide the solution.

The guard whose job was to prevent outsiders from wandering into the Armenian compound looked at me skeptically when I said I had an appointment with Father Enza Papakhanian. Reluctantly, he phoned the monastery, and he still looked skeptical when he told me that the father would appear shortly to escort me in.

Though he knew I was coming, Father Enza seemed surprised to see me. Perhaps he wasn't used to visitors from the outside world; perhaps my *kipah* startled him. Father Enza was tall and thin and very pale; with his black robe and short black beard, he seemed to be evaporating into his own shadow. His fingers were graceful, but he shook my hand limply. His vitality was concentrated in the passionate sadness of his big brown eyes.

He led me through the deserted cobblestone courtyard and into the monastic compound of the Armenian Orthodox Church, rows of newly renovated little apartments built around a stone courtyard. Father Enza's two-room apartment contained high vaulted ceilings, marble floors, Armenian tiles inlaid over the sink, a new refrigerator, and, most surprising of all, a big TV and a video player. It felt more like the apartment of a prosperous student than of a monk. Oddly, the only visible religious symbol seemed almost accidental: a painting of the Last Supper as backdrop to a clock.

I told Father Enza that I was on a search for holiness among the Christians, and he laughed. "I'm no holy man and I don't know any holy men in the Armenian church." As if to say: Why do you expect to find among us any greater miracle than survival?

Father Enza was the quarter's artist. He assumed I'd come to see his paintings, which were stacked in the kitchen, and he proceeded to display them on his easel. The paintings were mostly scenes from

Enza's village in the mountains of Armenia, where he'd lived before coming to study in the church's Jerusalem seminary seven years ago, at age twenty-three. He didn't paint religious scenes. There was no hope or faith or even anger in the portraits, only sadness and depletion. The faces, which resembled Enza's, were long and worn, the eyes round like full moons, distant with ghostly light. Children and adults shared those same big desolate eyes, their heads tilted, weighted with sadness. For Enza's Armenians, sadness wasn't acquired by the difficulties of life but inherited at birth. There was a gloomy clown, a farmer too tired to eat the potatoes set before him, village parents visiting their daughter at a university campus but showing no joy in reunion, only sadness at its brevity. A sad boy posed beside his sad snowman. "The boy made a friend," explained Enza, "but he knows his friend is going to melt."

"The tilted heads remind me of Jesus on the cross," I said.

"I'd never thought of that," Enza replied, and he smiled happily for the first time.

I asked him about the photographs of monks on the wall, assuming they were figures of religious inspiration. But he corrected me: They were heroes of the armed resistance against Turkey.

The lack of religious imagery perplexed me. And so I asked him, "Why did you become a monk?"

"I love my nation and my church," he said simply. The hierarchy of his loves was revealing: first the nation, then the church: faith as a consequence of nationhood. He was Christian because he was Armenian. And he was a monk because he had consecrated himself to the Armenian nation.

"And what about God?" I asked.

"For me it was the nation, not God," he said, shrugging. "But really it's the same thing."

Throughout my childhood, the people of Israel was my substitute for the God of Israel. In our survival through history I saw an approximation of eternity; taking pride in my people's miraculous endurance seemed to me the most accessible experience of divinity. I could no longer consider the nation—any nation—an adequate substitute for a personal relationship with God. Still, I respected the religious nationalism of an embattled people and realized that the warrior monks on Enza's wall were not just patriots but spiritual heroes, glorifying God by defending the suffering nation and denying evil the final say.

Two hefty young men in leather jackets dropped by. They were members of the planning committee for the annual commemoration of Armenian Genocide Day on April 24, and they'd come to consult with Enza about his design for the event's T-shirt. Enza showed them a sketch of a tree splintered by a bolt of lightning formed of the number 24. Though Holy Week had begun, the real passion was preparing for Genocide Day.

"You've come to the right person," one of the young men said to me when I explained why I was here. "Father Enza has a deep Armenian soul." Enza smiled painfully and turned away. However tenuous his relationship to God, he had the essential monastic quality of humility.

"Enza was probably too modest to tell you about the orphans," the young man continued. "In 1988, during the Armenian earthquake, Enza and his brother adopted two hundred orphans. He gathered them from the ruins and housed them and fed them. We raised money for him here in Jerusalem." So that is how Enza had begun his monastic life: After becoming a father to Armenian orphans, he'd become a father of the orphaned Armenian nation.

I asked the two men, both of whom had grown up in the quarter, whether they'd visited Armenia, and was surprised when they said they hadn't. "We're waiting for direct flights," one said lamely. Armenia, finally independent, was only a few hours away; and here they were, two Armenian nationalists, more engaged with their nation's crucifixion than its resurrection.

Enza tried to apologize for them. It was not a good time in Armenia, he explained. The country had achieved independence from the Soviet Union in 1991, but history had been stingy to reborn Armenia.

The landlocked country was surrounded and blockaded by Turkey and Azerbaijan. Unemployment was widespread, and corruption, a legacy of the Soviet era, only deepened the despair.

Enza looked at the clock on the wall with the painting of the Last Supper and said, "In five minutes, they will be locking the gate. I'm afraid you must go."

In the monastery's courtyard he pointed out a large stone cross: a *khatchkar,* the ancient Armenian cross of resurrection, whose extremities ended in flowers, resembling a tree in bloom. It was a beautiful cross. And it reminded me of the logo I'd seen of a Holocaust survivor organization: a row of barbed wire sprouting into a bud. Our two peoples shared the same religious impulse to invest suffering with meaning, the same expectation of a redemptive end.

"Armenian churches never display crucifixes," Enza explained. "We see the cross as the symbol of life, not suffering." It was as if some prophetic instinct in the Armenian soul had understood that a people destined for crucifixion would require a cross of comfort. Or perhaps it was an attempt to evade martyrdom altogether, the Armenian equivalent of Jesus in Gethsemani asking God to remove the bitter cup.

"The Armenian people are like lavash, Armenian bread," he continued. "It dries very quickly, but if you put it in water it becomes fresh again."

Yet where was the Armenian resurrection? Their joyless independence hardly seemed to qualify. Father Enza's paintings revealed a people too traumatized by crucifixion to celebrate or even acknowledge resurrection.

Enza escorted me out. The big iron doors shut behind me, and the quarter withdrew into itself, untouchable in its nightly ritual of self-incarceration.

The next night I returned to Father Enza. Word had gotten around that an Israeli journalist was visiting the monastery, and the room filled with curious young monks and deacons. But they weren't here only on my account. Enza's place was a drop-in center for fellow monastics, and also for the quarter's residents. Seminarians sought his advice about whether to enter the monastic priesthood, as Enza himself had done, or the lesser form of Armenian monkhood that permitted marriage. Parishioners confessed their personal problems because Enza listened more than he talked and didn't pretend to be more pious than he was. Most of all they came because Enza was what an Armenian monk was supposed to be: a repository of his people's passion.

Enza's sociability was a form of renunciation; he would have preferred to paint in solitude. But an Armenian monk, he explained to me, had two obligations: to perform the rituals and to serve the community. Once the Armenian church had valued asceticism and private devotion, but after the genocide, the spiritual imperative became the well-being of the nation. That survival strategy, combined with the murder of thousands of Armenian monks by the Turks and then by the Soviets, had depleted the church. A similar process had happened to the Jews after the Holocaust: Our spiritual energies were diverted into reconstruction.

Somehow the rumor had spread among the monks that I was writing a book about the Armenian genocide. I tried to explain that I was interested in religious experience, but I wasn't getting through. Maybe they were right after all; writing about Armenian spirituality meant writing about the genocide.

"I had to stand in church for six hours today with hardly a break," a young deacon named Edward complained to Enza. "These prayers are crucifying me."

Enza smiled but said nothing.

"Do you think about the Armenian tragedy during the prayers?" I asked Edward, whose lower lip protruded in permanent grievance.

"I always think of the Armenians," he said.

"So what does Holy Week mean to you?"

"It's a time to remember how Jesus forgives me. Every day, every hour, I do something wrong. I feel the relief of Jesus' forgiveness."

"And can you forgive the Turks?"

"Yes, when they accept what they've done. When they say, 'Forgive us.'"

"And until then, you will hate them?"

He smiled, as if caught in an act of mischief, at once apologetic and defiant. "I can't lie to you. I hate them when they deny the genocide."

"I think it's more important for the Turks to be forgiven than for us to forgive," said Enza. "We can survive without forgiving them."

I disagreed. "As long as you hate the Turks, they'll continue to control you and define you. I used to hate the Germans so much that if I touched a product made in Germany, I felt contaminated. My fantasy was that Germany would be plowed with salt, like Carthage. For me, part of becoming a free person was learning to relate to Germans as human beings."

Enza said, "You're lucky it was the Germans who killed you. They are civilized people. They know how to apologize."

He intended no irony. He actually envied our status as the twentieth century's preeminent victims, envied our Holocaust museums and movies, even envied us our murderers. And from his perspective, he was right. If I could move on past 1945, it was at least partly because the Germans had tried, however awkwardly, to compensate, and because the world remembered the Holocaust and didn't place the whole burden of memory on me. But the Turks with their brutal denial and the world with its thoughtless complicity had kept the Armenians caught in 1915, still trying to establish the mere fact of the genocide. The past refused to recede into history because history itself had been compromised.

The door was shoved open and a fat monk rushed in, threw himself onto a chair, sweating and heaving, and tossed his peaked hat onto the table, where it deflated and collapsed. "Give me time to breathe before you ask me any questions!" he shouted at me, though we hadn't exchanged a word. He obviously knew that I was the journalist who was writing a book about the genocide.

"Now you can ask!" he shouted a few moments later.

He seemed the kind of man who could take an up-front question, so I asked, "Does the Armenian church view the Jews as crucifiers of Jesus?"

"Let's put it in black and white," replied the monk, whose name was Father Avedis. "You're asking if the Armenians are anti-Semitic. I can tell you this, sir: We never had anti-Semitism in Armenia. Our liturgy doesn't say a word against Jews."

"But are the Jews responsible for the crucifixion?"

"We don't deny that Jesus said that his nation will crucify him. God wanted it to happen that way. But Jesus loved his nation; he praised his nation! When the Phoenician woman asked him for healing, he said he doesn't give the bread of his people to dogs."

"But the Jews killed Jesus," I said, insisting on the bottom line.

"Jesus had to be crucified, in order to be resurrected. And it had to be the Jews who did it. That is what I can tell you, sir."

He seemed to be saying that it was all a divine play: The crucifixion was necessary for Jesus to assume the sins of humanity and redeem it, and the Jews were simply fulfilling the role assigned to them by God.

Edward said, "Christianity is founded on the resurrection, not the crucifixion. The crucifixion isn't so important."

"Don't underestimate the crucifixion!" shouted Avedis, making a fist.

"But Father . . ."

"You just sit and be quiet and listen to what I tell you. There is no resurrection without crucifixion! Don't you ever forget the crucifixion!"

Evening came, but Enza didn't turn on a light. We sat in silence, watching the darkness. Somewhere in the quarter, members of the

Armenian scouts movement were beating on drums, rehearsing for the Easter procession.

4

In the quarter's cobblestone courtyard, a tiny bookstore sold prayer books with curling Armenian letters and dusty English-language pamphlets about Armenian history, theology, and of course the genocide. The Armenians were still living in the time when urgent ideas were contained in pamphlets, unable to abandon the early part of the twentieth century so long as its genocide was forgotten.

The pamphlets told a story of an industrious and intelligent and, above all, devout people. In the year 301, the Armenians became the first nation to declare Christianity its state religion. Saint Gregory the Illuminator, who presided over the final Christianization of Armenia, saw Jesus descending onto Armenian soil and pointing with a golden hammer to the spot he intended for his cathedral. In other lands, Armenians liked to say, Christianity was spread by Jesus' apostles, but in Armenia it was brought by Jesus himself. Religious and national identity were so entwined that the Armenian alphabet was invented to translate the Bible.

Armenians were among the first and most passionate Christian pilgrims to the Holy Land. The Armenian Quarter housed for many centuries the largest pilgrims' hospice in Jerusalem. Though Armenia obviously couldn't compete with the power of Rome or Byzantium, the Armenian Church, along with the Latin Catholic and the Greek Orthodox Churches, became one of the three main custodians of the holy places—divine reward, Armenians believed, for their tenacity and faith.

The pamphlets quoted accounts of non-Armenian pilgrims who were impressed by the piety and uprightness and even physical beauty of Jerusalem's Armenians. "The Armenians were the most civilized of the Orientals in Jerusalem," one pamphlet said, approvingly quoting a seventeenth-century French missionary. "Even non-Armenians" were moved by the Armenian service, noted another pamphlet, with a persecuted people's mixture of pride and insecurity.

Throughout their history, Armenians endured invasion and dispersion. In 451, an Armenian army led by priests fought a much larger Persian army who intended forcibly to convert the Armenians to Zoroastrianism. Though the Armenians lost the battle (along with "1,036 Armenian martyrs"), they won the guerrilla war that followed. Armenia lost its independence in the fourteenth century, and except for a two-year period beginning in 1918, didn't regain sovereignty until the collapse of the Soviet empire.

The genocide began in 1915. The Muslim Turks, who despised their industrious Armenian Christian minority and feared its secessionist impulses, tested techniques the Nazis would later perfect: state-organized mass deportations; secret coordination among the army, the police, and judiciary; and a campaign of deception to convince the victims that deportation was merely resettlement. Entire towns were emptied within days or even hours, their residents marched into the desert, where they died of starvation and thirst or were massacred by bands of convicts released for that purpose. Horseshoes were nailed to the feet of Armenian prisoners; some Armenians were nailed to boards, to simulate the crucifixion. A German Red Cross representative in Turkey, Armin Wegner, described the death march of the Armenian nation: "Children wept themselves to death, men dashed themselves against the rocks, mothers threw their babes into the brooks, women with child flung themselves, singing, into the Euphrates. They died all the deaths of the earth, the deaths of all the ages."

There seemed to me an eerie connection between the two key dates of Armenia's history: 301, when it became the first Christian nation, and 1915, when it became modernity's first martyr nation. The pamphlets offered no hints of how a religious people understood the relationship between assuming the faith of the cross and finally mounting it. Did Armenians believe they were chosen to suffer? And if so, for what purpose? Did they see themselves as a Christlike nation redeeming the sins of humanity through their suffering? Or had the nation been punished for its sins, which Jews had always believed was the source of their own historical disasters until the Holocaust exhausted their capacity for self-blame? Did Armenians believe that the closer a people got to God, the more exactingly it was judged? Besides anger at the Turks, was there also anger at God?

I was especially interested in stories of religious sacrifice. My own faith had been quickened by Holocaust-era accounts of spiritual resistance, like starving inmates in ghettos and death camps fasting on Yom Kippur and a Jewish mother circumcising her newborn son as they stood before a mass grave so that he could die a proper Jew. No doubt the Armenians had similar accounts. Those stories, I believed, would offer far better insight into the nation's soul than the pamphlets' apologetic paeans to the Armenian character.

My conversations with Father Enza and his friends had been intense when the subject was Armenia and the Turks but embarrassingly lame when we turned to God and belief and the meaning of suffering. One monk had suggested Job as a model of faith; a bishop who'd dropped by Enza's apartment admonished me that it was forbidden to question the ways of God.

And so I phoned George Hintlian, the historian of the Armenian Quarter, and asked him to meet me. History was the true spiritual passion of the Armenians, as it was for the Jews, the arena in which they measured God's closeness. Perhaps an Armenian historian would provide religious insights that the good men of the Armenian church apparently could not.

Even before he told me, I knew that George Hintlian was a fellow child of survivors. The moment of realization happened as we were walking to a café in the Jewish Quarter. (There were no cafés, of course, in the Armenian compound; that would have been too intrusive.) I tripped on the stone pavement, and George instinctively said, "Sorry," as if he were somehow responsible, not for the mishap but for failing to prevent it. He had the child of survivors' need to make the world right, to see life itself as an excessively generous gift for which he must continuously prove his worth.

Though in his early fifties, George wore the indifferent clothes of an old man, buttoned sweater and polyester pants. He was slight, balding, and soft-spoken. His eyelids extended diagonally across his brown Armenian eyes, as if to shield him from the atrocity photographs he'd spent a lifetime studying. The powerful anger within him was neutralized by decency, resulting in an enervating sadness.

George's father had come to Jerusalem as a refugee from the genocide; George was born and raised behind the compound's walls. He had studied in Beirut and now frequently traveled abroad, promoting genocide commemoration. Yet he remained a son of the quarter. "During the day I am fully a part of the life of modern Jerusalem," he said. "But at night I look forward to the moment when they shut the gates and we are left in our own Armenian world."

Like his father before him, George had helped administer the Armenian patriarchate. And like his father, he wasn't a churchgoer but was a believer. I suggested to him that we shared the same paradox: We belonged to peoples who were wounded by history yet who turned to history for confirmation of God's goodness.

We took a table on the café's terrace, overlooking the stone plaza leading to the Western Wall. Consciously or not, George had taken me to precisely the place where I would feel most comfortable discussing history and faith.

There was no need for preliminary small talk; we shared the same obsessions.

"For the Armenians," George began in a matter-of-fact voice, "the desert was like an ocean. There was no one to offer help, only you and your tormentors. An Armenian survivor told me about a woman who walked away from a death march. When a gendarme shouted at her, 'Where are you going?' she said, 'To a funeral.' 'Whose funeral?' he asked, and she said, 'God's funeral.'

"But you know," he continued, "there really is no such thing as an Armenian atheist. I interviewed many survivors in Jerusalem, but even those who said they lost their faith still believed somehow. No matter how far an Armenian drifts away from religion, he still believes in God, even if he doesn't admit it."

"After the Holocaust," I said, "my father refused to pray. But that was because he was angry at God, not because he stopped believing in Him."

"My father was in a Turkish prison, waiting for deportation. One day he noticed that the guards had left their posts. He and his mother and his brother simply walked out. He considered that a miracle. Most of the survivors I've interviewed considered their survival a miracle. One man was on a line of three hundred people. One by one, they put their heads on a block of wood and the executioner split their heads open with an ax. Can you imagine being on such a line and waiting for your turn? This man was at the very end, the second to last person on line. The man before him put his head on the block, the executioner raised the ax high—and suddenly he started to laugh. He simply went mad. He laughed so hard he couldn't bring the ax down. This survivor was convinced he was saved by a miracle. God sends disasters, but He is also generous in His miracles."

"What about the 298 people whose heads were split open?"

"God needs witnesses to tell the story," he said quietly.

"I always found stories of martyrdom more convincing testimonies to God's existence than miracles," I countered. "Do you know the photograph in Yad Vashem of the bearded Jew praying just before he's about to be shot? Corpses are wrapped in prayer shawls at his feet, and SS men are gathered around him, laughing. Even as a boy I felt that the Jew in that photograph knew more about how reality works than the SS men mocking him."

George said, "There was a group in the desert that wanted to take the last communion, but there was no priest. So they picked up pieces of earth and said the blessing themselves. People carried ancient Bibles and buried them in the desert when they were about to die, and survivors later returned to dig them up. One man who escaped the roundups carried the beautiful door of a monastery on his back from Turkey to Armenia. I saw the door in the Yerevan museum. Those people had a naive faith. Many times they ran into the church because they believed that God would protect them. The Turks said, 'These Armenians are really stupid, they make it so easy for us.' The Turks of course would just burn the churches."

"So what is the faith of those of us who know that God won't necessarily save you if you hide in a church, but who still believe in the God of the victims?"

"Faith in the survival of the nation," he replied. "God never allowed this people to perish. Throughout history we've been overrun and brutalized by conquering empires. We say that it takes us fifty years to recover from disaster. That's what history shows. Perhaps in future generations the miracle of survival will seem stronger than the genocide and will bring people closer to God."

"That's what happened to many Jews after the creation of Israel. It happened to my father and me after the Six-Day War. But why must the nation suffer, George?"

"Maybe we're supposed to be better. Not a light to the nations; we don't have that grand idea of ourselves. But a model, an example of a nation of faith. The first Christian nation should be on a certain level. But we became materialistic. We shouldn't be like all the nations."

"Could you face the people in the desert and tell them it's a punishment for their materialism?"

"Not a punishment. Maybe a test of faith, of strength. God takes you to the brink of the abyss and then you have to recover your God.

Part of the test is to go through terrible suffering and not become bitter. I don't get angry at God. If God had destroyed the Armenian people and left only one Armenian in a museum, then I would have been angry. But as long as the nation continues, I accept His will."

I watched the procession of tourists and soldiers and ultra-Orthodox Jews approach the Western Wall, symbol of Jewish endurance. At a younger age, I might have ended the conversation here, with George's affirmation of the survival of the nation as proof of God's benevolence. But that was no longer enough for me.

I said, "After the miraculous survival of the nation, we're still left with the simple question of human suffering. My problem with God isn't death. If we take the promise of religion seriously, then the soul doesn't just go to a better place but to its real home. One and a half million Armenians, six million Jews—everyone dies. The tragedy isn't death but suffering."

He said, "You can kill someone quickly, with a sharp knife at the throat, or you can prolong the death. I was sitting once with a survivor. My glass broke, and he started shaking. I asked him what was wrong, and he told me that he has a horror of broken glass ever since he saw a blind Turk cut up an Armenian boy. This blind Turk was a patriot, and he wanted to play his part in the great national effort of murdering the Armenians. So the gendarmes gave him a piece of glass and brought him a boy, maybe thirteen years old. The blind man tried to cut the boy's throat with the glass but kept missing. He cut him all over until the boy bled to death. So that's our question: Why a piece of broken glass instead of a sharp knife at the throat?"

His tone remained even; emotion was inadequate.

"Do Armenians identify with Jesus' helplessness on the cross?" I asked. "Or do you see it as a symbol for God's silence?"

"You know that our cross isn't a crucifix. Out of a hundred thousand Armenian stone crosses that have been discovered, only three are crucifixes. If we had emphasized the crucifixion, I don't think we would have had the strength to survive. When I see a crucifix, even in a museum as a work of art, I can't look at it. It's unbearable for me."

I explained my fear of the cross and that I'd come to the Armenians on Holy Week because I sensed I would be "safe" among them, that they wouldn't see me as one of the crucifiers but the crucified.

George said, "Menachem Begin once said that when he looks into the eyes of an Armenian, he sees a Jew. When I look into your eyes, I see an Armenian."

5

GOOD FRIDAY

In the Armenian Quarter's Saint James Cathedral, a bell rang in slow agony, pausing between reverberations. A symbolic casket was covered with crosses and flowers in little blue Armenian vases. The altar was concealed with a black banner imprinted with a simple yellow cross, terrifying in its starkness, the one day a year when the Armenians abandoned their flowered cross of resurrection. Today there was no way to evade the crucifixion, no comfort of a happy end. This was the day of the helpless messiah, the mystery of God's allowing evil to prevail, even against Himself.

The cathedral was dense with devotional objects. Hundreds of delicate silver lamps hung from chains, each lamp contributed over the centuries by another community whose name was engraved on its rim. Dark paintings of biblical scenes, especially Noah's ark, crowded the walls, as though unused space would evoke an unbearable emptiness. But high above, as the cathedral ascended toward its towering cupola, the walls became blank, peeling with neglect, conceding the human inability to encapsulate the sacred and leaving the upper reaches to God.

According to tradition, this church was the burial site of Saint

James, the first apostolic martyr, beheaded by Herod Agrippas in the year 44 and Armenia's patron saint. On the walls were paintings of a beatific face looking beyond the raised executioner's sword. I recalled the photo on the wall posters around the quarter, of Turkish soldiers posing beside severed Armenian heads. The Armenians' devotion to Saint James seemed like a premonition of a shared fate.

There were no pews, only Oriental rugs. Hundreds of Armenians, mostly middle-aged women and old people with long noses and sad eyes, filled the emptied space. Some sat on the floor against the wall. The monks happily mingled with their people. Their sociability surprised me. Even today? Especially today. This was when the comfort of community was needed most.

Father Enza greeted me, smiling warmly and taking both my hands, welcoming me into the inner sanctum of Armenian grief. No one stared at me or seemed surprised by the presence of a Jew in a *kipah*.

The service began, led by a choir of seminarians in green robes embroidered with flowers, so earnest and well groomed they seemed to come from another era. I suspected the old Armenians must be looking at them as miracles of life, delicate confirmations of the limited reach of evil.

One young man sang a dirge, while the others hummed in a sad key. Monks in black conical hats raised candles. One monk held a candle at its very tip, with only the wick protruding through his fist, as though he were holding raw fire.

I asked an old man beside me what prayers the choir was singing. "Praising the God," he said, and he turned his attention back to the service. Thanks a lot, I thought. But then I realized he'd given me the most appropriate answer. What was truly important about this service was that it existed at all, that the Armenians, like the Jews, had emerged from the twentieth century still praising God.

Saint James darkened. The pinpricks of light from the silver lamps failed to dispel the late-afternoon diminishment. From high above, a single ray of light penetrated the incense haze. The crowd pressed closer together. The choir chanted a deep winding hymn, so intricate it seemed eternal. The elderly patriarch, a large bent man in a purple robe embroidered with the sun, circled the chapel, followed by deacons clanging metal incense burners and black-hooded monks holding candles—a procession without beginning or end, an Armenian funeral for God.

6

On Easter eve, the stone plaza before the Church of the Holy Sepulcher filled with young Palestinian Christians. They seemed more interested in flirting than praying, and they reminded me of Jerusalem's Jewish teenagers, who chose Yom Kippur eve for an annual social gathering in the Western Wall plaza a few minutes away. Like them, these Christian teenagers didn't know how to honor the sacred except by their presence, but perhaps that was enough. Tonight they even wore crosses over their shirts; fear of their Muslim neighbors, who sometimes harassed them, otherwise kept the crosses tucked away.

The Holy Sepulcher contained a world about which I'd known almost nothing. Like most residents of this city, my reach of the sacred had been limited to my own faith. In Jerusalem, tolerance was measured by the space between religions; the less interest we showed in each other's holy places, the safer we were. Yet as I came to know the Holy Sepulcher, I wondered how I could have kept away, willfully diminishing myself as a Jerusalemite. Only those who loved all of this city's pilgrimage sites were truly at home here, could consider themselves citizens of united Jerusalem.

In recent months, I'd begun coming to the Holy Sepulcher, to meditate and watch. Aside from an elderly Greek Orthodox nun who'd stared at me, frankly convinced a Jew couldn't be up to any good here, I hadn't been made to feel like an intruder. Once, a young Greek Orthodox monk, speaking fluent Hebrew, offered to orient me. Another time, while meditating, I felt a touch on my shoulder and heard someone say "Shalom"; when I opened my eyes, I saw a priest hurrying away, sorry that he'd interrupted my devotions but unable to restrain himself from welcoming me into his spiritual home.

The cavernous, segmented building was a paradox of expansiveness and confinement. It contained the whole experience of Christianity, of religion itself, transcending human limitations and confirming them. Rooms led into smaller rooms, claimed and counterclaimed by rival denominations and cluttered with statues and paintings and crucifixes planted like flags, meant not only to venerate but to possess. Every morning around dawn, representatives of the three denominations that controlled the church—Greek Orthodox, Latin Catholic, and Armenian—together opened its great doors, a medieval ritual meant to ensure equal access to the building. Then, in the late afternoon, monks prayed along the route of their turf, a procession of ownership. Sometimes the territorial defensiveness actually caused violence. Jesus had urged the surrender of possessions, but here some of his followers tried to possess him.

In fact, the true spiritual custodians of this building were its anonymous pilgrims, who carved crosses into the stone walls because their own names no longer mattered and who fell onto the marble slab marking the stone that held Jesus' body and lovingly polished it with cloth, sprinkled it with rose water, or simply lay their heads on its smooth cool surface.

A noble exception to the interdenominational surliness was the reconstruction of the cupola in the mid-1990s, in which all the groups had participated. The new version was a dome with a gold sun emanating thick rays, lacking subtlety and grace and overwhelming the accretions of somberness below. The impetus for the sudden ecumenism was practical. The old dome had been in danger of collapse. Yet however uninspired the cause and however crass the result, the reminder of a common fate held an exalted message. Looking up from the dark alcoves to that glaring monument of ecumenical coopera- tion, a pilgrim was reminded of the reality of oneness beyond human grasping. High above, all our differences were dispelled in light.

The holiday crowds were cacophonous with expectation. From somewhere within the depths of the building came a rhythmic beat- ing on a wooden board like a tribal summoning, followed by the metal rattle of censers and the quivering of little bells and then more assertive bells and a clapping of wooden poles announcing the arrival of a church dignitary. Thousands of people, holding candles and video cameras, prayer books and guidebooks, were already inside, and thousands more waited patiently to enter. There were kerchiefed Russian women with faces as pale as the candlelight in their hands, Romanian foreign workers shabby even in their Sunday clothes, young Westerners not sure if they were tourists or pilgrims, Greek women in black dresses and slippers, Ethiopians in jeans taking each other's photographs.

I went up the stone stairs to Golgotha, an open, platformlike area overlooking the main hall and divided between the Catholics and the Greek Orthodox. The Catholic area was modest, with a stone slab for candles and a shimmering blue and gold mosaic of Jesus on the cross. The Greek Orthodox area contained a stone said to be the site of the crucifixion, kept under glass and guarded by a wary monk. A life- sized gold statue of Jesus on the cross was flanked by silver statues of Mother Mary and Mary Magdalene; their flat faces looked like paper cutouts. Silver engravings depicted the crucifixion, and I found myself scanning the scenes for Jewish faces; to my relief, I saw only Roman soldiers.

Two Armenian deacons, whom I recognized from the Good Friday service at Saint James, scattered incense, staking their claim here. Cer- tainly the Armenians wouldn't want to be excluded from Golgotha.

I returned to the main hall downstairs, where crowds waited for the procession to begin. At midnight, each of the Orthodox denominations would circle the domed structure in the middle of the hall that contained the empty tomb. Dozens of police mingled with the crowds, discreet and alert. A policeman, glancing at my *kipah,* asked me, "What are you doing in this party?"

"I'm interested in what happens in my city," I replied.

He shrugged: another Jerusalem lunatic.

"Why are there so many of you tonight?" I asked him.

"You never know what can happen here," he said. "If one procession intrudes even a centimeter into the procession of another group, it can come to blows. Last year there were injuries."

Outside, Israeli police with M-16s patrolled against Muslim extremists; inside, Israeli police armed with batons protected Christians from one another. On this night that Jews once feared, and in this place that was the source of that dread, Israeli policemen were keeping the peace. Yet they themselves seemed innocent of historical memory, concerned only with ensuring order. Cops doing a routine job. Their lack of historical self-consciousness was the subtle beauty of the moment, proof of how deeply Israel had healed us. Jews protecting Christians on Easter eve was our vengeance, not against Christianity but against Jewish powerlessness. I felt no gloating, only the joy of homecoming. This was my resurrection, the reason I could be here tonight without anger or discomfort.

The Armenians, I thought, would understand.

Upstairs on the roof, the Ethiopians were gathering. A large tent, whose black and yellow patterned cloth resembled leopard skin, had been erected to accommodate the hundreds of pilgrims who had come from Ethiopia, while hundreds more mingled outside in the cool darkness. A young man sold posters of Haile Selassie. People greeted each other Ethiopian-style, kissing repeatedly on either cheek. These were not poor villagers. Though almost everyone was dressed in the same white embroidered robes and sandals, some women wore high heels.

I found Germa at the entrance to the tent. Teasingly, I kissed his sleeve, as though he were a monk. "Get out of here," he said, and hugged me. Germa was the impresario of Ethiopian Easter: He had supervised the erection of the tent, negotiated with police, and escorted church dignitaries to the roof. But he wore no white robe and didn't join the prayers. Even on the roof of the Holy Sepulcher, as close as a Christian can get to the heavenly Jerusalem, he was an outsider to his people's joy.

We watched a circle of priests in white robes and turbans at the far end of the tent chanting Psalms. As a Westerner used to instant melodies, I couldn't decipher the leisurely musical progression. The chanters held each note for so long it sounded like moaning. They swayed together in and out of the circle, beating tambourines and waving horsehair brushes and ivory-tipped canes. "They believe that the Psalms must be sung and danced to," Germa explained, "because they think that is how King David recited them." They believe, they think—he sounded like an anthropologist.

Then he abruptly changed tone, confessing his longing for faith. "You see them praying, really praying, and you think, There must be some truth to it."

"So why don't you allow yourself to participate?"

"I'm like the person who goes to the beach but doesn't enter the water."

Traditional faith was a magic circle: Step outside, and its power dissipated. Germa was an exile from the circle, yet he remained bound by its pull. He was, in his way, a renunciate, organizing the ceremonies whose devotions were denied him. Among these pilgrims, I thought, Germa must be especially beloved by God.

"Why don't you go inside?" Germa offered, instinctively playing the host. Reluctantly, I stepped into the crowded, fluorescent-lit tent.

There was barely room to stand. I wanted to flee, but meanwhile others had entered behind me, and the exit closed up. I panicked in crowded places, and I was beginning to panic now. Perhaps it was an inherited memory from the Holocaust, that staged escalation of constricting space, from ghetto to cattle car to the final airless room. My claustrophobia now took an Israeli twist: What if a terrorist from an adjacent roof threw a Molotov cocktail into this tent? My ultimate fear was to be trapped in a small space with desperate fleeing bodies. And here I was, standing directly in the path of the stampede toward the exit. I selected a spot of refuge along the wall of the tent. When everyone rushed to the exit, I would head in the opposite direction.

I looked around. Hundreds of people stood or sat on the floor, yet no one pushed or squirmed or even seemed uncomfortable. Not like a crowd at all but self-contained beings who required only the space their bodies held. Some silently read from little Psalters printed in Geez. A woman with eyes closed was fingering prayer beads. They were heirs to an ancient dignity, a church that had preceded much of European Christianity by centuries. Whenever someone entered, the crowd parted, if just barely, accommodating another body. Here space was relative, expanding with a willingness to share. I recalled a legend of the Jerusalem Temple: When too many pilgrims came, the building simply widened. Perhaps the pilgrimage itself created a generosity that always had room for just one more. Even if disaster were to happen here, I realized, these people wouldn't panic.

I scanned the crowd for Haile Geiorgis, but I couldn't find him. He avoided all public displays of piety, and even tonight he was probably in his church, arranging the prayer books and sweeping the steps. Yet I felt his calm presence as I relaxed into this African crowd, felt him hovering behind me just as he did when I'd meditated in his church, protecting me from fear and blessing me with stillness.

7

EASTER SUNDAY

In the haze of a premature summer, *hamsin*—when the desert over-takes the city with a dry and gritty wind—Father Enza and his fellow monks gathered in the courtyard of the Armenian compound for the last ceremony of Holy Week, the Blessing of the Four Corners of the World. The idea was powerful: Jerusalem sending forth its blessings from the Armenian Quarter, repository of suffering and faith. But the concept was more inspiring than the actual rite. Perhaps a hundred bored and restless spectators had come to hear the monks drone their prayers. The old patriarch in his splendid robe with its rising sun was flanked by seminarians wearing their bright green and purple-fringed robes; but the majesty had been exhausted and the ceremony seemed forced. The Armenian soul, I suspected, like the Jewish soul, was still too wounded to bless the world.

Even the compound itself, which had its mysterious appeal, seemed merely cramped and depleted: weeds between the cobble-stones, stained and peeling walls, the houses with their little doors and windows crowded together in enforced intimacy. On the very day meant to reveal the glory of their faith, the Armenians were least able to conceal their brokenness.

I greeted Enza, and he whispered to me, "So many ceremonies. I'm so tired."

George Hintlian was in the crowd. He hadn't been in church on Good Friday, but he made a point, he said, of always coming to services on Easter Sunday. "Why go for the burial of God," he said to me, "when He rises two days later?" George could immerse himself in atrocity stories but refused to accept pain from religion, which was supposed to be the antidote to history and provide only comfort.

After the ceremony, Enza insisted I accompany him back to his room.

"I should let you rest," I said.

"I try to sleep as little as possible. We live maybe forty years, and half that time we waste eating and sleeping."

"Why forty years? I'm already forty-five, Father Enza. Where does that leave me?"

"Forty years is enough for me. I'm afraid of becoming old and helpless." He laughed. "But I'm also afraid of dying. I have too many fears. It's not good for a monk."

"There should be a way for us to use our obsession with death as a strength," I said. "We come from peoples who know that a whole world can end in an instant. That should give us a certain detachment."

"The Armenians say, 'When you feel giddy, go to the cemetery. When you feel angry or sad, go to the cemetery.'"

As soon as we entered his apartment, the phone rang. "I'm so important," he said to me, with self-deprecating humility.

Two seminarians named Vrej and Karen, both in their early twenties and wearing black collarless shirts, dropped by. They had come from Armenia to Jerusalem together with Enza to study to become monks. Though Enza wasn't so much older than them, they treated him with respect rather than intimacy.

Vrej was tall and very thin, with orphan Armenian eyes that widened in seeming horror but with the elastic mouth of a comedian. He was the first Armenian I'd met who laughed easily, without irony. He told me this story: Once, while vacationing on the Black Sea, a man approached him and asked if he was from Azerbaijan. Vrej, unhappy about being identified with the nation at war with Armenia, indignantly replied that he wasn't. "From your answer I understand that you are Armenian," said the man; he added, "Wait here." A few minutes later he returned with a bottle of vodka. "I am a Jew," he said. "You are an Armenian. Let's drink together because nobody likes either of us."

We all laughed.

"Why have our peoples suffered, Vrej?" I asked.

He'd obviously brooded over the question and didn't hesitate with his reply. "To refine gold, you put it through the fire. If God wants to lift up a nation, He has to give it difficult treatment. Through the whole Bible, God is testing the people of Israel. They were punished more than other nations. Not because they sinned more, but because God wanted something special from this people."

"I don't know the Armenians, Vrej, but I do know the Jews. Suffering doesn't necessarily make you more noble."

But Vrej didn't mean spiritual or moral refinement; he meant the nation's political cohesion. "Suffering helped our national characters," he said. "After the Holocaust, the Jews became stronger and better organized. The same with the Armenians. Now we are more together, more ready to sacrifice."

Karen, who had been listening quietly, said, "Satan showed Jesus this world and offered it to him, which means it is really Satan's world. God's people get punished because we don't belong here. I don't know if that's right, but I don't find any other answer."

He spoke with an intensity that surprised me. At first glance I'd dismissed him as uninteresting: He had slicked-back hair and an ordinary face whose only distinction was its even proportions. I looked at him more closely now: Thick eyebrows emphasized a seriousness beyond his years; a strong jaw suggested youthful defiance but also sturdiness. Despite his passion, he seemed calmer, less agitated, and therefore less Armenian than the other young people I'd met in Enza's room.

I asked Karen why he'd decided to become a monk, and he told me his story. He grew up in Etchmiadzin, the holy city of Armenia, whose main cathedral is said to have been built after a visitation by Jesus. As a boy, Karen had feared the black-cloaked men in their triangular hats and avoided even walking past the great cathedral. Then, when he was ten, his grandmother revealed that she had secretly baptized him as a baby; she hadn't even told his parents, who could have lost their jobs had the Soviet authorities who then ruled Armenia discovered the illicit baptism. Karen didn't know why, but he was pleased by his grandmother's revelation; he felt anointed.

Like all Soviet children, he had been taught in school that religion was voodoo and that God was created by man. Karen appreciated the theory of evolution but wondered how that alone could explain the origin of life. It seemed to him that the only notion more silly than that a great being had created the world with a purpose and a plan was that the world had created itself. For a Soviet boy, challenging the atheist inquisition was an expression of freedom; faith in God meant commitment to limitless possibility.

His grandmother's next revelation was the genocide. Like the Holocaust, the Armenian genocide was a forbidden topic in the Soviet Union, which feared national stirrings and so suppressed the histories of its subject peoples. Karen's grandmother revealed that his grandfather, who'd died when Karen was young, had been a genocide survivor who, at age twelve, had fled to Iran after his entire family was massacred. The secret genocide, the hidden God, the forbidden faith—all the elements that the Soviet state had tried to suppress now converged for Karen into a new identity. Suddenly, the invisible assumed a compelling vitality.

In 1991, the Soviet state collapsed and Armenia reemerged. Landlocked, impoverished, surrounded by Muslim enemies and at war with Azerbaijan, Armenia seemed like a parody of a country. "My father was pessimistic, like most Armenians," Karen said. "He didn't believe Armenia could survive. But then I saw soldiers with the Armenian flag on their uniforms. I'd never seen such a thing before: Armenian soldiers! At that moment I knew our resurrection wasn't an illusion."

I knew that emotion: My own break with the self-pity of the victim began at that moment when, as a fourteen-year-old tourist in Israel, I first glimpsed soldiers with "ZAHAL," the Hebrew acronym for the Israel Defense Forces, sewn on their shirts.

Though less than ten years in age separated Karen and Vrej from

Enza, the difference was decisive; the past ten years had been crucial for the Armenians, the first tentatively hopeful decade since the genocide. Karen and Vrej's formative experience was the collapse of the Soviet Union and the emergence of a free Armenia. Enza belonged to the forlorn faces of his portraits, to an Armenian nation where the generation gap was defined simply by those who came before the genocide and those who came after. Yet now there was a new potential generation gap: those who came of age before Armenian independence and those still young enough to have been transformed by the sight of Armenian soldiers wearing the Armenian flag. Karen and Vrej had entered an Armenian future, however uncertain, that honored the genocide but wasn't wholly defined by it.

Vrej said, "The Armenian resurrection isn't happening as fast as the Jewish resurrection. But it is happening. In 1991, the situation in Armenia was—oh my God, no light, no gas, no water. We had coupons for bread. And we were totally isolated. But now Armenia looks to me like Paris. New restaurants, new fashions, new mentality. Everything changed. People believe in the future."

And what, I asked, was the future of the Armenian church?

"When the seminarians get together, we sometimes say quietly that what the Armenian church needs is a Vatican II," said Karen. "To look at the liturgy and the theology and bring us into the modern world. An Armenian monk from Turkey told me a story about a cat that kept interfering in a church service. One monk decided to tie up the cat during prayers and then release it afterward. This became his job. Years later, after the monk died, people forgot the original reason and went out and looked for a cat to tie up during prayers."

Vrej: "And then centuries later a monk writes a treatise on the theology of cat-tying."

They laughed.

Karen: "But to change the tradition is a frightening thought. Who are we to do it? I know that's the wrong attitude, but it's deep in us."

Change was especially frightening for a survivor people entrusted with the rituals of its martyrs. To willfully alter the tradition meant in some way becoming complicitous with those who had tried to erase it. Nothing could be more horrifying to an Armenian, fighting against historical amnesia. Yet only the renewal of each generation's courage to claim the tradition on its own terms would save it from a fatal irrelevance.

I asked whether they foresaw a renewal of Armenian spirituality—that instead of totally identifying religion with the nation, an individual's relationship with God could again become the concern of Armenian monasticism. At first they didn't understand the question. Vrej said, "Religion is the vitality of the nation."

"But what about the vitality of the individual soul?" I persisted. "Religion pays a price when it becomes too closely identified with nationalism. That's what's happened to Judaism in Israel. Our rabbis became politicians."

Karen said, "A clergyman's job is to serve the people. But still, it makes us part of the world. It's very sad."

Karen spoke of a little band of Armenian ascetics who, like Saint Francis, wandered the countryside and repaired churches that had been destroyed or abandoned under the communists. They slept in the ruins and begged alms, which they then distributed to the poor. Karen clearly felt attracted to them. "Saints exist in every nation," he said. "They keep alive the nation's link with God."

Vrej said, "Last year when I was in Armenia, I saw two men playing guitar on the street. They had a sign that said, 'Whoever wants to, please give. Whoever needs to, please take.' It was wonderful."

"Is there an 'Armenian mission?' " I asked.

"To help other struggling peoples," Vrej replied. "I don't know how we can be in a position to help, but that's what history expects of us."

Whether or not that would happen, Vrej's sentiment was precious. His need to replace self-obsession with a relationship with other wounded nations was the first step toward healing. Perhaps the Armenian resurrection would happen after all, and someday Armenian monks gathered in the forlorn courtyard of their walled-in quarter might even find the strength to pray for the world with the same fervor they reserved for their own nation. I wished for the Armenians what I wished for my people: the wisdom to draw both generosity and strength from suffering.

8

APRIL 24, ARMENIAN GENOCIDE DAY

Perhaps a thousand people were gathered in the narrow road just outside the high stone wall of the Armenian compound. Once a year they emerged en masse, but quietly, without chanting or fist waving; the very act of demonstrating was so unusual for the reclusive community that any display of emotion was redundant.

Many held candles. An elderly woman, no doubt touched that a Jew had joined them, offered me her candle. I tried to explain that it was the Jewish Sabbath and that I was forbidden to handle fire, an elemental force of creation. She smiled at me, as if to say: I don't understand why you won't take a candle, but all that matters is your presence among us.

On the fence of the Armenian Seminary, just across the entrance to the quarter, hung blowups of black-and-white photographs, blurred and fading into time. A dead child, piles of skeletal bodies, familiar images of the century. The new Armenian tragedy was that the genocide had been overtaken by other atrocities, especially the Holocaust, before it had been acknowledged and absorbed into history. One photograph, though, still managed to shock: a dead woman, eyes open, with a cross etched into her chest.

Alongside the photographs were posters in English, Hebrew, and Arabic, appealing and demanding and accusing. "Shame!" read one sign in Hebrew. "Israel is encouraging denial of the Armenian Holo-caust." There was truth to it: Both left- and right-wing Israeli governments, protective of Israel's military alliance with Turkey, had surrendered to Turkish demands and excised the genocide from our school curriculum. It was outrageous, disgraceful, but entirely comprehensible. Given the precariousness of our geography, we couldn't afford to jeopardize our military alliance with a powerful Muslim state. Aligning with Turkey, even at the expense of a fellow victim nation, was part of the price of survival.

Still, my understanding for the Israeli position didn't lessen my shame. I had become complicitous in genocide denial. Here was a Christian community accusing the Jews of being indifferent to their suffering, the very sin we had accused Christians of committing against us. I had grown up resenting "the world," which didn't care if we lived or died. Now, for the Armenians, I was "the world."

A young woman at a booth was pinning commemorative tags on participants' lapels. The tag said simply, "April 24, Armenian Genocide Day," and was written only in Armenian. They were used to being ignored and speaking among themselves. In the center of the tag was a black cross, not the Armenian cross of resurrection but unadorned. Obviously, I couldn't put on that tag. Wearing the imprint of a cross while walking with my *kipah* through the Old City, past Jews on their way to the Western Wall? Unthinkable. Perhaps if it had been the Armenian cross, disguised with flowers, not really a cross at all . . .

I approached the booth and asked the young woman to pin a tag on my shirt. It happened so suddenly that I didn't know why I'd changed my mind. Maybe it was the role reversal I'd experienced confronting my complicity in genocide revisionism. Maybe it was the realization that this cross was "safe" after all, that it didn't represent the crucifixion of Jesus but of the Armenians. Maybe I was thinking of the cross carved into the dead woman's chest and saw that as the Christian equivalent of the yellow star.

The young woman smiled at me, acknowledging my goodwill but unaware as she pinned the tag near my heart that she was shattering centuries of inherited revulsion and fear. I surprised myself again: I felt free. I wanted to wear the tag not in spite of the cross but because of it.

The march began slowly and in silence, like a funeral procession. The route was a narrow road between high and curving stone walls leading from the Armenian Quarter to nearby Mount Zion. Old people and teenagers and mothers wheeling baby carriages all walked the same measured pace; scouts in orange scarves and khaki shorts beat drums. The old patriarch, bearing a gold crucifix, was held on either side by Karen and Vrej, who wore black cloaks and purple sashes, like medieval pages. For all their restlessness and hopes for change in the church, today they belonged entirely to the past, flanking the patriarch like the flowers of an Armenian cross.

Young people wearing the T-shirts designed by Father Enza—the date 1915 formed into a lightning bolt and splitting a tree—distributed leaflets to passersby. One leaflet approvingly quoted former British prime minister Lloyd George, "who described the Turks best as 'that human cancer—the only people who contributed nothing to enlightenment or progress.'" By contrast, noted the leaflet in damaged English, an Armenian scientist had helped discover a new medical treatment for AIDS: "This is not surprising to Armenian scientists all over the world who already had left their marks and contributions to world civilization."

We came to the Armenian cemetery on Mt. Zion, entering under a canopy of grapevines just beginning to flower. Poppies grew between the densely laid gravestones. Some of the stones, dating back hundreds of years, had been shattered and then lovingly reassembled like mosaics. A rally began around an obelisk memorial to Armenian soldiers killed in World War I, but most people ignored the speeches and gathered at family graves, covering the stones with bouquets of flowers still in their plastic wrappings. Here public and private mourning converged. For a people that had died in mass graves, cemeteries were precious, each grave a victory over anonymous death.

The sun was intense, and the Armenians, being practical people, didn't prolong their dutiful stay. We wandered back to the seminary across from the entrance to the walled compound. Families sat on the grass, boys ran around a tree shouting "Cowabunga!" and seminarians circulated with trays of Arab pastries and little cups of sweet black coffee. It seemed inconceivable that just minutes ago this had been a grieving people.

I found Karen, and we sat together on the lawn, listening to young men sing patriotic songs. Karen translated for me: "Hey, who are we? The strong Armenian people!"

"This feels like a celebration," I said.

"I woke up this morning and felt strangely happy," he confessed. "It bothered me. On this of all days to be happy. But then I realized: I'm happy because we're still here. This isn't just a sad day, it's also the day of the Armenian cross of resurrection. It is Good Friday and Easter Sunday combined into one."

Karen excused himself. The job of an Armenian cleric was to mingle with his people. I found George Hintlian speaking with a journalist, being useful for the cause. He noticed the cross on my chest, raised his eyebrows, but was too tactful to comment.

"So what are you praying for today, George?" I asked.

"That God should give the Armenians a proper burial. They're lying without graves in the desert; at least history should give them a tombstone. The denial has become our great tragedy. It is torturing us. No nation has experienced this. We should be moving on, but the denial keeps us stuck in the genocide. We're still at the primitive stage of trying to convey facts to the world. I'm a cultural historian, but I end up spending much of my time on the genocide. It's taken years away from my work. Maybe you'll be surprised to hear this, but I want to meet Turks, civilized Turks. I know they exist. Doctors. Pro-

fessors. I expect a cultured person to be able to deal with the problems of his own history. Every empire has its black pages. They
should have the courage to face it. I don't hold them personally
responsible anymore. You know, I'll go further: If they can't face it,
I'm willing to accept them anyway as human beings. So they can't
face it. Everyone has their weakness. I'll try to forgive even that. This
Turkish obsession is killing me."

I told him how reluctant I'd been to pin the commemorative tag
on my chest and how the Armenians had helped me overcome my
fear of the cross.

"You've taken a big step," he said, and in his voice I heard a trace
of envy.

five

Christmas

I

I crossed the border on Friday afternoon just before sundown. The drive from Israeli Jerusalem into Palestinian Bethlehem went past the army checkpoint of concrete blocks and barbed wire and a rough stone memorial for a Jewish woman stabbed on this spot: the stigmata of the land. Friday, the Muslim holy day, was fading into the Jewish Sabbath, and a rare calm settled on the border. The street leading from the checkpoint to Rachel's Tomb and beyond to the Church of the Nativity, normally crowded with pilgrims' buses and vendors selling hot chickpeas and broad beans, used shoes, and CDs without cases, was emptied. The Palestinian laborers, who during the week returned around now from their jobs in Israel as dishwashers and construction workers, stayed home on Fridays, and the young Israeli soldiers relaxed into the summer evening and became teenagers again, laughing and shouting at one another.

I didn't trust the peaceful atmosphere. I was now, after all, in Palestine, a hostile place. I removed my *kipah* to avoid resembling a West Bank settler and risk a rock thrown through my windshield. However justified the precaution, I felt humiliated hiding my Jewishness in Bethlehem. Jews in the Diaspora had once traveled dangerous distances to touch the grave of Mother Rachel and pray for their return to the land. At this moment, what remained for me of the endless debate over justice for the Palestinians and security for the

Israelis was the shame of failure, the inability to be a Jew in Beit Lehem. My regret wasn't political but religious, or perhaps simply personal: the sadness of a son whose ancestral home rejected him. I had become a foreigner here, like a Palestinian crossing in the opposite direction, from Bethlehem into Jerusalem, and confronting the density of apartment buildings rising from hills where Arab shepherds once led their flocks. Both Palestinians and Jews suffered the injustice of estrangement from the land.

In a few minutes, though, I would be among friends. I was on my way to celebrate Shabbat with the monks and nuns of the Beatitudes, a Catholic community devoted to reconciliation with the Jews and to restoring something of Christianity's Judaic roots, which the community believed would spiritually renew the church. Every Friday night the community's fifteen hundred members, living in seventy houses around the world, lit candles and sang the Shabbat service in as much Hebrew as they knew, then ate a festive meal. The Beatitudes' house in Bethlehem served as the community's international center for Judaic experience. Members came here to study rabbinic commentaries and Jewish mysticism, praying at the Western Wall and fasting on Yom Kippur, even as they continued to live a normative Christian life.

A Catholic community that celebrated Shabbat gave me a common language, not only as a Jew with Christians, but as a worldly person with monastics. Shabbat was the time when I tried to forgo ambition and anticipate my own death; I'd imagine those moments just before dying when you feel the shame of having consistently chosen the trivial over the eternal. Shabbat was the weekly opportunity to try yet again to commit myself to a God-centered life. Everything stopped—television, telephone, computer, car—and that fast from modernity stilled the electronic chatter and made me archaic, freed from time. On Shabbat I could dare presume that my cluttered life had something in common after all with the lives of monks and nuns, heroes of the war against mortality.

Sister Miriam greeted me at the door. She wore the community's habit: white robe overlaid with brown corduroy scapular, white kerchief, sandals. Yet there was nothing austere about Miriam, whose face revealed the precocious child she had been: high cheekbones pressing her eyes into smiles, nose sloping like a curtsy, firm chin delighting in its assertiveness. She was in her mid-thirties, like most of the monks and nuns here. In Beatitudes communities, men and women and even families with children shared the same houses, to create a contemporary form of contemplative life.

"Welcome home," she said, kissing me lightly on either cheek and then firmly hugging me. As I entered the building I restored the *kipah* to my head. Miriam was right; in a way this was home, a refuge in Palestine where I could be a Jew. Discovering a sense of home in unlikely places was also part of the experience of being a Jew in this land.

The house, a stolid building at the end of a narrow road off the main street, lacked the gardens and arched passageways of the Holy Land's other Catholic monasteries. Worse, it was on the wrong side of the checkpoint, isolating the Beatitudes from Jewish friends wary of entering Bethlehem and far from the synagogues where community members prayed on Friday nights. The community had tried to acquire a building within Jerusalem, but no suitable church property was found. And so, with monastic gratitude, members accepted this place as God's gift and tried to convince themselves that it really was for the best.

Inside the building, Jewish and Christian imagery coexisted, as if in this city where Christianity emerged from a Jewish womb, the parting of the ways between the two faiths hadn't been a traumatic rupture but an easily rectified misunderstanding. A seven-branched gold menorah stood on the stone altar in the chapel; its candles were lit before each mass. In the hallway hung a large sketch of Thérèse of Lisieux, "the little flower," the nineteenth-century French saint who died at age twenty-four; the image was blurred, as if the artist had caught the first stages of her absorption into God. Nearby hung an equally large photograph of an elderly Hasidic Jew in pre-Holocaust Poland, whose long, sad face seemed to sense imminent martyrdom. I wondered whether the monks and nuns saw in that face how Jesus might have looked as an old man, or perhaps how he'd aged on the cross. They were too aware of Jewish sensitivities to make any direct connection between the Holocaust and the crucifixion, but how could they resist a covert link between the solidarity they felt with Jewish suffering and the martyred Jew at the center of their faith?

The community's Judaica library would have been impressive even for a Jewish institution. It offered volumes of Hebrew and French translations of Mishna, Talmud, Hasidism, and Jewish philosophy; Maimonides and Buber; Rebbe Nahman and Levinas. Some Christian communities in Israel studied only New Testament–era Judaism, to connect to the life of Jesus; the Beatitudes studied all periods of Judaism, to connect to the life of the Jewish people. The community was undoing Christianity's original sin of attempted patricide, its insistence that Judaism's vitality and blessings had passed over to the church. The community functioned as a kind of reverse Christian mission: bringing Judaism to the church, rather than Christianity to the Jews. After the Holocaust, the Vatican had quietly dropped missionizing aimed at Jews, but the Beatitudes made that unspoken decision explicit. Ultimately, the community believed, God would bring all of humanity, including the Jews, to faith in Jesus; meanwhile, Jews needed to be as good Jews as possible, faithful to their spiritual calling of witnessing to God's presence in history.

Miriam was fasting. Community members, she explained, fasted every Friday, reliving the Easter cycle: Friday was the time of crucifixion, Sunday of resurrection.

"And where does Shabbat fit in?" I asked.

She went silent, reluctant to discuss her private devotion. Finally, she said, "For me, the highest expression of Shabbat is when I recall Jesus resting between the crucifixion and the resurrection. That's how I understand the idea of God resting on Shabbat. But," she quickly added, perhaps sensing my unease over her Christianization of Shabbat, "everyone in the community has his own way of connecting. Usually, just being in Shabbat is enough, and I don't have to explicitly link it with Jesus. But when I first joined the community, taking on Shabbat didn't feel quite authentic to me. It seemed like playacting. I thought, 'I'm a nun, not a Jew; I need a Christian justification for this.'"

Miriam took me to my room. It belonged to Genevieve, who would be moving in with Miriam for Shabbat. Genevieve hadn't yet decided to become a nun, though she was already living as one. The room was far too large for her few possessions: desk, cot, night table, an unframed photograph of the marble slab in the Church of the Holy Sepulcher marking the spot where Jesus' body was said to have lain. The room's aesthetic longings were concentrated on a makeshift altar: straw stool covered with white cloth, on which was mounted an Armenian-style cross, whose arms ended in the shape of flowers, and a vase filled with thistles, imparting the hard beauty of the land. Nothing diverted one's attention from devotion; even the few books at Genevieve's bedside were religious. The single-mindedness both enticed and frightened me. Here love of God wasn't merely an enhancement of life but life itself. How long would I last in God's presence without the relief of distraction?

I unpacked: silver-and-white-striped prayer shawl, Hebrew prayer book, a history of Christian spirituality—everything a Jew needed for Shabbat in a monastery. I laid the articles in a symmetrical pile, inspired by the precision with which Genevieve's meager things were arranged. The randomness of daily life slipped away, replaced by a rhythm in which every act had purpose.

In the bathroom I found a pile of toilet paper that Genevieve had torn for me for use on Shabbat. Jewish tradition prohibits cutting anything but food on Shabbat, to restore creation to its natural state, and so part of an Orthodox Jew's Friday preparations is ensuring a supply of precut toilet paper. My own observance wasn't nearly so exacting, but I was touched by Genevieve's gesture of respect and surprised by her insider's knowledge of the smallest details of Judaism, a measure of how deeply the Beatitudes were committed to reconciliation with the Jews.

Genevieve's room overlooked an olive grove. The land was dry and faded. The rainy season had ended several months earlier, in the spring. Just beyond lay Bethlehem to one side and Jerusalem to the other. Building cranes hovered over both cities; half-built houses crowded the hills. The building frenzy was a new war of stones between Arabs and Jews, staking their competing claims. I felt the relief of Shabbat in the fading light, peace returning to the quarried land.

In the dining room, the table awaited Shabbat: silver candlesticks, rose-colored glass cup for blessing the wine, two home-baked challahs covered with a hand-painted cloth depicting Jerusalem's arches and domes. Sister Gabrielle was rushing about, like a Jew in the final moments of preparation before candle lighting. In her early forties, Gabrielle was the elder among young enthusiasts. She also had seniority because she'd lived in Israel for sixteen years, longer than any other community member. She had just returned from the Galilee, she told me, where she'd led a group of visiting priests from Beatitudes communities. "It was *kef*," she said in Hebrew, using the slang word for "fun." "They really got it." She meant: They'd connected not only to the Holy Land but to the Land of Israel. Christian pilgrims to the Galilee usually sought an encounter with the Christian Jesus; Gabrielle, though, took her groups to the "Jewish Galilee"—Talmud-era excavations and modern kibbutzim—restoring Jesus to his people and faith.

The room began to fill: African priests from Gabrielle's group,

Eastern European seminarians spending the year studying Judaism, Gabrielle and Miriam and the half-dozen others who ran this house. Brother François de Sales motioned me to sit beside him, at the head of the long table, and I took a seat between him and Gabrielle. François de Sales, who despite his name was German, was "shepherd" of the house. I thanked him for the community's hospitality, and he said, in his formal English, "On the contrary, it is we who thank you for coming." Then he added with a wry smile, "It is not every Shabbat that we get to have a real Jew with us." I laughed. It was a measure of the Beatitudes' ease with Jews that a German could allow himself to joke about his own Jewish obsession, rather than be solemnly polite toward Jews, like some Germans I knew.

I looked around at the faces turned toward me: expectant, welcoming, grateful. I would have felt more embarrassed had I not realized that the appreciation wasn't directed at me personally but as a representative of Judaism. A real Jew, coming to share Shabbat with the Christians.

Sister Rachel lit the candles. She waved her hands, beckoning the light toward her eyes, then opened her palms to disperse it. Rachel was beloved here for her modesty, her shy smile, which seemed unaware of its generosity. She looked surprised whenever someone paid attention to her and would probably have preferred an invisible job in the kitchen to the role of bringing in Shabbat for the community. Perhaps for that reason she was given public tasks, which she accepted without complaint. Modesty, after all, could be an excuse for an undeveloped personality, or even become a matter of subtle pride. Sometimes the spiritual life required the surrender not only of your worst traits but of those you considered your best. In a surprisingly strong and steady voice, she said the Hebrew blessing, thanking God for sanctifying us with the Shabbat light.

Brother Johann, the community's accordionist, played *Yedid Nefesh*, "Friend of the Soul," the love song to God sung in synagogues on Friday evening. "My soul is sick for your love," we all sang in Hebrew. Then we began chanting the traditional service, singing key phrases to Hasidic melodies: *Lehu neranana*, "Come let us sing to God, let us raise our voices in joy." Those who knew Hebrew fluently prayed from the Shabbat prayer book, others from transliterated sheets. Beside me, Gabrielle swayed with the rhythm of the synagogue.

They sang briskly, even when the melody required restraint, marching with the accordion from one prayer to the other with barely a pause. It was disorienting to hear my prayers and melodies through another tradition's interpretation. Slow down, I wanted to say, you've got it wrong. But then I began to appreciate the sensation of strangeness. Suddenly these prayers I knew from memory weren't so familiar anymore; freed from rote, the words seemed to reclaim their pristine urgency.

"Shake the dust off," they sang, "arise, wear your glorious garments, My people." I looked around at the avid gentile faces singing our synagogue prayers and wondered what my father would say. He wouldn't believe what he was seeing. Here in this room was the measure of distance between his generation and mine. My father had felt so abandoned during the Holocaust that long afterward he still wondered whether Jews would ever be accepted as part of the human race. In their reverence for Judaism, the Beatitudes were saying the exile of the Jews was over.

However moved I was by the service, I was brooding over what Miriam had said to me earlier, about celebrating Shabbat as Jesus' time of rest between crucifixion and resurrection. Wasn't Christianizing Shabbat just another expression of the church's old inability to appreciate Judaism on its own terms and of reducing its spiritual validity through Christian fulfillment? Wasn't there a danger that community members would equate the inner—the "true"—meaning of Shabbat with Jesus? Were the Beatitudes revering my tradition or co-opting it?

I whispered my concerns to Gabrielle. "When people started

speaking about bringing Jesus into Shabbat, I didn't like it," she replied. "Why do we have to bring Jesus into everything? Why can't we just appreciate the grace of celebrating Shabbat with the Jewish people? But now I think there is a logic to it. If we don't find a way of integrating Shabbat into our Christian identity, I'm afraid the community will eventually lose Shabbat. Celebrating Shabbat is the most tangible expression of our communion with the Jewish people. We used to pray for the Jewish people. Now we also pray with the Jewish people. But this process is so new that we need patience. What is the right way? I don't know."

Gabrielle's ambivalence reassured me. The community had taken on the mission of healing the deepest religious wound in history. We were an experimental generation; there were so many sensitivities. Jews and Christians needed to give each other room to make mistakes.

"Why do you need Shabbat at all?" I asked.

"Our whole week is like a wave. From Thursday night through Sunday we try to live with Jesus: Gethsemani, cross, grave, resurrection. Then we discovered twenty-four important hours in the middle of that—Shabbat—a time of hope and quiet, of returning to Eden. Through the cross, Jesus brought us into Eden. And he of course celebrated Shabbat. We're returning to our womb, renewing our faith through a living relationship with the Jewish people. It's a decision of the heart, not of theology."

"Is Jesus a central part of your own Shabbat devotions?" I asked, trying to avoid judgment.

"More the Virgin Mary," she said. "She was the Jewish mother; she was never anything but a Jew. She was the one who watched over Jesus on Shabbat, waiting for the resurrection. I think she is a way of connecting Jews and Christians. What does a mother want if not peace between her children?"

As for Jesus, she added, "Some Christians who celebrate Shabbat feel they need to consciously bring in Jesus as a kind of 'protection,' to ensure that they're still good Christians. I feel Jesus is with me all the time. I don't have to make a special point of it."

We sang *Shalom Aleichem*, welcoming the angels of peace who come on Shabbat. Then we sang *Eishet Hayil*, the hymn to the woman of valor. "Strength and glory are her garments; she laughs at the last of days." Gabrielle closed her eyes and sang to the Virgin Mary. I closed my eyes and sang to Gabrielle and Miriam, Rachel and Genevieve.

2

Gabrielle phoned me, distraught. For Gabrielle to concede vulnerability violated the premise of her being, which was to be among those who give comfort rather than seek it. Her brothers and sisters in the community routinely confided in her; they knew they could trust her because she'd learned to turn her considerable capacity for judgment inward, against herself, leaving mercy for others.

"Did you hear the news?" she said to me. "We're going to have to buy gas masks from the government."

She was referring to the Israeli government's decision to provide free gas masks only to Israeli citizens; foreign residents, including monks and nuns, would be offered the option of buying theirs. Saddam Hussein was threatening to renew missile attacks against Israeli cities, and the Israeli government was distributing updated gas mask kits, which contained medicines and injections against unspeakable assaults. Once again apocalypse co-opted Israel's daily life. The army opened gas mask distribution centers in schools and shopping malls, and TV commercials urged viewers in absurdly upbeat Hebrew to "refresh their kits," a euphemism for trading in the old gas masks from the Gulf War era, which we kept hidden in closets and under beds, trying to forget our mortality.

I knew Gabrielle wasn't upset about the cost of the gas masks but about the principle of not being treated as an Israeli, especially during crisis. Being a part of Israel was essential to her spiritual identity, her vocation as a nun. It didn't matter whether Jews acknowledged her presence among them; learning to emulate God's love, which sought nothing in return, was part of her renunciation. Gabrielle did ask one thing of the Jews: the chance, if necessary, to suffer with them. As a younger nun, she'd sometimes imagined herself in Nazi-occupied Europe, either rescuing Jews or sharing their fate. Yet now the Israeli government was telling her, symbolically but unequivocally, that she was extraneous, and no rebuke could be more devastating. The Jews might be facing another assault—with gas, no less—and she would be considered a stranger, an outsider to Jewish fate.

I tried to reassure her by foolishly stating the obvious. "You're not citizens, Gabrielle. The government is obligated to provide free gas masks only for Israelis. It's not discrimination against non-Jews; Arab citizens also get gas masks."

"But we're part of Israel, we belong here!" Her soft voice, which usually resisted emotion, turned anguished and indignant. "I know Christians volunteering in hospitals, working with Holocaust survivors. Are they going to be excluded, too?"

In fact, Gabrielle had tried to become an Israeli citizen, but the process proved so arduous that she soon gave up. Israeli citizenship wasn't confined to Jews; 20 percent of Israeli citizens, after all, were Arabs, and hundreds of thousands of Russian immigrants weren't Jewish according to Judaic law but spouses or descendants of Jews. Yet it was rare for a foreigner without Jewish family connections to receive citizenship.

For Gabrielle, becoming part of Israel was a tangible expression of the identity of the church, which was, as the apostle Paul put it, a branch grafted onto the olive tree of Israel. The church, she believed, would never fully become "spiritual Israel" without a reconciliation with the people of Israel, a "conversion" to its own Jewish roots—a belief she acknowledged was implicit only in the church's new thinking on Judaism and the Jews. The gentiles who'd entered the church, she insisted, had brought with them persisting traces of paganism; Gabrielle saw Christian anti-Semitism as a subliminal pagan revolt against Jesus, disguised as hatred for the people that had fathered him.

I said, "Why don't I raise some money from friends to provide the community with gas masks?"

I made the offer only to console her; I was certain she would reject it. But she accepted with gratitude. If the gas masks wouldn't be provided by the Jewish state, at least there would be some Jewish recognition of her place among us.

My offer turned out to be unnecessary. The Jerusalem municipality decided to provide gas masks to Christian clergy in the city. But the experience deepened the trust between us. We were now not just friends but—far more important to Gabrielle—spiritual allies in the same frontline unit.

Gabrielle was beautiful with a vigorous purity, which made her look younger than her forty-two years. Her head was slightly tilted, forced permanently upward by the habit of aspiration. Her long struggle against judgment was imprinted on her features: chin curved to soften its sharpness; big brown eyes, which once mocked the world and now pitied its flaws.

She had grown up Protestant in a Catholic town in northern France. Though not devout, she'd learned the stern morality of her Huguenot ancestors. Asked in high school to write about the subject that upset her most, she chose injustice. She despised stupidity, weakness, all the human failures on which evil fed. Mercy seemed to her an indulgence of those failures, inadvertently reinforcing evil. In class she was usually the lone Protestant, defender of "pure Christianity" against the Catholic Church, flawed with statuary and pomp. One of her favorite places was a museum that chronicled the Catholic persecution of the Huguenots; she felt proud to belong to a heroic faith.

While still in high school she discovered the Holocaust. She read whatever she could about the camps, survivor memoirs and historians' accounts, trying to understand. Until then she had considered evil a manageable opponent, easily defeated by uprightness and resolve. But here was a revelation of evil before which her own strength and notions of justice were helpless.

She found her weapon in prayer. After Auschwitz, only the counterrevelation of God's presence could challenge the power of evil. She joined a Protestant charismatic prayer group, which taught that God was constantly speaking to us and that if we stilled distraction and listened, we would learn to hear Him. The group would enter silence, and after a while someone would speak in unintelligible words or simply weep. Once Gabrielle felt the urge to ask God to help her surrender to Him. But she stopped herself, cringing at the notion of exposing herself before others, fearful of the vulnerability of prayer.

Then she met the Beatitudes and, drawn by the power of their prayer, eventually became a Catholic. The Beatitudes had undergone a similar transition from Protestantism to Catholicism. The community had been founded in France in 1974 as a Protestant charismatic movement by a preacher known simply as Ephraim, who was regarded as a kind of prophet by his followers. When Ephraim became Catholic, he brought his style of charismatic prayer with him into the church, and that is what initially drew Gabrielle. The community, said Ephraim, aimed to be a force of "love at the heart of the church." It built houses for contemplative retreat in France, offered medical assistance in Africa, and spread the Gospel in Eastern Europe, ambitiously combining tasks normally divided among the church's various orders. Through the Beatitudes, Gabrielle discovered the saints and especially Thérèse of Lisieux, who taught "the little way of spiritual childhood," which meant trusting God's love like a child toward a parent and aspiring to serve Him with small acts of devotion rather than great deeds, which belonged to Him alone.

She came to Israel in summer 1982, just as the Israeli army invaded Lebanon in its war with the Palestine Liberation Organization. She hadn't intended to stay; like other novice nuns and monks of the Beatitudes, she'd come only to experience a taste of Judaism. Gabrielle, of course, shared the community's vision of reconciliation with the Jews, but that wasn't the center point of her devotional life. In fact, she was sure that love of God was a Christian innovation and that real intimacy with Him was possible only through the church.

Sometimes on a Friday night, members of the community living in Jerusalem would exchange their habits for what they called "civilian dress"—men in white shirts and knitted *kipot,* women in long-sleeved dresses and colored kerchiefs—and pray in a Hasidic synagogue. Though Gabrielle didn't know Hebrew, she felt strangely at home there. Initially, she'd sat among the Hasidic women in the upstairs gallery and quietly prayed to Jesus, because that is what a nun was supposed to do. But it didn't feel right. If Jews prayed to the Father, maybe she should do the same, at least here. To whom, after all, did Jesus pray in the synagogue if not to the Father?

Gabrielle felt privileged to pray with the Hasidim, Holocaust survivors who could still praise God. Among them she felt shame for having equated love of God with Christianity alone. In her Jewish studies, she discovered that Jesus' insistence on the primacy of love was only a more radical formulation of already existing rabbinic ideas. In trying to distinguish itself from Judaism, the formative church had distorted the truth about Jesus' relationship with Torah. Like the story of the disciples picking corn on Shabbat: The point, Gabrielle realized, wasn't that Jesus permitted a minor violation but that he was trying to purge pettiness from Halakhah, which doesn't mean "the law" but "the way," dynamic and flexible. When he said that "the Sabbath was created for man, not man for the Sabbath," he was affirming Shabbat observance, in fact repeating a saying of the rabbis. Gabrielle began to see the Jewish life around her as the context for her devotions, sharing the experience of the early Christians as a minority among a Jewish majority. She entered the rhythm of a religious Jew, pacing her days by their proximity to Shabbat.

If Christianity's uniqueness was no longer love, and if Judaism also offered intimacy with God, then why remain a nun? For Gabrielle, the answer was the cross, God's willingness to share in man's mortality and thereby help him transcend it. That idea was powerful enough, she decided, to justify Christianity's separate existence from Judaism. Yet paradoxically, it was precisely at the cross where she most intensely encountered the Jewish people. Of all faiths, Christianity, founded on martyrdom, should have understood long ago that the suffering of the Jews wasn't a sign of God's rejection but of His intimacy. For Gabrielle, being prepared to follow Jesus on the cross meant sharing Jewish fate.

Like most monastics, she experienced times of spiritual depletion, feeling detached from prayer. At those vulnerable moments, she would wonder why she'd become a nun, sacrificing home and family and remaining in a kind of suspended childhood, a "sister" rather than a parent and a spouse. My life is like a broken bottle of perfume, she thought, a lovely, wasted scent. When she could no longer bear the sense of failure, and even the works of the saints couldn't inspire, she would turn to books about the Holocaust. Rather than increase her depression, the Holocaust galvanized her. Renunciation wasn't just a matter of individual salvation but a commitment to the war against evil. She would recall the shock when she first discovered the Holocaust as a high school girl and remind herself that her spiritual life, from joining the Evangelical prayer group to entering the Beatitudes to becoming a nun, was in part a response to that moment when she encountered Satan in Auschwitz.

Gabrielle became the Beatitudes' Jewish expert, its Jewish conscience. She helped uproot residual incursions in the community of the old theology of Christian triumphalism, like the prayer for the "illumination of Israel," which members had routinely recited when she'd first become a nun. What right, insisted Gabrielle, did we have to pray, however obliquely, for the reconciliation of the Jews with Jesus? The only reconciliation we did have the right—the obligation—to pray for was that Jews forgive us and that we honor our Judaic roots. And what exactly did we mean by praying for the "illumination of Israel": that Jews lived in darkness and Christians in light? Gabrielle won that argument, and the prayer was quietly dropped.

In resisting Christian triumphalism, Gabrielle was also trying to uproot any lingering judgment within herself. But often she had to confront her frustration at the church's slow pace of change toward the Jews. Be patient, she rebuked herself; the church is a clumsy body, and we are only beginning to undo centuries of distortion. Nor should a nun think she knew best, even when she really did.

Yet it was so hard to be generous to those who themselves lacked generosity. One year, Gabrielle had approached the Latin patriarch of Jerusalem, Michel Sabah, a Palestinian, suggesting that the church present a wreath at the official Israeli commemoration on Holocaust Memorial Day. Sabah refused her request, saying that the Holocaust was a Western event and that the Eastern church wasn't responsible. He did, however, give her permission to bring a wreath in the Beatitudes' name. Gabrielle tried to understand the patriarch. No doubt he feared encouraging sympathy for the state of Israel at the expense of the Palestinians; no doubt the Holocaust personally pained him. But after all the rationalizations, what remained for Gabrielle was shame. On Holocaust Memorial Day, she and Miriam attended the official ceremony, with a wreath bearing the names only of the Beatitudes and several other "Western" monasteries, rather than the name of the Catholic Church.

Sometimes one of her brothers or sisters would make some remark that depressed her, like the need to use their love for Judaism to draw Jews to Jesus. And once again Gabrielle would try to educate the well-meaning offender toward a truer love of the Jews that sought nothing in return.

And that was more or less what Gabrielle received. She prayed for a pure love that would be tested by adversity and make her worthy of standing with the Jews, and God, receptive to that kind of selfless request, was especially generous to Gabrielle. The more she intensified her love for the Jews, the more she was ignored and even abused. One priest wrote her an angry letter accusing her of syncretism; Gabrielle wrote back that the real danger for Christians and Jews wasn't blurring the differences between them but not knowing the other. There needed to be at least some Christians, she insisted, who loved the Jewish people so intensely, so unconditionally, that they took on as much of Judaism as Christian faith could accommodate. To draw Christians and Jews close, mere apologies weren't enough. Only an act of reckless love could challenge our pathological estrangement.

In the community's early years, it had naively idealized the ultra-Orthodox as the ultimate Jews, embodying Judaism's spiritual vitality. That is why the members went to pray in Hasidic synagogues, where they were mistaken for secular Jews searching for roots. Then, in the mid-eighties, they moved to an old stone house adjacent to Meah Shearim, Jerusalem's ultra-Orthodox ghetto, with courtyards and narrow alleys and more yeshivas and synagogues than shops. Not surprisingly, the ultra-Orthodox saw the Beatitudes as invaders, Jew-haters and missionaries, who had come to steal the souls of their children. The ultra-Orthodox were committed to preserving the world that had existed before 1939; Jews needed to remain the same Jews, Christians the same Christians. The concept of a monastic community in love with Judaism violated ultra-Orthodoxy's dare against time.

Gabrielle and other members of the community were spat on by Hasidic children; neighbors ignored their greetings. When some in the community became discouraged, Gabrielle tried to comfort them.

How could the ghettoized Jews of Meah Shearim possibly know that we aren't the same Christians who murdered their parents and grandparents, that we haven't come to preach to them but learn from them, that we are precisely the wrong Christians to blame for the past? And yet maybe we weren't the wrong Christians after all; maybe God wanted us to suffer, refine our love until it became selfless. Maybe the way to atone for the baseless hatred of the past was with baseless love. We are the generation of Christians to whom God has entrusted the work of penitence. If we condition our relationship to the Jewish people on reciprocity, then our love is merely sentimental. What did we expect—to dispel two thousand years of wounds with our accordion and Hebrew songs? If we aren't ready for a little rejection, then we aren't worthy of this work of healing.

Once, though, even Gabrielle lost her forbearance. Children in the neighborhood began calling the nuns prostitutes, and after much hesitation, Gabrielle summoned the courage to approach one of the Hasidic mothers. You see how we live, Gabrielle appealed to her. We pray throughout the day. We never missionize. We don't play the radio on Shabbat, out of respect for you. How could your children possibly think of us as prostitutes? But the woman, unmoved, said only that there were two kinds of people, Jews and goyim, almost as if they were different species.

Yet rejection and disappointment didn't undermine Gabrielle's love. During the Intifada, which was accompanied by media images of Israeli soldiers shooting and beating Palestinian rioters, the wife of a French diplomat posted in Israel had indignantly asked Gabrielle, "How can you still talk about loving Israel?" Gabrielle replied, "If your son does something wrong, do you disown him, or is that the time when you draw him closer and pray for him even more?"

Like most Jews, I'd tended to minimize our resentment of Christianity as self-defense, the residue of a traumatized history. Yet meeting

Gabrielle forced me to confront my "Christian problem." Jewish jokes about priests and Jesus no longer seemed so innocent, while anti-Christian traditions, like the ban on even entering a church, became outright offensive. Because the sisters and brothers of the Beatitudes were so understanding of Jewish resentment toward the church and so intolerant toward Christianity's failures, they inadvertently challenged me to stop indulging the inexcusable in my own tradition. Most of all, I wanted to protect them from being hurt by my people. For a Jew from Brooklyn, that was a radically disorienting notion: I needed to defend Christians.

Through Gabrielle, I began to realize the extent to which the Catholic Church was evolving in its attitudes toward Judaism and the Jews. She became my teacher, introducing me to the subtleties of the new Christian theology. We would meet in the Beatitudes' library, surrounded by Talmuds and rabbinic commentaries, the reassuring proof of a penitent Christianity, and she'd explain the significance of the remarkable Vatican documents outlining the "correct way," in church terminology, to teach Judaism in Catholic schools. The church, explained Gabrielle, was in the process of not merely repudiating its anti-Jewish theology but reversing it. The Jews weren't cursed but blessed. The very fact that a monastic community that adopted Jewish rituals could remain in good standing, endorsed by leading clerics in the French church, proved how far the church had come. Still, Gabrielle readily conceded that the implications of the new theology hadn't yet been fully absorbed by the church itself. "The old theology continues in subtle ways," she explained. " 'Thank you, Jewish people, for giving us the Bible. Thank you for being the people of Jesus.' But that's archaeology. Am I ready to encounter Judaism as it is or just for nostalgia?"

I came to meetings with Gabrielle equipped with long lists of questions. At times our discussion resembled an interrogation. But she responded patiently to the most provocative challenges.

"Gabrielle," I said, "you've convinced me to stop worrying about the church's hostility. But what about the church's love? How can you as a nun not hope, even passively, that I'll accept Jesus?"

"I believe that Jesus is the messiah of the nations and of Israel," she said. "And I believe that Jesus will have a new appointment with his people. But that will not be a 'Christian victory': It will be a reunion of two lovers."

She continued, "I never pray for Jews to accept Jesus. It's not a question of theology but of where a soul is spiritually fulfilled. It is arrogant to assume that Jews have no spiritual life of their own and can only be fulfilled in the church. We have to reach the point where we see each other as allies. On the Christian side we haven't freed ourselves from 'the truth.' And on the Jewish side, they're still seeing Christianity as a threat. There is a verse in the Psalms that says that mercy and truth have to embrace. I like that prayer very much. For two thousand years we said that the Jews weren't faithful to truth. But we weren't faithful to love. And the Jews were faithful to their calling."

"What about Edith Stein?" I asked. I assumed that Gabrielle must surely identify with the Jewish-born nun martyred in the Holocaust.

As usual, she surprised me. "I don't feel any personal connection to Edith Stein," she said curtly. "She didn't consider herself part of the Jewish people." Here was Gabrielle, distancing herself from a fellow nun because she wasn't sufficiently sensitive to her Jewish identity. That kind of unexpected irony was part of the pleasure of our encounter.

"So you oppose her canonization," I said, rather than asked.

She surprised me again. "At first I didn't like it and shared the Jewish unease. I thought, what's the point here? It seemed to me a kind of return of the old theology. But now I think that maybe it's something else. It's not directed at the Jews but at the Christians. It is telling Christians that any attack on Jews is also an attack on the church."

At our next meeting, Gabrielle said happily, "I've been reading about Edith Stein, and I was wrong. She did identify very much as a Jew, even after her conversion. And she wanted to share in the fate of her people."

I asked Gabrielle whether she thought that Stein had seen herself as a sacrifice for her people's rejection of Jesus, and she said, "She belonged in some ways to the old theology. I read in a French Catholic newspaper a quote from Edith Stein about how she weeps for her people living in darkness. I felt so embarrassed."

And yet, added Gabrielle, "I think her canonization can be a blessing. So many Christians are turning to her in prayer. Maybe she is linking Jews and Christians together in heaven. She is praying for us; I feel it. When you believe in the power of the unseen world, it's hard to know the effect."

3

"Gabrielle," I said, "I'm afraid."

We were sitting, as usual, in the Beatitudes' library.

"Can you imagine the reaction," I continued, "when my friends and relatives in the Orthodox community find out I've been going to monasteries? Do you know how that's going to play in my old Brooklyn neighborhood? A Jew entering churches to experience Christmas and Easter. There's nothing worse than that. I'm about to become a Jewish traitor."

Of course she knew. Who better understood the risks of crossing the Christian-Jewish divide than Sister Gabrielle? She said, "We have to go on, and whoever will understand, will understand. We won't be able to take along everyone we love."

"Gabrielle, I need to learn from your courage."

She said quietly, "I'm afraid, too."

"You?" I said, unable to hide my surprise. The nun who prayed in Hasidic synagogues, who offered herself as a sacrifice to reconciliation?

"I'm afraid of being considered too different," she confessed. "Even within my own community. Of course people there share my love for the Jewish people, but I worry that they'll see me as an obsessive. 'Yes, celebrate Shabbat, but why overdo it?' I'm afraid of being considered a nun who thinks she's getting her assignments directly from God."

Gabrielle told me about a slide presentation she'd assembled on the history of Christian-Jewish relations, which she'd shown in churches around Germany and France. Recently, she'd screened her slides for a group of church theologians active in interfaith dialogue, and it had been a disaster. The men used the event as a pretext to attack the Beatitudes for observing Shabbat and other Jewish rituals. Who do you think you are, they demanded, to enter an area in which we interfaith specialists have worked for decades? "I felt like I was standing before the Inquisition," she said to me. She had wanted to tell those experts: Don't you understand that the original sin of Christianity was to relate to the Jews with theology and "truth," and that the only way to heal this wound is with a love as total as the hatred had been? But she'd kept silent, intimidated by those powerful men.

Gabrielle said to me, "I felt so weak, so silly. How can I be among all those important people? I should just be a good nun and leave this work to the experts. But whenever I show the slides to people who are simple believers and go to church every Sunday, there is a very good response. Ordinary people also need to know about the dialogue; it can't just be for the experts. You need a simple person for that work, and that's my job."

Listening to Gabrielle struggle with herself encouraged me: Even as we try to take a step forward, we carry our flawed selves along. She continued, "We have to make our statements and let God worry about the consequences. We think we have so much time, but really there is very little time. We have to live as intensely as possible."

Then she added, more to herself than to me, "Whoever touches this work must be ready to suffer."

4

On Shabbat morning, I was drinking tea with the brothers and sisters around the big wood table in the community's dining room. A young King David playing the harp looked down at us from a framed reproduction of a medieval Jewish Psalter.

Miriam said, "Once I led a group of Christian pilgrims to Elijah's Cave in Haifa. We arrived during a Jewish prayer service. Afterward, one of the women in the group said, 'It's amazing, they say 'amen' and 'hallelujah,' just like us!'"

We all laughed.

"I explained to the woman that those were actually Hebrew words," Miriam continued. "Then I said to her that Jesus was not a Christian but a practicing religious Jew, and so were all the apostles. I could see her getting more and more confused. I didn't tell her that Joseph and Mary had also been religious Jews. I thought she'd figure that one out for herself."

"It's not only a Christian predicament," I said. "Jews need to make their peace with Jesus. We're still angry and afraid of him. My father used to blame Jesus for all our troubles. But until we welcome him back as a brother, we'll continue to treat Christianity as inauthentic. Jesus was the divine instrument for fulfilling the Jewish goal of spreading the word of God through the world. Thanks to Jesus, I have a common spiritual language with half of humanity. Now that the church is changing the old theology, I can allow myself to feel parental pride in Christianity."

Everyone looked at me, startled. No one here had ever asked me what I thought of Jesus, and I hadn't volunteered. We'd all understood that establishing trust between Christians and Jews meant removing the missionizing impulse. It was a measure of the trust that had grown among us that I felt I could violate our unspoken pact.

Genevieve said, "For three years I've been living a one-way relationship with the Jewish people. I was resigned to thinking I am no different for Jews as a Christian than if I'd been a pagan. It's so important for me to hear what you've just said."

"If I'd stayed a Diaspora Jew," I explained, "I don't think I would have been able to talk to you like this. But becoming part of a Jewish majority—and meeting Christians like you—made it possible for me to stop fearing Christianity."

I told them that I hadn't actually read the New Testament until I moved to Israel and was already in my thirties. As an American Jew, I'd feared any intimacy with Christianity. But Jesus spoke to me as an Israeli. Reading the New Testament sometimes felt like reading an Israeli newspaper. We also faced a religious establishment that often lacked humility, and I found myself wishing we had someone in Israel today like Jesus, an implacable visionary who would take on the religious bureaucrats. Jesus joined my pantheon of spiritual heroes—Jesus the Jew, not the sacrificial lamb assuming the sins of the world. Like the prophets and the kabbalists and the early Hasidim, he had tried to reinvigorate Judaism with the love and presence of God. I knew Israelis, including Orthodox Jews, who felt that same simple connection with Jesus. But fear of being tainted by the deepest Jewish horror—*shmad,* the Yiddish word for conversion to Christianity, with overtones of destruction—kept them silent.

Even the New Testament's anti-Jewish passages lost their menace for me. Partly it was discovering, through Gabrielle, the church's attempts to reinterpret the New Testament as a philo-Semitic book, emphasizing the relatively benevolent voice of Romans, which reminded gentiles that salvation is of the Jews and that God's promise to them endures. And exposure to Israel's bitter public discourse helped me realize that the New Testament's language reflected how Jews argued with one another when they were the majority in their own land. Israeli rightists and leftists, secularists and Orthodox, routinely denounced each other as betrayers of Judaism and Jewish history who threatened the nation's survival with their suicidal policies and treasonous ideas. Jews could argue that way and still remain a family, however dysfunctional, because on some level we all realized we were guilty of hyperbole. But when the New Testament passed into the hands of outsiders, an internal feud among Jews became the language of demonization against "the Jews."

Now, though, a combination of Christian contrition and Israeli self-confidence was transforming the New Testament, or at least the Gospels, into a familiar Jewish book again. Modern Israel had returned Jesus to his natural landscape. One of the astonishing features of the state of Israel was the similarity of its debates to those of the Second Temple period, as if we'd resumed our national life at the point of its severance. Once again we were arguing about messianic hope and apocalyptic dread, political zealotry and defeatism, religious stagnation versus innovation.

"How do you see Jesus?" Genevieve asked, tentatively, curiosity just barely overcoming tact. I appreciated the Beatitudes' dilemma: Devotion to Jesus and reconciliation with the Jewish people were the two foundations of their spiritual lives. They had taken an implicit vow to renounce expectation that the Jews would reciprocate their interest, accepting that Christian crimes had imposed on them an unrequited love affair. Still, if any Christians needed some sign of a changing Jewish attitude toward Jesus, it had to be them.

"I have a great deal of respect for Jesus," I said, suppressing the frightening words I really wanted to say. Then I forced myself to say them anyway: "I feel love for Jesus." I quickly added, "Obviously, I don't love Jesus the way you do. For me, Jesus isn't the world redeemer, but he did bring a measure of redemption into the world by drawing so many souls to God. Maybe there is no single world redeemer. Maybe God will send each religion the messiah it needs and is waiting for. Sometimes I think that the *Mahdi* will come to the Muslims, the Buddha *Maitreya* will come to the Buddhists, the Jewish redeemer will come to us, and Jesus will return to you."

Miriam, who was struggling with the relationship between Catholic dogma and religious pluralism, said, "Some of our brothers would put you before the Inquisition."

"I'm a Jew, Miriam. I'm supposed to be a heretic."

Everyone laughed, except for one brother, who sat gloomily as his fellow monastics seemed to enjoy my theological deviations. Perhaps he was one of Miriam's inquisitors.

"I don't know how," blurted Genevieve, with the exaggerated urgency of youth, "but I'm sure that some day Jews and Christians will be one. Not through conversion, but somehow."

"I'm sure we'll be one," I said. "Not only Jews and Christians— everyone. That's the messianic hope."

But that, of course, wasn't what Genevieve meant. I wondered whether I'd made a mistake in being so honest with them, assuming these young people could keep their twin enthusiasms for Jesus and for the Jews from becoming too entwined. Perhaps it was too much to expect that I could confide my love for Jesus as rabbi and reformer without rousing expectations that I would accept him as messiah.

On Shabbat afternoon, while waiting in the living room for a session with Gabrielle, I was approached by Johann, the community's accordionist. "May I speak with you privately?" he asked.

Johann embodied the suffering of German rigidity. He held his head stiffly, and his voice, extraordinarily deep, seemed to startle him, as if he wondered how bass notes could emerge from his thin, flute-like neck. Yet when he played the accordion, he seemed almost physically transformed. A gracefulness surged through his long fingers and animated his head, which kept time with the music. Before joining the community, he had studied classical composition, but the conservatism of his teachers depressed and stifled him, until composing became unbearable. Then he met the Beatitudes and discovered Hasidic melodies. Through their deceptive simplicity he retrieved his joy in music. He became the community's Hasidic troubadour, a German soul freed by the music of East European Jewry.

He asked me now, with visible discomfort, "You are, it is right, a religious Jew?"

"I try to be," I said.

"And religious Jews, is it right, don't travel on Shabbat?"

I nodded.

"Yet you did travel on Shabbat to be here," he said, confused and, it seemed to me, a little angry.

"I slept here last night, Johann."

"Oh!" He actually laughed with relief. "I thought you . . . I didn't know . . . I see!" He was as happy as a Catholic monk once would have been to encounter a Jew ready to be baptized. All that these monks and nuns expected of me, I realized, was that I be a "real Jew." The Beatitudes' version of provoking Jews to jealousy: By loving Judaism, they would force us to be better Jews.

It was time for the evening prayer. This was when the community tried to invoke the Holy Spirit, prepare itself to receive intuition, the community's term for divine direction. They were Catholic charismatics, who spoke directly to God through prayer and believed that He sometimes responded through the Holy Spirit—what Jews call *ruach hakodesh,* the animating force of prophecy.

Walking toward the chapel, I was approached by a young woman, a lay member of the community from Germany named Gertrude. Desperate and garrulous with guilt, she insisted on apologizing to me personally for the Holocaust. It was so terrible, and she was so sorry, and she felt so ashamed even to speak with a Jew. I tried to reassure her that I didn't hold her responsible and that those who felt most guilty were usually the most innocent, but she was too absorbed in her misery to register the absolution. I thanked her for her sympathy and fled.

The little chapel filled with white-robed monks and nuns. Gabrielle and Miriam sat on their knees on the stone floor; in their hooded robes they resembled little tents. I sat cross-legged beside them. They began with a French hymn, soft and sad with longing. They sang Christian hymns delicately, unlike the sharp, almost militant way in which they sang Jewish songs. Perhaps that was a reflection of how they understood the role of the Jewish people in history: asserting through adversity the presence of God.

I sat in silence. To borrow the language of Christian prayer would have been inappropriate, mere mimicry. But if I couldn't pray with them, I could still be with them in prayer. I closed my eyes and tried to focus on God's name. Meditation was my way of striving toward intuition. The stilling and focusing of the mind offers those souls who watch over us an opening for more direct intervention in our lives.

Yud, heh, vav, heh. The black Hebrew letters press as if branded but without pain, a neutral pressure that spreads along the forehead like a band. The more intensely I observe them, the stronger they press, animated by attention. The two *hehs* form gates, the *yud* and *vav* pillars. I am pulled into the opening, as if into a House of God. The letters turn white, gold, burn with clarity—

The harmonious singing around me abruptly dissolved. Each voice was now singing a different wordless melody, creating a dissonance that resembled musicians tuning up. What happened? It seemed like a reenactment of the exile from Eden, unity shattering into fragmentation.

Then I realized. They were turning inward; this was the time of the Holy Spirit.

The more intensely they prayed, the quieter they became. My notion of charismatic prayer was American: arm-waving hysteria. Yet these were European monastics, both culturally and spiritually averse to demonstrative piety.

Finally, the singing stopped entirely, and the brothers and sisters entered meditation. After a while someone spoke, reluctant, almost whispering. "Thank you, God, for being with Your people in the desert . . ."

It was Gabrielle. She abruptly stopped, overcome by silence.

"Amen," people whispered. It sounded like breath.

Another voice: "Forgive us, God, for what we did to Your people, the Jews."

Gertrude. I braced for another assault of German guilt. Yet her voice was steady, without hysteria. "Strengthen our efforts for reconciliation," she continued calmly, and I wondered whether the Holy Spirit could bestow not only exuberance but restraint. "Amen," I said, and meant it.

The cacophony of disparate song began again, a slow crescendo. And then, suddenly, the harmony resumed, without any evident signal; the voices that knew each other so well in prayer had rediscovered their delicate oneness. This ability to dissolve and form again seemed to me the real miracle of their prayer.

Gabrielle rose to speak. She read the passage in Luke about the Prodigal Son who leaves his father's house and then seeks to return, though he is so unsure of his welcome that he offers to be a servant. The older brother, who'd remained at home, resents his sibling's reappearance, perhaps fearing his own usurpation. The two brothers, said Gabrielle, misunderstood the essential point: the father's unconditional love for them both. The brothers were Christianity and Judaism, and the Father wanted them both at His feast.

In the Torah, continued Gabrielle, a repeated motif is the rivalry between two brothers. Cain and Abel. Isaac and Ishmael. Jacob and Esau. "Each brother needs to realize that the other has something unique that he needs. That not everything is contained in your own faith. To introduce a third component, besides me and God, protects me from becoming enclosed in myself."

They sang a hymn in French, and Miriam whispered to me a Hebrew translation of the simple words: "Father, we are coming to You." By invoking the Father instead of the Son, they were trying to accommodate my presence, allow me as a Jew to find my place in their prayer. I joined them. It was one of those rare moments when I felt I was making God happy.

After the service a priest approached me. He was visiting from New Zealand, one of the community's few native English-speaking people. He had spent years as a merchant marine before joining the Beatitudes, and his expansive smile carried the camaraderie of the sea. He was smiling now. "I bless you in the name of the Father," he said, and he pressed his palm against my heart.

5

It was a few days before Christmas. Miriam and Rachel were setting up the crèche of little domed houses and shepherds and sheep; traces of that biblical landscape were still visible in the hills outside the window. François de Sales was decorating the tree with green crystals that resembled giant pine needles. He wanted to be sure, he said half-jokingly, that no one tried to Americanize the tree by overwhelming it with colored balls.

Sporadic gunfire sounded in the distance. Palestinian rioters were throwing rocks again at Jewish worshipers at Rachel's Tomb, just up the road from the Beatitudes' house. Israeli soldiers were responding with tear gas and rubber bullets. Those sounds weren't unusual here, and we all tried to ignore them.

Gabrielle and I went upstairs to the library. Perhaps it was the imminence of Christmas that made me wonder now what these books on Jewish theology and philosophy really meant to the Beatitudes. I asked Gabrielle why Jesus' Jewishness was so important to her. If God had become man for the redemption of humanity, wasn't his Jewishness incidental, just as the church had insisted for centuries?

Gabrielle paused, even though she knew exactly what she wanted to say. She often hesitated before answering a question, stifling an inclination to proclaim and instead silently invoking God's presence. Finally she said, "God is trying to tell us something in the way He chose to incarnate. If He became man to join us in our humanity, then it has to be all the way. He didn't incarnate among the Jews as an accident. He is telling us that the Jewish people is crucial for redemption."

"In what way?"

"It's written in our community rule that we are to wait together with the Jewish people for the messiah. The issue isn't whether to recognize or not recognize Jesus. We have an image of a Catholic Jesus in our minds, but I think we're all going to be surprised when he comes. The messiah will be so different from what any of us expect that no one will be able to say, 'We were right and you were wrong.' For me, what matters in the time before his arrival is the anticipation. The waiting together. Jews and Christians don't express it the same way, but we are both waiting for a time when there will be no suffering. Our job is only to try to prepare the way. Maybe it is to share the suffering of longing."

Through all my encounters with Gabrielle and the Beatitudes, I had tried to understand the possibilities and limitations of a new Jewish-Christian relationship. Yet only now did I finally realize what Gabrielle's Jewish passion was really about. Though she loved the Jews, she wasn't drawn to us by mere emotion. Nor was she motivated by guilt or even anguish over the Holocaust, or by a search for Christianity's Judaic roots. Her focus wasn't the past at all but the future. If the two faiths that had most in common and had been most estranged could form an alliance of messianic expectation, that in itself would be a redemptive act, perhaps even the messianic trigger. Gabrielle's boldness was to try to transform the center point of conflict between Judaism and Christianity—the messiah—into our potential common ground. Whether or not the messiah was coming a second time, she was saying, mattered less than the fact that he was coming at all. And those who awaited his coming belonged to the same side.

I was tempted by Gabrielle's vision. But I also feared it, precisely because I had once been a passionate messianist. Either of the two major Jewish events of the twentieth century—the Holocaust and the creation of Israel—would have been enough to spiritually convulse us; coming together, they created in my generation the first messianic upheaval among Jews in centuries. The survivors had been too broken for messianic ecstasy, and so the delayed reaction happened among us, their children. Some of my friends from Brooklyn became West Bank settlers, focusing their messianic enthusiasm on the reclamation of biblical lands, as if the distance separating the unredeemed world from perfection could be measured in kilometers. I knew Lubavitcher Hasidim who believed that if enough Jews would light Shabbat candles and wear tefillin, the accumulation of small gestures of holiness would force God to release the messiah; finally, they lost patience and placed ads in the *New York Times* announcing that their rebbe was about to reveal himself as the redeemer.

My old messianic beliefs hadn't been so precise. I wasn't even sure that I believed in an individual messiah. Instead, I'd seriously contemplated the notion that the Jews themselves were collectively the messiah. God had ingathered us back into Israel from a hundred exiles to prepare us for our messianic mission: to overcome our divisions and create a mini-humanity that would teach the world oneness. Ironically, it was Israel itself that freed me from that fantasy. No political state could fulfill such grandiose spiritual expectations; illusions of Jewish unity were impossible to sustain in our strident society. Finally, delusions about Jewish chosenness became untenable for me. Zionism had intended to "normalize" the Jewish people, and it had succeeded in proving our painful ordinariness.

"It's not easy to live here and stay romantic about the Jewish people," Gabrielle conceded. "But I can't accept your rejection of Jewish chosenness. Why did the Nazis *davka*—especially—single out the Jews?" Her tone was more imploring than challenging. "Anyone who wants to destroy God, first has to destroy the Jewish people. The great shock of the Holocaust for the church was that we'd thought the Jews weren't faithful to God. But suddenly we discover that God's enemies are also the enemies of the Jews. The new theology didn't emerge only from Christian guilt; it came from the realization that we had misunderstood the role of the Jews in history."

"I don't deny that there's something special about the Jews," I said, appreciating the irony of a nun trying to convince me that my people was chosen. "I believe that God preserved us and brought us back here for a purpose. I can accept the Jews as a chosen people but not *the* chosen people, the heart of God's plan for redemption. There are other chosen peoples who've been martyred for God. Like the Armenians. We need a little humility. I know what an obsession with chosenness can do to the Jewish ego. You start thinking that no one really matters but the Jews."

"So you're saying that there are many points of light, even if the Jewish people was the first that God set aside, as a promise for humanity's destiny."

"Not only aren't we the only light, sometimes we're not a light at all."

Gabrielle said quietly, "We've also taken big blows to our ego. We're not the church we once were. We're finally facing our sins. And we're not living in a Christian world anymore. It's not such an honor these days to be a nun. When I walk around Paris in habit, people laugh at me and call out sexual insults. The church is supposed to live the life of Jesus, and maybe this is the time of the crucifixion. Maybe now, when Jews and Christians are both on the floor, we can start to realize that neither of us on our own can bring redemption. Maybe we can come together in our brokenness."

6

On Christmas Eve, shortly before two in the morning, after mass and exchange of simple gifts, the monks and nuns of the Beatitudes began walking across Bethlehem toward Shepherds' Field, where a host of angels is said to have informed shepherds of Jesus' birth. I was the only one who seemed concerned about the distance. "Maybe an hour's walk, maybe two," Miriam said to me, and laughed. It was Christmas Eve in Bethlehem; what else mattered?

Hooded against the wind, which filled their white robes and blew clouds across the black sky, the sisters and brothers seemed to skip through the sleeping streets. Johann on the accordion led the way. Gabrielle accompanied him on the tambourine, allowing herself to look foolish by banging on an instrument made for those who can't play anything else. Tonight they all seemed young enough and happy enough to believe that sainthood could be achieved through joy alone, without suffering. In celebrating the baby Jesus, they were celebrating their own child-essence and monasticism's gift of eternal youth: owning nothing and aspiring to nothing, delighting in the company of your brothers and sisters, and surrendering to the Father's will.

A nun dropped a sheaf of song sheets, and they scattered in the wind. Everyone gathered around, laughing and singing, as they tried to retrieve the pages.

I walked with Rachel. I was surprised to see gray hairs slip through her kerchief; her shyness made her appear so young. "What does it mean to you to be here tonight?" I asked her. She seemed startled by the question, as if wondering why I was interested in her opinion. Reluctantly, she said, "I'm thinking of all those people whose minds are turned to Bethlehem tonight but aren't privileged to be here. I have to remember their devotions with every step I take."

"And what does it mean to you, Rachel, that Jesus was a Jew?"

"It shows how much God loves His people. First He gave them

the Torah, His word. Then His spirit lived among them in the Temple. And finally, He appeared among them as a fellow Jew. A nun is supposed to try to love like God. That means I have to try to love the Jewish people just as He does."

"Some Christians would say that means you have an obligation to help the Jews realize that God had incarnated among them." It was a trick question, ungenerous and unfair. After all this time, a part of me still probed for the hidden catch in the Beatitudes' love.

Rachel, though, was unfazed. "God loves the Jews well enough for Him not to need my advice on what their relationship should be," she said.

There seemed to me no more appropriate way for me to enter Christmas than with these people in this place. Back to the source, with Christians who loved Jesus' people. In returning here together, we could dare imagine that it was possible for Jews and Christians to begin again.

We passed Rachel's Tomb. The white-domed building was hidden behind a high concrete wall built by the Israeli army to protect Jewish worshipers from Palestinian rock-throwers. "Remember the old photos of Rachel's Tomb?" Gabrielle said. "A little building in a field."

Several Hasidim emerged and averted their faces when they saw us. Suddenly I was part of the enemy camp. But the two soldiers standing at the entrance smiled at us, perhaps at our naïveté, or else just pleased to see a happy, neutral presence.

Gabrielle shared this story: One Friday during the Muslim holy month of Ramadan, she was waiting in the community's van at the checkpoint into Jerusalem as thousands of Palestinians approached on foot, hoping to reach the Al Aksa mosque for prayers. Three terrified Hasidim who had just come from Rachel's Tomb knocked on her window, pleading for refuge. Throughout the ride to downtown Jerusalem, the three men sat, silent, eyes downcast, terrified by their proximity to a nun. "Did they at least thank you when they got out?" I asked. Gabrielle laughed and acknowledged that they hadn't.

"Another beautiful story about Gabrielle's romance with the Jewish people," I said.

"Maybe we'll meet in heaven," she said, "and I'll remind them that I was the one who gave them a lift."

We walked the deserted streets of downtown Bethlehem. The Christmas displays were paltry, a mere recollection of joy: some colored lights on apartment buildings, a few Santas in the windows of tourist shops selling olive-wood carvings of biblical figures. The gray stone walls were stained with graffiti left behind by the Intifada and with posters of Yasser Arafat's face.

We walked into the hills, along the edge of a valley, dark with olive groves. A spotlight mounted on a church steeple probed the sky, as if seeking a portent.

"Hallelujah!" the young people sang.

Miriam kept time by striking a triangle. "So tell me about Christmas," I said to her.

"For me this is the day of God's fragileness. God being born as a baby. Incredible. You can't imagine such a thing. Sharing in our vulnerability. Absurd." She spoke with the tenderness of a mother. Tonight she wasn't the bride of Christ but the mother of Jesus, nurturing the fragile opening to redemption.

"Imagine being unable to protect yourself. To be at everyone's mercy. And we did kill him." I liked the "we." Christians were finally accepting the consequences of their own theology, that it was absurd to blame the Jews when humanity's sins were responsible for Jesus' voluntary sacrifice. Miriam's understanding of Christmas transformed the baby Jesus from sentimentality into tragedy: He was entering mortality, beginning his journey to the cross.

"God becoming human is what allows us to get close to Him," she continued. "There is no other way."

"No other way, Miriam?" That wasn't the kind of theological language I'd come to expect from her.

"I don't mean that only a Christian can reach God," she said. "Any person who sincerely tries to serve God achieves salvation. But I've come to believe that somehow, even if you aren't conscious of it and even if you don't believe in him, Jesus is involved in the process. Maybe he escorts the soul to heaven at the moment of death."

"But why insert Jesus into every spiritual drama? Why can't God relate to each faith on its own terms?"

"If Jesus isn't the only Son of God, then giving him my life and giving up a husband and children make no sense. Why can't you accept what I'm saying as coming from a place of love? That it's not something aggressive but tender? Is there no way to overcome the anger over the past?"

I wasn't responding with Jewish anger, I explained, but with impatience at our monotheistic tendency to confuse one God for one way.

Still, I wondered whether she was right. I could happily join the Beatitudes in singing Shabbat songs and praying to the Father and celebrating Jesus the Jew who had brought the God of Israel to the nations. But I had avoided the "Christianness" of the Beatitudes, and now that was no longer possible. This was the night of the Christian Jesus, savior of humanity and lamb of God. Was I capable of accepting the Beatitudes in their tradition as they had accepted me in mine? Appreciate them not because they celebrated Shabbat but because they celebrated Christmas?

We came to Shepherds' Field. Foolishly, I had imagined an actual field, some pristine spot where in the early hours of Christmas and in the company of giddy young monastics you could imagine angels so overwhelmed with joy that they would share their glad tidings with anyone who happened by. Instead, Shepherds' Field turned out to be a walled compound with little plastic Palestinian flags strung over the gate.

A van pulled over and unloaded a dozen monks and nuns wearing the Beatitudes' robes. They were members of the community's other house in the Holy Land, located midway between Tel Aviv and

Jerusalem. I knew only a few of them cursorily; my connection was with Bethlehem. The Bethlehem contingent greeted the newcomers with the effusiveness of a camp reunion. Holding hands, they entered the compound, singing the song of the heavenly host, "Gloria in excelsis Deo!" Glory to God in the highest. Absurdly, I felt neglected, like the camper at the reunion no one is glad to see. But that was merely an expression of a deeper unease: Even among the Beatitudes, I was feeling the superfluousness of a Jew at Christmas. For a moment, I wanted to be one of them, celebrating the possibility of redemption.

An elderly Franciscan, disgruntled with sleeplessness, reluctantly unlocked the door leading to the grotto chapel for an impromptu mass. Inside, a foamlike ceiling was made to simulate stalactites. Embedded within the rough stone walls were glass-encased exhibits of shepherds in kaffiyehs and fat sheep. Before the altar was a crib holding a plastic doll, meant to recall the baby Jesus. The face was pudgy and careless, yet the monks and nuns knelt with reverence. I didn't share the Jewish aversion to sacred imagery; exposure to Eastern religions had taught me the difference between pagan idolatry and images that inspired devotion. My problem with the plastic doll wasn't theological but aesthetic. It seemed to me silly, a violation of the mystery it intended to evoke. Why the need to make myth explicit, to so mistrust the imagination?

Gabrielle found me in the crowd. Though I didn't mention to her my discomfort over the doll, to my surprise she sensed it. "It may seem absurd to treat a doll as something holy," she said. "But for me, the essence of Christmas is suspending the skeptical mind and making yourself a child for God, just as God made Himself a child for us."

Gabrielle's words were an implicit plea to me: Let's not judge each other's devotions. Any device that helps us turn inward should be appreciated by people of faith.

The mass began. The singing was led by a monk from Zaire, whose young brother, I'd been told, had recently been killed with a machete in an obscure civil conflict. The monk sang in a strong baritone, dredging joy from the depths. Though it was close to four in the morning, no one seemed tired. I had planned to meditate through their service, as I usually did during the community's prayers, but now I stood with them, roused by their excitement. "Gloria in excelsis Deo!" they sang, with the delicate forcefulness of proclaiming angels. I felt an old, almost forgotten thrill: the sense of God made real in this land.

I had never before seen people take communion. No Christian ritual was more alien to Jewish sensibilities than the notion of imbibing the flesh and blood of Jesus. Yet watching their reverence as the sisters and brothers approached the priest, I felt the absurdity of how we judged each other's faiths, as abstract theologies rather than lived experiences. They chewed slowly, reluctantly, savoring this moment of mutual renunciation. Jesus had given his life to them, and they were offering their lives in return.

I watched Gabrielle. She covered her mouth as if to protect the Divine Presence. Her head fell forward, impelled by the force that had entered her. Or perhaps it was the weight of responsibility: She was imbibing not only redemption but the cross. I felt privileged to be here. Only now, stealthily sharing her most intimate moment, could I truly appreciate her as a Christian.

And then, as I watched her, she began to change. She became thinner, sharper, very pale. Then she changed again: softer now, almost transparent. The physical transformation was so total that I wondered whether it really was Gabrielle. Could I have confused her for someone from the other Beatitudes house? But I'd seen her rise from the bench, approach the altar, and return to her place! I felt so disoriented that I no longer trusted my own senses. And then, just as suddenly as she'd disappeared, Gabrielle returned.

Maybe I was tired. It was, after all, nearly dawn. Or maybe I'd glimpsed the soul of Gabrielle?

We walked the steep hills toward Manger Square. The happy

energetic group became silent with fatigue. Even the relentless Johann had stopped playing the accordion. "Don't tell me you're tired," I said to him. He began to apologize, then realized I was teasing and gave me an ironic smile.

The muezzin sounded with the first light, rousing the day. Gabrielle said, "He's especially loud now. He wants to remind us on Christmas who really controls Bethlehem." She was probably right. Muslim extremists often used the call to prayer to intimidate Christians and Jews, just as Muslims had built minarets that deliberately towered over Christian and Jewish holy places.

"I wouldn't want to be a Muslim," added a nun. "To have someone shouting at me in my sleep." Her friends laughed.

"It's Ramadan," I said. "The first call to prayer is also a signal to begin the day's fast."

"They eat at night," the nun replied, shrugging. "I'm sure there are those who do it sincerely . . ." But if so, she clearly implied, they were wasting their devotions in a false, even absurd faith.

Listening to the nun disparage Islam, I realized why I couldn't fully accept Gabrielle's offer of a Christian-Jewish alliance of messianic expectation. That would allow Jews and Christians to pretend to evade the hubris of chosenness: If neither of us could be chosen alone, we would be chosen together. The two biblical faiths, exalted above all others: the Muslims with their distorted scripture, the Hindus with too many gods, the Buddhists with no god at all. Jews and Christians would learn to deal with each other through love rather than theology, as Gabrielle had beautifully put it during one of our sessions. But that wouldn't apply to our relations with other faiths.

We came to the low stone entrance in the massive walls of the Church of the Nativity. Gabrielle explained to me that the opening had been deliberately lowered in the Middle Ages to prevent Muslim horsemen from looting the building. "I like the result," she said. "You have to bow your head to enter."

We walked down the marble steps to a long, narrow room, whose walls were covered with black cloth imprinted with faded paintings. Incense and candles singed the air. Brass lamps hung thickly from the low ceiling, blackened by centuries of smoke.

A silver star embedded in the floor of a marble-coated alcove marked the spot of Jesus' birth. From here the message of the God of Israel had been released to the nations: history wasn't random or cyclical but a story with a beginning and an end. The young people of the Beatitudes knelt around the star the way homeless people on a winter night gather around an urban bonfire. Then they dispersed through the room, joining the handful of people sitting on the stone floor. One young woman held her head as though in pain. Near her sat a priest with eyes closed tightly, almost wincing, perhaps trying to keep the young woman out of his thoughts, or perhaps trying to gather her in.

I sat down and tried to meditate. But the silence in the room felt restless. Someone had been here, tantalized with a vision of imminent redemption, and vanished. Two thousand years later, those who loved that vision were still awaiting the end of the story. For Christians, of course, Jesus was a living presence, readily accessible through prayer. Still, I sensed disappointment. Perhaps the people here were simply exhausted from their all-night vigil. Or perhaps they were acknowledging the suffering of humanity, the tragedy of a redeemer born for the cross.

I looked up and noticed Gabrielle, who had stopped kneeling and was sitting cross-legged on the floor. She reminded me of a mourner in synagogue on the Ninth of Av, when the Divine Presence was exiled and the Temple became a remnant wall, no longer a place to celebrate our intimacy with God but to mark our distance from Him. A day beyond prayer, beyond hope. Precisely the point, I thought, where Jews and Christians could begin to wait together.

7

At Yad Vashem, the Holocaust memorial, they were preparing for the wreath-laying ceremony. It was Yom Hashoah, Holocaust Memorial Day, and Israelis gathered from around the country on this Jerusalem hilltop surrounded by pine forest. There were representatives of *landsmanschaften* groups from vanished European communities, the army, the police bomb squad, the national airline, the post office. A determined little man in a beret carried a wreath from a ghetto fighters' group, spiritual grandfather of the young people here wearing the uniforms of Jewish rebirth: paratroopers in red berets, Golani infantrymen in brown berets, women soldiers in short olive-colored skirts, and police in Israeli blue and white. Like the Hindu practice of meditating in graveyards, this was Israel's annual ritual of death recollection. But unlike the Hindu mystics, the Jews weren't here to become ethereal but to affirm their return to concreteness. For survivors, the true mystical experience of the Holocaust was the nation's resurrection. And so the post office workers and the national airline representatives and especially the soldiers were as much the point of this gathering as the martyrs they had come to commemorate. On this day, the dead and the living honored each other.

I was waiting for the monks and nuns of the Beatitudes. They came every year, bearing a wreath. Today, though, Gabrielle wouldn't be among them. She was leading a group of pilgrims in the desert, teaching them about Judaism, one of the few reasons she would consider legitimate for not coming here on this day.

Although the community members had never been harassed at Yad Vashem, they were surely vulnerable. They didn't know whether they'd be received with indifference or silent gratitude or made to feel like intruders, relatives of a murderer at the funeral of his victim. At any time, a survivor might get unhinged and lash out at these unwitting symbols of historic Christian crimes. In fact, it was a measure of how much the Catholic Church had changed that the main arguments left between the Jews and the Vatican concerned the past, like Christian guilt for the Holocaust and the canonization of Edith Stein. For survivors, of course, those were the most emotional issues, and it took courage for the young people of the Beatitudes to appear in habit at Yad Vashem.

They were coming to be with my people; I had come to be with them. Probably nothing would happen, but I didn't want to leave their goodwill exposed without a Jewish escort. Still, it wouldn't be easy for me. By appearing with monks and nuns in this place and on this day, I was violating the Jewish need to gather in private and recall our sense of aloneness. I was challenging the child of survivors within me on his most tender ground, where intimacy with Christianity was unthinkable.

The Beatitudes' van arrived. Miriam and Rachel led the half-dozen sisters and brothers from Hungary, Austria, Zaire. Their white robes flapped like flags in the wind. Oddly but tellingly, I'd never quite noted until now the wooden crosses that hung on their chests. For a cowardly moment I wished they'd come incognito. Then I made a point of kissing each of them, including those I didn't know, perhaps to refute that unworthy impulse; I also hoped to ease their discomfort and to signal Israelis who might be watching that these were friends.

"I wasn't sure if I should come in habit," Miriam confided to me. "I know that people don't want to be reminded of the church on this day. In past years I sensed that some survivors didn't want us here. But I felt it was important for the church to be present in some way. It's not easy to be here, but it's also not easy not to be here. If I'm hurting anyone, I'm sorry."

We headed toward the plaza where the ceremony was being held. Rachel carried the wreath that bore only the community's name, conceding the futility of consoling words. The monks and nuns huddled close and looked at the ground, avoiding eye contact with passersby. People stared, but they were more curious, it seemed to me, than hostile.

We walked through the "Avenue of the Righteous," a grove of carob trees, each tree accompanied by a little plaque bearing the name of a gentile who had rescued Jews in the war. Choosing fruit trees for this place had been a wonderful idea, and it seemed to me that my ability to be here with monks and nuns was the fruit of those rescuers who had helped Jews to avoid despairing of the human race. When I was a boy, we had a bitter saying in Brooklyn: If you want to know how many good gentiles exist, count the trees on the Avenue of the Righteous. At the time, there weren't many. But as survivors established themselves and recalled the generosity of their rescuers, the trees had multiplied, and now there were thousands. Even that proliferation didn't tell the whole story. For every rescuer, there were at least several accomplices who either actively helped or aided with their silence. And many thousands of rescuers went unrecognized. My father had hidden in the Transylvanian woods and was kept alive by an elderly forest keeper who brought him food when he could. My father had intended to contact the man—or his family, since the old man himself was almost certainly dead—and plant a tree here in his honor. But my father had died before he could manage it.

I said to Miriam, "I feel you're here representing the rescuers. You belong to the same spiritual denomination."

"I think we're here in place of all those who could have helped then but turned away," she replied. I was trying to comfort her, help her feel she belonged. But she had come to stand here in grief and shame and wasn't going to make it easy on herself.

We entered the stone plaza. An honor guard of paratroopers stood beside six iron cauldrons filled with oil and awaiting lighting. However cynical Israelis had become toward Zionist rituals, here it was still possible to feel the old thrill at the mere sight of Jews in uniform and recall what it was like when we didn't have our own soldiers in color-coded berets.

An elderly woman approached us. "Excuse me," she said, "but may I ask you a question?"

Her face had the stunned expression I knew from survivors; it recalled that moment when, as a teenage girl, she'd first encountered Auschwitz.

"Are you related to them?" she asked, pointing to the Beatitudes. She meant: What could we possibly have in common?

"We're related through the soul," I replied, wary.

"I'm a secular person," she continued, "but when I saw someone with a *kipah* kissing nuns and monks, I thought, It must be the time of redemption." She smiled, embarrassed, and quickly left us.

Miriam said to me, "More and more I realize that love means just being present."

I led the brothers and sisters to a row of folding chairs; I was their host in the house of mourning. As we waited for the ceremony to begin, they sat in silent prayer.

Miriam said, "Today is my anniversary. Exactly eleven years ago, on Yom Hashoah, I came to Israel."

"What does that mean to you?" I asked.

"Maybe that my personal renewal has something to do with the renewal of the Jewish people. Gabrielle always used to tell me that I have a special relationship with the Jewish people, and I always denied it. When I first came I knew nothing about the Jews. I barely realized that the Holocaust had anything to do with Jews. I suppose I knew that Jesus was Jewish, but that fact meant nothing to me. And here I am, eleven years later. I feel it's my birthday."

It had never been easy for Miriam in Israel, and she often wondered whether she'd ever feel at home here. She'd been hit in the head with a stone in Meah Shearim, spat on and cursed as a missionary. Her kerchief had been ripped off her head by Jewish children and then by Muslim children. Miriam tried to accept the humiliations as a gift, a way to purify her love from the need for reciprocity. Freeing her love from emotional whim, from dependency on attraction and aversion, was the struggle of her monastic life. As an aspiring actress in Montreal, she had equated emotional expression with personal fulfillment. She had loved the volatile camaraderie of the theater, the attention of the stage. Becoming a nun required negating a lifetime of instincts, seeking anonymity instead of fame, self-criticism instead of applause.

She said, "We don't fit in anywhere. For Jews, we're missionaries; for Muslims, we're Zionists. A Palestinian Christian accused me of not being sensitive to his people's suffering. I know I should be open to everyone in equal measure, but I can't do it. I stand with the Jewish people. Sometimes I say to God, 'Why do you expect me to be an instrument of peace?' And the answer I sense is, 'Your suffering over your failures is what I need.'"

"Why is suffering necessary, Miriam?"

"The saints of every religion say the same thing: that suffering is a gift from God that enhances and purifies the soul."

"Can you say that here?"

"No," she said, without hesitation. "Free will brought the Holocaust, not God's will. It's not my place to tell the victims that their suffering was useful. But someone who suffers and doesn't fall into bitterness, his heart opens. I knew a monk who was dying of cancer. He said, 'The only right that suffering gives you is the right to love.'"

On the other side of me sat Father Issaie, a Beatitudes priest with a sharp face and pointed beard. His body was still, almost rigid, hands folded on his lap. I asked, "What do you say about the meaning of suffering, Issaie?" He replied carefully, "Suffering can purify. But there is some suffering that is so great that the only decent response is no response." He looked straight ahead and resumed his posture of silence.

An announcer asked us to stand, and a few moments later the memorial siren sounded, hoarse rather than shrill. Two sirens intertwined, like a braided havdalah candle used in the ceremony ending Shabbat, separating sacred from profane time. I imagined myself a point of light in an endless field of light, each point another soul. Knesset Yisrael, the assembly of heavenly Israel. I sensed my smallness but also my secure place in the familiar vastness, which formed a single body of light. I felt loved and embraced: Israel above protecting Israel below.

Afterward I asked Issaie what he had been thinking about while the siren was sounding. He replied, "I said to God, 'Seigneur, here I am, among my brothers and sisters.'"

PART III

six

Feast of the Transfiguration

I

It was early summer 1999, and the Three Weeks were approaching. The Hebrew calendar knew no greater time of dread than the Three Weeks, which commemorated the Roman siege against Jerusalem. The rains stopped until late autumn, and the desert sky outside my window became white and remote; the land lost its subtle beauty and turned harsh, hostile. The Three Weeks began with the fast of the Seventeenth of Tamuz, when the Romans broke through the walls of besieged Jerusalem, and culminated with the fast of the Ninth of Av, marking the destruction of both the First and the Second Temple and the exile of the Divine Presence from Israel.

In this religious season of defeat, Israelis would turn sullen and pessimistic, pressed by heat and history and insoluble conflicts over land, identity, morality, and faith. This year, especially, fears of external threat combined with a growing sense of internal incoherence. The peace process with the Palestinians was close to collapse, and in Israel's recent elections, the ultra-Orthodox parties had attained unprecedented power. Friends of mine from the secular left and the religious right repeated, if for opposite reasons, the same refrain: The state is no longer viable. Casual apocalypticism penetrated our daily conversation. One friend, a writer who usually avoided morbid speculation, said to me, in a matter-of-fact tone that frightened me even more than his words, "Maybe the Arabs were right after all, and we're just a passing phase in the Middle East, like the Crusaders."

For the first time since moving to Israel, I'd begun to wonder how the Zionist dare of collecting Jews from a hundred nations could possibly succeed, whether we could fashion the most minimal common identity among the competing ideologies and ethnicities ingathered into this strip of coast and desert, where even the topography clashed. With each passing year we seemed to be drifting farther away from national cohesion. What common vision could possibly unite a Russian immigrant who had come to Israel only because this was the farthest west he could manage and an Ethiopian immigrant who had walked through jungle and desert to reach Zion? A secularist who saw little relevance in Judaism, and an ultra-Orthodox Jew who saw little relevance outside of Judaism? A settler whose dream Israel was the biblical heartland of Judea and Samaria and a leftist who refused on principle even to visit the West Bank?

And those were merely the Jewish conflicts. Even if we managed one more Israeli miracle and fashioned the Jews into a people that learned to respect its own diversity, how would we integrate the one million Arabs among us? For Israeli Jews, the founding of the state was an act of redemption, a movement from holocaust to rebirth; for Israeli Arabs, that process was in effect reversed. How could we create one nation from Jews who celebrated Israeli Independence Day and Arabs who mourned it? Our notions of the Israeli future were hardly less antagonistic. Arabs were demanding a de-Judaized Israel, a state that would accommodate its citizens into a neutral national identity; Jews insisted on an Israel that remained heir of the Jewish story and protector of the world's Jewish communities. Both expectations were just, but they were irreconcilable.

The land was too crowded and intimate to sustain such contradictory visions of its most basic nature and purpose. In my better moments, I could appreciate the vital insights of each of our ideological camps. Israel's contradictions, after all, were being fought within me. I loved the biblical landscape but was ready to share it with the Palestinians; I hated the occupation but didn't trust the Arab world to let us live in peace. I was at once a religious Jew and a democrat; I wanted a Jewish state that honored its roots and a modern state that honored all its citizens.

I believed it was no coincidence that Israel was an intense meeting point between democracy and tradition, East and West. Our contradictions were the stuff of our spiritual work, perhaps the purpose for which we had been returned to this land. Somehow, we had to overcome our absolutist instincts and learn to contain opposites. And so I refused to take sides, nurturing my confusion and inhabiting an uneasy center in which Israel's paradoxes clashed. I saw in my journalistic work an extension of my spiritual challenge as an Israeli: to find truth in every voice.

But now, as the Three Weeks impinged, I found myself losing the patience, the empathy—the open heart, as Sheykh Ibrahim would put it—needed to balance Israeli realities. Instead, I felt contempt for the whole self-righteous cacophony, dragging us to the abyss. I tried to detach, not take each Israeli failure so personally. But that strategy wasn't working. Every issue was life and death; the fragile land offered no margin for failure.

I needed a break to remind myself how to sustain my love in the midst of intensity, how to stay open even to those closed off from each other. When Israelis reached this desperate point, we often went abroad for what we called vacations but were in fact escapes. Yet through my encounters with Christianity I had discovered local escape routes, places of silence in which to draw on the renewing power of the land. It was time to get to a monastery.

2

"Go to Lavra Natofa," said my friend Yehezkel Landau, a religious Jew active in reconciliation efforts among Arab and Jewish Israelis. "It's run by Father Yaakov Willebrands. He's one of the few Christians living here who manages to keep his heart open to both Arabs and Jews without taking sides. And he's got this wonderful church in a grotto he dug out himself. It's a great place to meditate. Besides," added Yehezkel, "he may be a saint."

Yehezkel explained that Father Yaakov lived with three other monastics on an isolated hilltop in the Galilee. A Trappist monk in his native Holland, here he joined the Melkites, Catholics who follow Byzantine rite and whom Yaakov believed were descendants of the first Jewish Christians. He went by two names, the Hebrew *Yaakov* and the Arabic *Yakub*, both derivatives of Jacob, encompassing in his own identity the two peoples of this land.

Without knowing anything more about Father Yaakov, or Abuna Yakub, I was drawn by his refusal to choose either side of the Arab-Israeli conflict, or rather his ability to choose both.

In the Holy Land, Christian love was often selective. Foreign Christians living here tended to embrace either the Jewish or the Palestinian narrative. Each appealed to a different facet of the Christian soul: the prophetic fulfillment of Jewish homecoming, the Palestinian struggle for justice in the land of Jesus. Well-meaning but one-dimensional outsiders became either Christian Zionists, who despised the Palestinians and tended to see Islam as a satanic opponent of God's plan for Israel, or else Christian liberationists, whose "anti-Zionism" merely updated the old theological contempt for Jews as enemies of the good. It was perhaps inevitable for Jews and Arabs to turn their life and death struggle into a passion play; but for spectators similarly to trivialize one of the world's most morally ambiguous conflicts meant squandering an opportunity for a neutral loving presence.

Yehezkel said that if I wanted to see Father Yaakov I'd better do it soon, since he was in his early eighties. Father Yaakov had no phone, so I wrote him a letter, addressed to a post office box in a Galilee Arab village, explaining my journey into Christianity and Islam and asking whether I could spend a few days with him. To my surprise, he wrote back immediately. "Almost every four months we are approached by the Israeli television to be presented in some program," began the note, which was written in the dull letters of a manual typewriter and on a page that had been frugally cut in half. "We steadily refuse, because we don't seek to attract crowds. But you are aiming at something very recommendable. Therefore we look forward to know one another better and to cooperate. We need mutual assistance on the way to salvation, and God is providing new opportunities with the creation of Israel and the existence of a 2,000-year-old Palestinian church."

That enigmatic last statement was partly explained in a pamphlet about his hermitage, Lavra Natofa, which he enclosed. ("I need it back but you may make a copy.") Father Yaakov saw the Melkite church, supposed descendant of the ancient Jewish church in Jerusalem, as a potential bridge for Arabs into Israeli identity, beyond the formalities of mere citizenship. And he believed that, through the Melkites, Christianity as a whole could find its place within the Jewish state.

I wasn't going to meet Father Yaakov for his improbable ideas but for the spirit behind them. Here, it seemed, was a man who accepted Israel's spiritual challenge of reconciling opposites and dared to take on our most insoluble paradox: the inability of Israeli identity to contain both Arabs and Jews. Perhaps Father Yaakov could impart to me something of his wisdom of balance, teach me how an open heart can contain more than one truth.

Driving to the Galilee, I heard a radio interview with an ultra-Orthodox spokesman about what he called the "missionary threat" of the new millennium. Thousands of Christian missionaries, he insisted, were planning to converge on the Holy Land in the year 2000 to convert the Jews. The bemused interviewer said, "All these years you people are warning about missionaries, but how many Jews in this country have actually become Christian? Don't you think you're exaggerating?" The spokesman replied, "Our fear of Christianity is so deep that it will never go away."

A narrow mountain road without railings ended at the security fence of Hararit, a village of practitioners of Transcendental Meditation, or TM. The village was a single street of pastel-colored houses and signs advertising Lakshmi's Tea House and Satva Industries. The quiet was astonishing. Hararit seemed deserted; maybe everyone was meditating.

I parked at the end of the street, walked through an olive grove, and entered a wooden gate into Lavra Natofa. A dirt path shaded by carob trees was marked by trails of stones, and carob pods covered the ground. Forest extended in every direction; the sharp smell of pine mingled with dry earth. In the distance lay the still waters of the Sea of Galilee, and then the brown hills of the Golan Heights, fading into mist.

The path led to a little church, built of rough-hewn stones of all sizes and fitted together like a reconstructed ruin. It seemed as if a random pile of stones had miraculously cohered. A steeple, likewise made of ill-fitting stones, was capped by a stone cross. A vine grew over the arched wooden door.

Behind the church was a stone hut. I knocked on the door and was greeted by an old man, tall and slightly stooped. "You must be Yossi, hmm," he said. "We've been waiting for you, yes, hmm."

Father Yaakov wore a blue knitted skullcap that entirely covered his head, sandals, and a plain blue robe with a large monastic belt that sagged on his fragile frame. His white beard was thick but carefully rounded, and his deep-set eyes carried the blue of the sea. Though the late-afternoon sun wasn't strong, he squinted, a permanent impress of his years on the mountain. His face was kind but not tender: fierce chin that even the thick beard couldn't entirely conceal, high forehead and stubborn nose like a cannon protecting a walled city. Only the lips were delicate, receding from disuse: Though no longer bound by Trappist rules, he still lived mostly in silence. He smiled and searched for words but couldn't find them—a solitary monk who loved people but sometimes forgot how to interact with them. In the awkward silence he reached for a comb and smoothed his beard, the touching gesture of an old hermit who refused to surrender to a shabby eccentricity, insisting on representing the dignity of faith.

"Would you like to see the church?" he finally asked. Whatever I needed to understand about Father Yaakov, he seemed to be saying, would be explained by the church he'd hollowed from the earth.

We descended on uneven stone stairs into a cavernous room with moss-covered limestone walls on which hung oil lamps and icons. It felt like a hothouse, moist and invigorating with growth. The air smelled of kerosene and incense, a mingling of heaven and earth. Thin light penetrated from an opening in the corner of the high ceiling. A stone ledge along the walls offered the only seating. On a rough stone altar was mounted a gold menorah and a plain wood cross.

Father Yaakov told me the story of his church. He had obviously repeated it many times before, but he still managed a sense of wonder at God's hard generosity and at his own persistence. In 1964, he began negotiating with the Arab who owned the land on which Lavra Natofa now stood. The man refused to sell. The Arab villagers suspected Father Yaakov of being a front for a Zionist plan to settle the area with Jews. And so every day for three years Father Yaakov drank coffee with the landowner, until he relented. But then the Melkite church reneged on its promise to fund the hermitage, and he had to raise the money from friends in Holland. Finally, the Israeli authorities, who suspected him of being a missionary intent on converting the Jews, refused to grant him a permit to build, insisting that the mountain was intended for military use. Yaakov decided that if he couldn't build on the ground, he'd burrow beneath it. "God had enough proud churches with their noses in the air," he said to me. "This land needed a humble church, like the first churches."

But just as he was about to start work expanding a little cave into his underground church, Yaakov's partner, Toma, a former American Trappist, raised the final obstacle. Toma wanted the cave turned into a cistern. "He's a pragmatic American," Yaakov said, trying to laugh though clearly still annoyed. "I said there must be a proper chapel. This is essential. So we decided not to interfere in each other's work." Toma planted trees and covered the bare mountain with forest. Meanwhile, Yaakov began digging. He had no machinery, so he dug by hand. It took three years. "But limestone isn't such hard rock," he said, trying to temper his justifiable pride.

I asked Yaakov why he'd come to Israel. It had begun with his uncle, he explained, a Catholic bishop in Holland who was sent to Auschwitz for denouncing the deportation of the Jews. Because of an infection in his leg, he was chosen for Dr. Mengele's medical experiments and was turned into a cripple. Shortly after the war, he came to speak at Yaakov's monastery. God is planning a "great witness" through the Jews, he prophesied, and the entire world would be transformed. Yaakov was deeply affected by his uncle's vision. He'd never heard even the most sympathetic Christians speak that way about the Jews.

When the state of Israel was established, Yaakov's uncle wanted to move there but was too physically broken to travel. Yaakov resolved to go in his place, but his superiors denied him permission. Every year he would ask again, with the same persistence he would later apply to carving his underground chapel from stone; every year he was turned down. Finally, in 1961, his superiors relented. "They gave me their blessing," he said to me, "but not much more."

Yaakov's goal was to help revive ancient Christianity in the Holy Land, which had, after all, begun as a humble minority among the

Jews. The reborn state of Israel allowed not only Jews but Christians, too, to dream of reclaiming their lost biblical glory, their intimacy with God.

But then he encountered the plight of the Arabs. The Galilee's Arab villages often lacked electricity and even water. In those years, Israeli Arabs lived under military rule and needed permission just to leave the village. Yaakov understood the besieged state's fears of an Arab minority emotionally aligned with the Arab world, so he didn't judge Israel but resolved to ease its dilemma. Perhaps God had brought him to the land for a calling he hadn't suspected: not just to help make peace between Christianity and Judaism but to help unite Arabs and Jews in a common Israeliness. He became a pastor to the Arabs, walking from village to village because public transportation hadn't yet been extended to Arab areas. And he joined the Melkites, partly to encourage an Israeli Christian identity and partly in solidarity with the Arabs, though they themselves couldn't understand what he was seeking among them. "The Arabs like power and authority," Yaakov explained to me. "They said, 'Why don't you stay with the Latin Church? They're the ones with the power.'" He laughed. He loved the peoples of this land but had no illusions about us.

Yaakov continued, "I look at the prosperity in some of the villages, and I can't believe how far we have come. There is still injustice toward the Arab minority, but they are the freest Arabs in the Middle East, and they know it. When they visit Arab countries they boast about living in a progressive state. The Christian Arabs especially know how lucky they are to be living in Israel. The next step is for Arabs to find their place in Israeli identity. That is my dream."

But how, I asked, could Israel neutralize its Jewish identity? I had exchanged life in the United States for the Middle East to participate in the reconstruction of the Jewish people. My most moving moment as an Israeli was watching the barefoot and white-robed Ethiopian Jews descending wide-eyed and silent from planes onto Zion. Yet if we defined ourselves simply as a "normal" Western nation rather than as a Jewish state responsible for protecting the world's Jews, we would never have dispatched the Israeli air force into an Ethiopian civil war to retrieve thousands of illiterate African tribesmen. And that was an Israel I wouldn't want to live in.

Yaakov said, "God certainly wants His people back in His land. Yes, hmm. But there must be a message here for the Arab people, too. I'm convinced that the spiritual meaning of the Jewish return won't be fulfilled until the Arabs find their place in it."

We walked up the hill to the guest house, a surprisingly ugly concrete building that violated Lavra Natofa's harmony. My room was so small that Yaakov had to wait outside while I entered. It contained only a cot, desk, bookshelf, and kerosene lamp; there was no electricity in Lavra Natofa. The communal bathroom held buckets of rainwater for flushing toilets, collected from cisterns in the winter months—"from the heavens," Yaakov explained. There were showers, but signs urged guests to use them sparely.

In other monasteries I'd visited there was invariably a cross or an icon in the guest rooms. Here, though, the walls were bare. It was in fact a deliberate omission, an act of religious restraint: Jews and other non-Christians, Yaakov explained, sometimes came on retreat here. The only religious exhortation was a Psalm posted on the door: "Shout unto the Lord, all the earth. Serve the Lord with gladness; come before His presence with singing. For the Lord is good; His mercy endureth forever; and His faithfulness unto all generations." Yaakov's ecumenism was evident, too, in the selection of books on the shelf: manuals for spiritual development by Sri Auribindo and Rabbi Moshe Haim Luzzatto, the autobiography of Saint Thérèse of Lisieux, a comparative study of Zen and Christian mysticism—and the collected writings of Snoopy.

I joined Yaakov and Toma for dinner. Two young monks lived here too, but they were off hiking in the Golan Heights. We ate noodles and green beans on the kitchen veranda under a corrugated roof. Just beneath us was a grove of fig trees, then farther down the hill an olive grove, and in the valley brown and green patches like a bedouin rug unrolled to the Sea of Galilee. Arab villages, identifiable by their flat roofs, spread comfortably through the hills, while the red-roofed houses of the Jewish villages were symmetrically arranged.

Toma had a long, untrimmed gray beard and long gray hair, and he wore a torn T-shirt and shorts. He spoke in a barely comprehensible Midwestern mumble and hunched, trying to minimize his substantial height. It seemed to me that Yaakov, with his careful grooming, had used the casual American as a model of how not to live as a recluse. Toma didn't sit with Yaakov and me, but ate alone. He acknowledged my presence with a nod but didn't seem interested in knowing who I was or what I was doing here. Compared to Toma, Yaakov seemed garrulous.

A Christian Arab named Elias, who had grown up in a neighboring village but now lived in Germany, dropped by to see Abuna Yakub. Elias made a point of coming to Lavra Natofa whenever he was back in Israel visiting family. He had married a German woman and ran a Middle Eastern restaurant in Bonn. He was short and sturdy and, like me, in his mid-forties. With his trucker's cap and money belt, he looked like a tourist, a foreigner.

"The people in the village don't know what they have ten minutes away," he said to me. "Who comes up from Deir Hanna to pray in this wonderful church? You don't know what you have until you lose it."

"If there was peace, it would be a real paradise here," I said. That was the kind of inane remark that well-meaning Jews and Arabs were expected to say to each other.

"But there is peace," Elias insisted. "Between you and me there is peace."

I sensed Father Yaakov's pleasure: a Jew and an Arab speaking in Hebrew at Lavra Natofa.

Elias continued, "You see those olive groves? They belong to my family. And I am living in Germany. Why? I don't feel at home there, and I never will. Here family is so important, but there it's different. My wife's parents invite us to dinner, and if we're fifteen minutes late, we find them already eating. We have two children; we're not always in control of events. The first few times it happened, I couldn't believe it. Finally I realized that it's not rudeness but a cultural difference. But who wants to live in such a culture?"

Yaakov said, "I was at a funeral last week in Deir Hanna and the whole village came. You tell that to people in Europe and they say, 'Arabs must have a lot of time on their hands.' They can't understand the social solidarity that exists here. One of my regrets is that we don't have Palestinian monks in the Melkite church; all the monks are Westerners. Palestinians couldn't bear the separation from their families. Elias's uncle is the archbishop. When he visits a village, the whole family comes out to greet him."

They laughed.

"Why don't you come back?" I asked Elias.

"My wife is afraid of the conflict. And my children don't know Arabic or Hebrew. They feel at home in Germany."

Elias knew he belonged in this land, with its warm, overheated people, not in that cold, distant place. But he also knew that it was too late for him to return. I had heard the same lament from Israeli Jews living abroad, watching home recede.

I felt the sadness of his exile, not just on the human level but as a fellow Israeli. What a loss to this society, I thought; we so badly needed people of goodwill like Elias. In truth, I had never before regretted the notion of Arabs emigrating from Israel and certainly hadn't considered their voluntary departure an Israeli tragedy. Another Palestinian has decided to leave Israel? That's one less voter to undermine the Jewish state from within. For all our mutual protestations of coexistence, Arab and Jewish Israelis still secretly wished for the other's disappearance. This land was too small; we threatened each other's most basic aspirations. The Arabs resented their transformation into a minority; and we warily watched their national loyalties, wondering whether they would demand autonomy and perhaps even secession for the Galilee, leaving Israel truncated and untenable. Yet sitting with Elias, I experienced the same regret I'd felt toward Israeli Jewish expatriates. Elias was stretching my sense of Israeliness.

He'd been away seventeen years, precisely the period I'd lived here, as though we'd traded places. What was it about this restless land that continually created exiles? Israel allowed no respite: Even now, contemplating the sun setting over the valley and the sea, we were tormented by our contradictions.

"Come home soon," I said to Elias, and meant it.

"*Inshallah,*" he said in Arabic, with God's help, and then he added the Hebrew equivalent, "*b'ezrat Hashem.*"

After dinner, Yaakov scattered the leftovers for a dozen cats that gathered around the kitchen shed. He stood over them as they ate, ensuring that the smallest ones didn't get eased out. Then I joined him in the kitchen; I washed, he dried. I tried to emulate his careful gestures, the determined gracefulness that reminded me of Sheykh Ishak Idriss Sakouta. He noticed my efforts and said, "Hmm, very good. When you leave here, we'll give you a certificate in dish washing."

We walked to the guest house. Toma was sitting on the porch, drinking beer. Toma and Yaakov sat here every night after dinner and watched the twinkling valley reflect the full night sky.

"Yaakov," Toma said, "why don't you celebrate the tranquillity with a beer?"

Yaakov took a beer from the cooler and told Toma about a monastery in Jerusalem that the Franciscans had leased to the Melkites twenty years ago and now wanted back. The Melkites, who had turned the neglected monastery into one of the most beautiful in Jerusalem, had nowhere to go, but the Franciscans seemed determined to reclaim the property anyway. "What would Saint Francis say about that?" demanded Yaakov.

"Saint Francis was the first and last Franciscan," said Toma, and he made a muffled sound that resembled a sneeze but was in fact laughter.

"It's no better with the Greek monasteries," said Yaakov. "Santa Katarina has become a tourist center."

"They can get rich if they want, God help them," said Toma. "And bring in a few old men from Greece to light candles."

Yaakov told a story of two Ethiopian monks in Jerusalem who had been caught shoplifting. Just as they were about to be deported, they suddenly recalled their Jewish ancestry and demanded the right to immigrate to Israel.

Toma snickered, delighting in Yaakov's tales of monastic hypocrisy.

I asked Yaakov how he balanced the tension between solitude and openness to the world. He was after all a man with a mission, determined to help Arabs, especially Christian Arabs, enter Israeli identity; it must have been hard to isolate himself from Israeli society. Yaakov acknowledged that the early years had been a struggle. "I was very restless. I'd hear about an interfaith conference in Jerusalem and wanted to immediately go. But now I appreciate the solitude. I love Deir Hanna and Tel Aviv, but I'm glad I don't live in either place. To be a monk means to be separated from all and united with all."

"I'll sign up for that," said Toma.

I asked Toma why he came to Lavra Natofa. He replied that he'd been a member of a Trappist monastery in Tennessee called Gethsemani, heard about Yaakov's attempt to found a hermitage in the Galilee, and got in touch. "Looked to me like Yaakov was doing something important for God. Thought I could make a contribution. Nobody needed me in Tennessee."

"Wasn't Thomas Merton in Gethsemani?" I asked, referring to the late monastic writer.

"Think I saw him walking around once. My brother came to visit and said, 'You got a poet living here?' That's how I heard Merton was at Gethsemani." Clearly, proximity to fame held no interest for him.

For all of Toma's appreciation for Yaakov's efforts, it had never been easy between them. Even now tensions remained between the laid-back American recluse, a Trappist by nature as much as faith, and the stubborn visionary Dutchman who dreamed of transforming Israel. Yaakov wanted to bring in new monks; Toma was content to let things be. Yet they had grown to respect and even love each other in their own taciturn ways. They had overcome the odds against Lavra Natofa and against the success of their improbable friendship. Every morning Toma tended his trees and planted saplings; twice a week he shopped in Deir Hanna. ("Used to have a tractor, before that a donkey. Now we got a jeep. Movin' up in the world.") Yaakov puttered around the church, cooked and cleaned in the kitchen, and answered correspondence, maintaining Lavra's circle of supporters. Two old monks, hardened by struggle and softened by silence.

Toma offered a grudging "good night" and left. Yaakov said, with a respect that Toma had worked hard to earn, "He has a very fine theological mind. Outsiders don't see it; he keeps his true personality to himself."

In the distance were the lights of Safed, the town of the medieval kabbalists, and of villages along the shore of the Sea of Galilee; perhaps we were seeing the lights of monasteries in Tabgha and the Mount of Beatitudes. In every direction, a sacred landscape.

Yaakov said he was certain that Jesus had walked the hills around Lavra Natofa. And he believed that the Transfiguration—Jesus' appearance to his disciples as a body of light, reputed to have occurred on Mount Tabor—likewise occurred in these hills, perhaps on this very mountain. He offered proof from the New Testament, which I couldn't follow. "But the last thing we need are tourist buses," he said. "If we find any archaeological evidence that this was the site of the Transfiguration," he added, laughing, "I'll destroy it."

3

The bell rang at 4:15 A.M., muffled by silence and wind and the fog that had settled on the mountain. I went to the kitchenette of the guest house to prepare tea and found Toma, drinking coffee. "Do you always get up so early?" I asked. "Been up since 3:15," he said. "Got to shake off the sleep, be awake to pray."

I walked to the underground chapel through a field of young carob trees planted by Toma. In the mist, the lights in the valley looked like fire; a chilly wind blew black wisps like smoke.

The chapel, though, was immune to wind. I took a seat on the stone ledge and felt enveloped in mildew and kerosene fumes. I closed my eyes and tried to outwit exhaustion with a higher alertness. Toma sat nearby, wearing the torn T-shirt and shorts in which he worked the fields.

Yaakov descended the stone steps into the grotto imperceptibly, as if his body had taken a vow of silence. In his long white beard, blue knitted skullcap, and black robe, he looked like a cross between a monk and a rabbi. *"Adonai rahem, Adonai rahem, Adonai rahem, Adonai rahem,"* he chanted in Hebrew, deep and melodic. God have mercy. Even if we don't have mercy on each other, I silently appended, even if we don't have mercy on ourselves. *"Adonai rahem, Adonai rahem, Adonai rahem, Adonai rahem."* Any other prayer seemed superfluous.

He chanted selections from the Psalms, some in Hebrew, some in Arabic, resolving the conflict between Jews and Arabs by blessing them both. Toma picked through a Psalm in hesitant Hebrew: "Why should the nations say, 'Where, now, is their God?' Our God is in heaven, whatever He desires, He does . . . Israel, trust in God, their help and their shield." Yaakov held high a candle and proclaimed, as though rousing a crowd, "Behold Christ, light of the universe!" It didn't matter that only Toma and I were beholding the light in the predawn hiddenness of this underground chapel. Even if the people in the valley couldn't hear him, he was on the watch for them, dispensing light. He waved a censer; incense smoke enveloped his black robe, as though he were dematerializing.

After sunrise, Yaakov and I walked around the mountain. He held a roughly carved walking stick and crossed the slopes with slow but unstoppable determination, a man used to imposing himself on his surroundings. In our skullcaps, beards, and sandals, we could have belonged to the same sect.

We came to a grave, so far the only one on the mountain. The grave belonged to a Dutch volunteer, Yaakov explained. "We buried him at this particular spot to establish the border with Hararit," he continued, referring to the neighboring village of TM meditators. "They were claiming part of our land, and we knew that Jews wouldn't dig up graves."

Every step had been a struggle. Even the meditators at Hararit had resented Yaakov's presence. They'd tried to expand into the government lands on the mountain, but Yaakov had resisted, arguing that Lavra Natofa would turn into a besieged island without its buffer of forest. When Toma planted trees on government land, Hararit dispatched forestry officials to uproot them. Finally, the Jewish head of the regional council, who realized that Lavra Natofa embodied an essential Galilee quality, awarded Yaakov custodianship of the government lands, and now he lived at peace with Hararit.

Even relations with his own Melkite church had sometimes been turbulent. Yaakov's vision of the Melkites as a bridge for Arabs into

Israeli identity was never taken seriously by the Melkites themselves. The notion that a tiny church caught between the Muslims and the Jews would dare create a new Arab Israeli identity seemed naive, one more fantasy to be devoured by this land. In fact, the Melkite church had produced the most traumatic incident in the history of Israeli-Christian relations. In 1974, a Melkite bishop, Hilarion Cappucci, was caught by Israeli soldiers running guns in his car for the Palestine Liberation Organization. It was the heyday of PLO terrorism against Israeli buses and schools, and a priest who armed the murderers of Jewish children reinforced the most traumatic memories of Christianity. The Cappucci incident reverberated even now, undermining Jewish-Christian relations: Security personnel at Ben-Gurion Airport, recalling the terrorist priest, often subjected outraged clergy to stringent searches.

The arrest of Cappucci had been Yaakov's most trying time. He wrote an anguished letter to the Melkite archbishop: It was one thing to be sympathetic to the Palestinians, but how could a follower of Christ smuggle guns? Yaakov had intended the letter to remain private, but the archbishop, perhaps to discredit the eccentric foreigner, published it in his church bulletin. Suspicions against Yaakov now seemed confirmed: He was a Zionist agent planted within the church. Yaakov endured the cold distance of his fellow Melkite clergy just as he'd accepted all the obstacles that God had set in his way since he'd first dreamed of coming to the Holy Land so many years before. He consoled himself with a quote from the rabbis: "The land of Israel is won by suffering." So he suffered and persisted. Now, too, forgiven by the hierarchy and beloved in the villages, he remained an outsider, silent at church meetings and deferring to the Arab clergy even when he knew he was right.

But Yaakov didn't resent his position in the church. He appreciated the spiritual discipline of reticence, the humbling role of lonely European under an Arab hierarchy. "It's good to be a minority, hmm. Also for the Christians in this land. One hundred eighty thousand

Christians among five million Jews and two million Muslims. It teaches us humility. We're not the only ones who have an admission ticket to heaven."

"What about the New Testament's assertion that the only way to the Father is through the Son?" I asked.

"There are Muslims in the villages who have complete confidence in me; some have even named their children after me. I can tell them to become Christian and they would. But what then? They would become totally cut off from their families and their villages, and in Arab society, that means you are lost. Is God to just abandon them? And how can Jews accept Christ after all that has happened in history? Are they not to be admitted into the Kingdom? The God of love can't possibly work that way. So He creates other ways to approach the Kingdom. Jesus said to Pilate, 'Whoever listens to My voice, he is on the side of truth.' I have been at the deathbeds of Muslim and Jewish friends; I saw how well their religion had prepared them for passing over. I didn't feel there was anything I needed to add as a Catholic priest."

"How has living in the land of Israel changed you, Yaakov?"

"I used to be very impatient. I had definite ideas about how things should be done, hmm."

He paused, that final syllable a passage from speech into silence. Clearly he wasn't used to such extravagant speech. I urged him to continue; I sensed that he sometimes forgot that his thoughts weren't audible.

"Hmm, yes. In Holland I fought with my superiors against the class system that existed in the monasteries of that time. There were two classes of monks, the choirmasters and the lay brothers. The lay brothers were poorer boys who did the more humble work, but I felt they had more life wisdom than the immature choirmasters. I was in charge of the two groups, and I insisted on only one class of monks, which is what finally did happen."

"Weren't you right to fight for your ideas?"

"Yes, but you also have to know when to let go. Stand up for what you believe in, but leave the results to God. That way you allow room for His ideas, not just your own. We have to do our tasks but not be too worried. God always has the last word. I used to suffer very much if things didn't go fast enough. But God taught me patience. Now," he laughed, "I'm a bit more mature."

Yaakov's great monastic challenge had been impatience, which is why, he believed, God tested him on the mountain with the years of waiting and digging and conflict, like his namesake Jacob, working seven years and then seven years again for the elusive Rachel. The goal of the spiritual life was a stilling of the separated self, first its needs and desires and then even its higher aspirations, until you became an instrument for God's will. That had been Yaakov's true struggle, and like the patriarch Jacob, all his battles were a great wrestling match in which God had tried to subdue and possess his lower self.

"Sometimes God gives you refusals," he said. "But rejection can be the best affirmation. That we understand only afterward. Like the Jews in the desert, God has tested me, and God has fed me."

In the late morning I found Yaakov in the kitchen, chopping celery. He was making soup: pieces of celery in a powdered imitation chicken broth. At least it wasn't noodles and green beans, which we'd eaten for the past two days.

"Yaakov," I said, "I was wondering how you kept your love for Israel even when you discovered the reality of relations between Arabs and Jews. I know Christians who came here very pro-Zionist but became disillusioned and turned against Israel." With Yaakov there was no need for preliminary small talk; you simply approached him with whatever was on your mind.

"I also came to Israel one hundred percent pro-Israeli," he replied.

"But you didn't become one hundred percent pro-Arab at Israel's expense."

"I never lost my love for all the people of this land. Even when I saw injustice, hmm, I never stopped understanding the fears of the Jews. And I never stopped believing that God had a purpose for bringing the Jews back. We don't know His purpose or His timetables. I'm against apocalyptic Christianity. But I believe that God has something special in mind for this land. It's God's secret. But it could be a new youth for all the people of God."

Unexpectedly, he laughed, and for a moment I glimpsed the young and vigorous monk, setting out to conquer the mountain and transform Christianity in its native land.

"How did you keep your heart open to Arabs and Jews? How do you keep loving people even when they act in awful ways?"

"Each person is unique. God doesn't repeat Himself. So I want to know: Who are you? What unique aspect of God do you have?"

"And when that unique aspect of God is covered up?"

"Then I try to think of what this soul will be like in the future. All souls will be redeemed. We are created in the image of God, yes, but just as important, we will all share in His glory."

By focusing on our common future, Yaakov was reversing the logic of the interfaith movement, which promoted dialogue based on our common origins—children of Abraham, created in God's image. Yaakov was implicitly saying that evoking the past wasn't enough. We needed to see each other not as static beings but as souls on the way to perfection. Life was the process of exposing the true identity of each person, his unique divine quality. If you really lived like Yaakov, you couldn't allow yourself to get angry or disappointed at human failures. To identify a person with his flaws was to arrest a soul at an awkward moment of its evolution. Solidity was the great illusion; all life was prelude.

I returned to my room and read an essay Yaakov had lent me that he said expressed his own ideas about faith. It was from an American Christian intellectual magazine and was written by a theologian named Paul Lakeland. "Faith is a primal force," wrote Lakeland, "imagination on the move. Faith is the dynamic element in life, what keeps us in process, in becoming, in possibility. There is no such thing as faith in the past. . . . A faithful people is not marked by its jealous preservation of relics, but by oneness with the faith in the future that its own dead bequeathed to it. . . . It is a looking forward, not a looking back."

Yaakov, I realized, didn't love this land only for the past but for the future role he believed it would play in revealing God's glory. That same anticipation had allowed him to maintain paradoxes that lesser believers found untenable, like loving the Jews even when they didn't act justly toward the Arabs and loving the Arabs even when they denied the homecoming of the Jews. He could accept paradox because a part of him inhabited a redeemed future in which failures were revealed as mere stages of growth, preconditions of perfection.

In the evening I sat on the guest house porch with Henk and Esteban, the two young monks who lived at Lavra Natofa and had just returned from hiking on the Golan. With their ponytails and stiff black skullcaps they looked more Greek Orthodox than Catholic. Henk, a Dutchman, had met Yaakov as a teenager and eventually followed him to this mountain. Esteban, an Argentinean, had come to Lavra Natofa after living in an Indian ashram.

I asked what they thought of Yaakov's vision of Arabs and Jews and the Melkite church. Henk, smoking a cigarette, said, "Those are Yaakov's ideas. I'm a Melkite because I like the ritual and the music. It has more spirit than Western Catholicism."

I asked Esteban why he'd decided to leave the ashram and come to Lavra Natofa. "I liked Eastern religion," he replied, "but there isn't salvation in it. As a Christian, I have salvation just by accepting Christ."

"Don't we need to spiritually work on ourselves?"

"You can't be lazy," he conceded. "But God is generous to those who believe. In the East, the goal is to get rid of bad karma. But if you believe in Christ, he takes away your karma."

Esteban and Henk depressed me. Somehow Yaakov had failed to imbue his young monks with his own commitments to pluralism and to Arab-Jewish reconciliation. He had tried to become a living model of spiritual peace, and no other Christian I knew had so fully absorbed both Jewish and Arab identities, praying in Hebrew and Arabic, celebrating Israeli Independence Day with prayers of thanksgiving, and mourning the Palestinian tragedy with the Melkite church. Yet that experiment had remained a private obsession. No one understood the old man on the mountain, not even those who shared his life.

4

The fast of the Seventeenth of Tamuz, the beginning of the Three Weeks, coincided with my last morning at Lavra Natofa. I asked Yaakov for permission to pray in his chapel while wearing tefillin. I was sure he'd be pleased, but the request was so unusual that I needed to ask anyway. For many Christians, bringing tefillin into a church would invoke the horror of syncretism; for many Jews, it would be an abomination. For me, though, it seemed under the circumstances the most natural act. I needed a place to pray, and here was a house of prayer, sanctified by sacrifice and devotion. We religious people needed to begin seeing each other's synagogues, churches, temples, and mosques as variations of home, refuges from the secular world.

Not surprisingly, Yaakov was delighted. "Hmm, yes, very good, very good," he said, as close as he could manage to effusiveness. For Yaakov, a Jew in tefillin praying in his grotto would fulfill something of his vision of Lavra Natofa as a place of reconciliation between the faiths.

I descended into the hothouse, dense with humidity and prayer, entered the depths of the Holy Land. Light peeked from a gash in the rock ceiling high above. I fastened prayer-filled boxes on my head and on my forearm opposite my heart, uniting thought and feeling and action in God. I placed the prayer shawl over my head and felt the earth rising and the heat settling. *Adonai rahem, Adonai rahem, Adonai rahem, Adonai rahem.* My prayer shawl absorbed the smells of mildew, incense, and kerosene.

"Sound the great shofar of our freedom," I recited from the Hebrew prayer book, "raise a banner to gather our exiles, and bring us together from the four corners of the earth into our land. Blessed are You Lord, Who gathers the dispersed of His people Israel."

The prayer offered no comfort. Yes, we had been physically ingathered, but we remained in exile from each other. How could this chaos of contradictions possibly become Israel?

I knew how Yaakov would reply: Faith and patience, Yossi, hmm. Patience nurtured by faith, an active patience, striving for the goal but renouncing its fulfillment to God. Yaakov's active patience was embedded in his church. To carve this grotto from rock required a hollowing of himself, an emptying of his own will that created an opening for God. Sitting in Yaakov's cathedral of renunciation, I felt the relief of accepting my own insignificance. Each of us was entrusted with a minuscule piece of God's plan. Impatience was futile; only the massive accumulation of small acts of good would ultimately ensure the plan's success. Like the Jews wearing down the exile with prayer, like the monk chiseling against the rock.

I tried again: "Sound the great shofar of our freedom, raise a banner to gather our exiles . . ." For centuries, religious Jews had recited that prayer three times a day. Where did they get the strength to believe in it? The return to Zion was the fantasy that allowed Jews to resist the pressures and taunts and allures of Christianity and Islam, which compellingly argued that God had shifted his love from the exiled Jews to their triumphant successors. And now here I was, living in a sovereign Israel, my daily life the fulfillment of prayer. The Seventeenth of Tamuz, it seemed to me, should no longer be a day just of mourning but also of quiet celebration of persistence and faith. I offered an impromptu prayer: "Thank You, God, for bringing us home, for fulfilling Your promise at the moment of our brokenness; thank You, God, for allowing us to believe in You again." It occurred to me that Father Yaakov, who'd come to Israel in place of his uncle, the Auschwitz survivor, must have offered variations of that same prayer in this place.

I went to Yaakov's room to say good-bye and thank him for his gift of patience. His stone hut was at once intimate and austere. An Arab carpet covered the stone floor, bookcases held works on Christianity and Judaism, an arched window opened to the Sea of Galilee. Kerosene lamps hung on the wall, and a kerosene heater awaited winter. Over his crowded desk hung a rough wood cross, balancing a branch of thyme; over his cot hung an icon of Jacob's ladder, from which angels descended to earth. A grandfather clock was the room's single extravagance, reminder that Yaakov once had a life beyond the Middle East.

I told Yaakov how I'd been dreading the Three Weeks and struggling with the fear of Israel's disintegration and with my own frustrations toward Israel's rival camps, and how he had inadvertently helped me cope. I added that I intended to use the Three Weeks to try to renounce impatience, to remind myself that my job wasn't to change the world or even Israel but to ensure the purity of intent behind my limited acts.

He smiled and nodded. I asked him for parting advice, and he said,

"Don't try to force things. If there's a day when you're not inspired to write, put it aside. If your imagination is attracted to something sinful, think of something else that is beautiful. If you can, do it in a gentle way."

"Yaakov, have you achieved an end to restlessness?"

"There are always tests, hmm. I'm not afraid of dying. I'm ready to be taken right now. But I would be more at peace if I had someone to pass my work on to. Henk and Esteban are fine fellows. Esteban is a marvel with his hands. He can enter a store and within seconds be in rapport with the shopkeeper. And Henk: He has a real feel for the Orthodox liturgy. But they aren't my successors." He didn't need to elaborate. Even from cursory conversation with the two young monks, I'd realized they didn't resonate with Yaakov's dreams.

"I'm waiting for my Isaac, my heir," he continued. "I tell you frankly, it keeps me awake nights."

He knew that, after his passing, nothing would remain of his vision but the memory of a wonderful hermit who'd had some eccentric notions about the Melkites and an expansive Israeli identity accommodating Arabs. He had reclaimed his little patch of the Holy Land with fierce self-sacrifice, and now Lavra Natofa was in danger of slipping away. In his way, he too shared the essential experience of this land: the fear of uprooting, of impermanence.

"Yaakov," I offered, "maybe it's God's will that your work here was meant for a certain period."

"Yes, yes, hmm. Certainly if it happens that way, yes. Maybe Lavra Natofa will be something else after I'm gone. That is also a possibility I have to consider. It is in God's hands, not mine." He paused, wrestling with himself. "There was a fine young man who was considering coming here. He wanted to work for coexistence. But then he decided to join the Jesuits. It was a great loss."

Nothing was more understandable than the desire of an old man to see his work survive him. And what, after all, was Yaakov working for if not the glory of God and peace in the Holy Land? When he told visitors to the mountain the story of the grotto, he wasn't boasting of his own labors but extolling the wonders of God. Still, a subversive thought chiseled away in him: With all that God has done here, how could it be allowed to simply dissolve?

In his best moments Yaakov knew the answer: A monk was supposed to renounce physical continuity, not only through children but also through works. A monk's prayer was simply: Thy will be done. Yaakov knew his struggle wasn't over, that God was still testing him, forcing him to confront what remained of his stubbornness and self-directed will. Perhaps his real suffering came from the awareness that his anxiety over the fate of Lavra Natofa was unworthy of a monk. He had reached that point on the spiritual path when even your finest qualities and aspirations had to be surrendered. To feel God's presence in meditation and prayer was the easy part; the real challenge was to feel God's presence in failure, and even more, in the seeming failure of a job done for God. Yaakov's victory over mortality now depended on accepting the failure of Lavra Natofa, renouncing the fruits of his renunciation. This was his ultimate wrestling match, his final attempt to transform from Yaakov to Yisrael, Jacob to Israel. A rabbinic word play turned the name *Yisrael* into *Shir El*, song of God. To become Israel, then, meant focusing your being into an instrument for God's song, unobstructed by even the most noble self-will.

We embraced. He kissed me on either cheek, so softly I hardly felt his touch.

"Pray for me," he said, with a humility that shamed me.

On my way down from the mountain, I stopped at a grocery in the Arab village of Arrabe and bought a liter of local olive oil in a plastic soda bottle. Like other urban Israeli Jews seeking "authentic" connections with the land, I bought Arab oil whenever I could. But now I had an additional motive: I wanted to bring home olive oil from Father Yaakov's neighborhood, bring something of the peace of

Lavra Natofa to Jerusalem. Olive oil symbolized not only peace in ancient Israel but also divine anointing. On Friday nights at our family table, we dipped bread in olive oil, to symbolize renouncing the ambitions of the week and surrendering to God's will. As it happened, this coming Friday night we would be hosting an Arab family; the daughter worked with my wife, Sarah, in her university research lab. We had intended to invite the family for months, but somehow it had worked out that they'd be coming the day after I returned from Lavra Natofa. I wanted Yaakov to be represented at that encounter. The oil from Arrabe, then, would be Yaakov's oil, symbolizing his hopes for Arab-Jewish rapprochement, as though he were blessing our table.

5

The Joulani family was nervous and tentative. "We've never been to a Shabbat dinner before," admitted Umaya, Sarah's friend from university. Nadal, Umaya's father and a lawyer, tried to conceal his anxiety with jokes. "Are we allowed to drive home on Shabbat, or do we have to sleep here?" His wife, Nadia, offered, "I like Hasidic music very much." Clearly, they'd never been to the home of religious Jews, whom Arabs tended to identify with settlers, the hard face of Israel.

Sarah and I were scarcely calmer: seventeen years in Israel, and this was the first time we'd hosted a Muslim family for dinner. That was hardly unusual; Jerusalem wasn't the Galilee.

The Joulanis were Arab Israelis who had left their Galilee village and moved to Jerusalem to provide their children with a better education. When the Palestinian Authority was created after the 1993 Oslo Accords, the Joulanis became increasingly nationalistic; the family had even considered moving to Palestine. But Nadal had since become so disillusioned with the corruption and repression under Arafat's regime that he now saw his family's future firmly linked to

Israel. Nationalist passions, he'd decided, weren't as important as living in a decent society. "Palestine is a mafia state of bullies and thieves," he said. "You can't buy a bottle of cola without having to bribe someone. There is no hope for that country."

Umaya, a nationalist, was offended. "Rich Palestinians will invest in the economy," she said to her father. "The situation will improve."

"Who would invest in a corrupt dictatorship?" demanded Nadal.

"Palestinians will come from America. Like Yossi and Sarah came to Israel."

"Yossi and Sarah came to a democracy," countered Nadal.

The Joulanis lived the political and cultural paradoxes of an Arab Israeli identity. They seemed in constant flux between secularism and tradition, East and West, Palestine and Israel. No identity could hold any of them fully; one logical choice negated the other. It was precisely those contradictions, it seemed to me, that made them a vital part of Israeli reality. Sometimes Umaya almost felt Israeli, singing along with Hebrew songs on the radio and identifying with Israeli feminism. She felt culturally smothered in Arab society but politically smothered in Israel. She compartmentalized her emotions: She was genuinely warm toward her Jewish friends but bitter and unforgiving when conversation turned to politics, repeating ethnic generalizations that the better part of her should have despised. Lately, she'd begun exploring Islam, fasting by day on Ramadan and then partying after sundown in Ramallah nightclubs—a Muslim feminist. Nadal, too, now fasted on Ramadan, though he considered himself an atheist and fasted only in solidarity with his fellow Muslims.

"I'm an Israeli, and my future is in Israel," Nadal said to me. "The question is, does Israel want me?"

"What does Israel need to do to make you feel part of it?" I asked.

The answer was unequivocal: dismantle itself as a Jewish state. The national anthem, which invoked a Jewish soul longing for Zion; the national flag with its Star of David; the Law of Return, which granted Jews automatic citizenship: All would have to go. The good news was that Nadal wanted to be part of Israel; the bad news was that Nadal could only feel part of an Israel that for me would lose its soul.

But Nadal's list of demands wasn't over. For Israel truly to accommodate Arab sensibilities, he continued, it would have to accept the return of Palestinian refugees. "Poor Ahmad has been sitting in a tent for fifty years, waiting to come home," he said. "If you bring in Russian immigrants, why not Palestinians?"

"That would be the end of Israel," I said, my voice rising. "By insisting on the demand of return, you're saying that Israel has no right to exist."

"I accept Israel's existence. There was a time when bastards were stoned to death in religious societies. Can anyone imagine doing that now? The same thing with Israel. In today's world, this bastard state has the right to exist."

Nadal's attempt at rapprochement only depressed me more. If he could do no better than accept Israel as an illegitimate child, then what chance did we have of creating a common national identity between Arabs and Jews?

"Why don't we begin the meal," Sarah said sensibly. She and I sang the Shabbat hymn to the angels of peace, whose presence among us we badly needed. Then I blessed the wine. Umaya had reassured Sarah that her family wouldn't be offended by the presence of wine. Though she and her mother wouldn't drink, in deference to Muslim law, her father, the heretic, would gladly join us.

Sarah blessed the challah. She broke off pieces, dipped them into the olive oil I had brought back from Arrabe, and passed them around the table. Both Nadal and Nadia said almost at once, "Where is this oil from?"

"The Galilee," I replied. "I just got it yesterday."

"Where in the Galilee?" demanded Nadia.

"Arrabe."

She gasped.

"That's our village!" shouted Nadal.

"There is a God," said Nadia.

Their connection to the land was remarkable: Just by tasting the oil they'd known it had come from their region.

But I was more amazed by another, less visible connection: I had offered this olive oil as a link with Father Yaakov, and somehow he had responded. God's friends created invisible patterns. Whatever happened to Lavra Natofa, I realized, the effects of Yaakov's work would endure. Perhaps not in ways he envisioned or could even claim, but the prayers had gone forth, the pattern formed. However indirectly, Father Yaakov, Abuna Yakub, had blessed us with his peace.

6

A month later, I returned to the Galilee for a vacation with Sarah and our two-year-old son, Shahar. One evening, which happened to coincide with the Feast of the Transfiguration, we visited Lavra Natofa. I was struck again by the peace of the hermitage, surrounded by Toma's forest, the land of Israel cherished by silence.

Yaakov greeted us with his awkward warmth: "Very nice, hmm, very nice." It was dinnertime: noodles and green beans. Tonight, though, bits of meat had been added to the dish, in honor of the Transfiguration, celebrating Jesus' revelation to his disciples in a body of light. "We're ordinarily vegetarian," Yaakov told me, "but it's not good to be dogmatic about anything." Still, he understood that Sarah and I wouldn't eat nonkosher meat and took no offense when we didn't join him for dinner.

He brought us to the grotto and told Sarah the saga of its construction, with the same enthusiasm and wonder with which he'd related the story to me. A stand displayed an icon of Jesus, who was mounted on a white star and flanked by Moses and Elijah, who were said to have been present at the Transfiguration. "In our Eastern tradition," Yaakov explained, "the meaning of the Transfiguration is that the disciples' eyes were opened, and for the first time they could see who Jesus really was. We pray for illumination on this day, to see God's presence in the world."

Then he said, "Tonight is also a great event for us at Lavra Natofa. A young man is coming from Italy. He is interested in the monastic life and in peace work between Arabs and Jews." Decades of solitude had suppressed his ability to raise his voice; still, he could hardly contain his excitement, and he smiled for emphasis. Clearly, Yaakov was hoping that God had chosen this auspicious day to send Yaakov's spiritual heir and save Lavra Natofa.

It was time for evening prayers. Yaakov suggested that Shahar ring the bell. He understood Shahar's soul, which longed to make a great impact on the world. Yaakov held him and together they pulled the cord, summoning the faithful: Toma, Esteban, and Henk. I asked Yaakov to bless Shahar. He laid his hands on the boy's head and said, "May you be a good boy and grow up to serve Israeli society, all of Israeli society." He meant: Become a peacemaker and help Arabs feel at home in the Jewish state.

We walked toward our car, which we'd parked at the entrance to Hararit. A taxi approached. "Is there some kind of monastery here?" the driver asked us. "I have a tourist, straight from the airport." I looked in and saw a young man, dark and round-faced: the Italian. I was tempted to hug him. You can't imagine what your arrival means for Yaakov, I wanted to say; you are an incarnation of his prayers.

I controlled my enthusiasm and said only, "So you're planning to stay a while?"

"Yes," he replied, "perhaps for three days."

I pointed toward Lavra Natofa and walked away, mute with Yaakov's imminent disappointment.

"Maybe he'll fall in love with the place and stay," Sarah offered.

"Poor man," I said, "being set up by God for another disappointment."

But then I thought: Maybe this was Yaakov's final test. Maybe this was the setback that would free him from all earthly hopes, leave him with nothing to anticipate but the will of God. Maybe he was right, then, and this really would be a great holiday for Lavra Natofa: the night of Jacob's transformation into Israel.

seven

Lailat al-Miraj

I

Sheykh Abdul-Rahim, spiritual leader of the Rifa'i Sufi order in the Palestinian areas, lived in the Nuseirat refugee camp in the Gaza Strip. Sheykh Abdul-Rahim was the beloved teacher of my Sufi friend, Sheykh Ibrahim. According to Ibrahim, Abdul-Rahim's followers would pierce themselves with swords during states of ecstasy and then be instantly healed by Abdul-Rahim's touch. When Abdul-Rahim had prayed at the grave of the Prophet Muhammad during a pilgrimage to Medina, said Ibrahim, a hand extended from the tomb and presented him with an Islamic green robe.

Eliyahu McLean, my Jewish guide into the Sufi world, was determined to make a pilgrimage to Abdul-Rahim, the "sheykh of sheykhs." Ibrahim offered to help persuade Abdul-Rahim to receive Eliyahu. It was no simple matter for a sheykh, even a Sufi, to host a Jew in a Gaza mosque. Gaza's refugee camps were the heart of Palestinian extremism. Hamas was headquartered in Gaza; the suicide bombings had emerged from there. Ecumenical contacts with Islam became increasingly difficult the deeper you penetrated the Palestinian tragedy: Dialogue was possible with the Palestinian citizens of Israel, rare with West Bank Palestinians, and, with Gaza refugees, almost inconceivable. Precisely for that reason, Eliyahu was keen on meeting Sheykh Abdul-Rahim, as an opening into Gaza's Islam.

I, too, wanted to meet Sheykh Abdul-Rahim, but Gaza terrified me. An Israeli's definition of vulnerability was to be caught alone in a Gaza refugee camp. And of all of Gaza's camps, none frightened me more than Nuseirat.

In the summer of 1991, my reservist infantry unit spent a month in Nuseirat. It was the time of the first Intifada. We were middle-aged men in ill-fitting uniforms, many of us new immigrants with minimal Hebrew and even less military training. We patrolled the camp mornings and evenings to "demonstrate a presence," in army parlance, but in reality we controlled nothing. We walked in a nervous line through the shantytown of cinderblock houses with corrugated roofs, while Palestinian teenagers ambushed us with rocks and broken glass and iron bars and then disappeared through the impenetrable maze of houses. We responded with futile chases and barrages of tear gas, which the wind often blew back in our faces. Not long before our arrival in Nuseirat, an Israeli reservist named Amnon Pomerantz was driving back from leave to his base in a nearby Gaza camp, made a wrong turn, and was surrounded by a mob and burned to death. Nuseirat's teenagers delighted in taunting us with his name: "Amnon bisalem aleik," they chanted, Amnon sends you his regards.

The walls of Nuseirat were covered with hate graffiti, Arabic letters leaping in rage. Just to make sure that we understood their intent, the graffiti was accompanied by explanatory drawings: a sword piercing a Star of David, a machine gun firing a line of bullets at an Israeli flag, swastikas.

Late one night, our unit was sent to find Palestinians to erase graffiti. We knocked on a random door, and a large balding man in a nightgown appeared, roused from sleep. Our officer ordered him to bring paint. "No problem," he mumbled wearily in Hebrew and returned a few minutes later with two sons, a sullen teenager and a man in his twenties, large and double-chinned like his father. We aimed the lights of our jeep on a graffiti-covered wall and watched them cover it with white paint. No one spoke or even looked at one another. It was so quiet we could hear the brushes stroking the wall.

The occupation corrupted through small abuses. The first few times that I'd enter a bedroom in the middle of the night to make an arrest—the suspect could be a terrorist or a tax evader—I'd avert my eyes, feeling the shame of mutual violation. But then it became routine. Or the degradation of language: Initially I resisted the mocking terms of the soldiers, like calling Nuseirat "Amsterdam" because of the open sewage canals running through its alleys. But fear and rage undermined the good conqueror, and finally I used those expressions, too.

A Palestinian teenager, caught throwing stones, was brought into our tent camp, bound, and blindfolded. A crowd of soldiers instantly formed: the curious and the smirkers and the few who sought either to abuse or to protect the prisoner. The boy was limp; even his lip drooped, lacking the will to remain upright. The blindfold, tightly bound, forced his eyebrows up into a look of permanent, dumb surprise. A soldier told the boy in Arabic, "Repeat after me: '*Wahad humus, wahad ful, ana bahbib Mishmar Hagvul.*'" One order of humus, one of beans, I love the Border Police. The boy repeated it, phrase by phrase. There was laughter.

Nuseirat embodied Israel's insoluble dilemma: We couldn't occupy the Palestinians, and we couldn't make peace with them. The dream of Gaza wasn't to expel us only from their homes but from ours. Undoing the occupation of 1967 was only a step in the negation of 1948, the creation of Israel. The maps of Palestine drawn on the walls told the truth of Nuseirat's deepest longing: They included not only Gaza and the West Bank but Israel, too. Gaza mocked the fantasy that peace could be reached by a compromise that offered the Palestinians two truncated pieces of territory with Israel like a dagger between them. For Gaza, justice and vengeance were interchangeable.

And so we were ambivalent occupiers, veering between repression and retreat. One night a grenade was thrown into the walled army compound of the Gaza town of Deir el Balah, and our unit was summoned as backup. Arab men gathered for questioning waited on a corner under guard. Some men were told to face the wall; others were allowed to watch. Some were told to stand, others to sit. We paced aimlessly, awaiting orders while our officers debated the next move. One said, "The grenade didn't explode. Let's forget about it and no one has to know." Another countered, "By tomorrow morning everyone will know anyway. If we don't react, they'll rise up and celebrate." The hard line won. We were divided into small groups, each of which was to enter homes and collect the identity cards of seven random men, who would then be sent to the military compound to reclaim their documents. Just to let everyone know we were on the case. We entered alleys lit only by the half-moon. A rat ran by, then another. A breeze carried the smell of garbage. *"Iftah, jeish!"* our officer shouted in Arabic. Open, army. The houses were almost identical: a courtyard with a fig or olive tree in its center, circled by rooms without furniture, filled instead with numerous children sleeping on striped wool rugs. In one home there was a plastic truck missing two wheels; I saw no other toys in all the houses we entered. Most families had a television; many had burners; some had refrigerators. On the fading green walls were gold-lettered quotes from the Koran.

We lived in a tent camp on the side of the road. Every night we debated among ourselves whether we should be here at all. We imposed on Gaza the wisdom of our varied exiles. For Wolfie, a South African immigrant who had fled apartheid and who became increasingly listless as our month of duty progressed, Gaza was Soweto. For Shimon, an Ethiopian immigrant who limped through patrols because a Sudanese soldier had smashed his steel-tipped boot on Shimon's bare foot in the refugee camp he'd lived in on his way to Israel, Gaza posed no moral dilemma at all: The Palestinians wanted to turn him and his family back into refugees, so it was us or them.

Gaza presented me, a child of the Holocaust, with an unbearable paradox. I believed that history imposed on Jews two inviolate demands: Never do to others what was done to you, and never underestimate the intentions of your enemy. Yet freeing Gaza from occupation meant empowering the enemy that wanted to destroy me. The Israeli left anguished over the occupation of Gaza but ignored its expansionist dreams; the Israeli right warned of Gaza's malevolence but dismissed the corruption of occupation. I was cursed with an openness to opposing truths; the result was shame for being an occupier even as I felt that I had no choice.

I would return home on leave from Gaza, enraged at the normalcy of Israeli life proceeding in proximity to the Intifada. And I was enraged at the Palestinians for rejecting every compromise they'd ever been offered, provoking the wars that ended in their expulsion and occupation. Gaza deprived both occupiers and occupied of innocence; all of us were implicated in this abyss.

One morning we were sent into Nuseirat's outdoor market to "demonstrate a presence." We had never gone to the market before; that was considered a provocation. But for some unexplained reason, the orders changed. The rocks—"rain," in Israeli army parlance—began falling as soon as we entered the market, where stalls sold used tin pots and onions and prickly pears from crates. Despite the "rain," people continued to buy and sell, like in a dream where you are caught in some desperate activity that passersby don't even notice.

While the rest of our unit tried to take cover along a wall, our officer, a combat veteran who considered mere stones an insult, strolled toward the rioters. Since I was carrying the unit's radio on my back, I had no choice but to follow him. Finally, the rocks were falling so thickly around us that even our officer had to concede the danger, and we took shelter in a tiny corner pastry shop.

Almost as soon as we entered the shop, a rock flew through the open door and into my helmet, just above my eye. I momentarily blacked out. When I revived, I found myself leaning against a display case holding trays of baklava; my gun had apparently cracked the glass. The grim little man who ran the bakery offered me a glass of water. "You, me, little people," he said in broken Hebrew. "Leaders make the trouble." I apologized for the cracked glass and gave him what money I had in my pocket to fix it. We avoided eye contact even as we wished each other, *"Ma'a salaame,"* the Arabic farewell for peace.

Long after I'd physically healed, I felt a sense of violation, as if my forehead were imprinted with the mark of Gaza's hatred. I thought often of the terrible verse in Deuteronomy, warning the Israelites that the land would vomit them out. The weapon of Gaza was pieces of earth, expelling us with the land itself.

Since then, everything had changed. The Palestinian Authority now ruled most of Gaza, and Israeli soldiers no longer patrolled the refugee camps. The Palestinians were well on their way to forming a state in Gaza and the West Bank.

Yet, in another sense, nothing had changed at all. Despite Israel's voluntary territorial contraction, Gaza refused to reciprocate with a contraction of its hatred. Hamas continued to operate openly in Gaza's refugee camps, where would-be suicide bombers marched in white shrouds, and crowds of thousands cheered the symbolic burning of cardboard Israeli buses. No attempt was made by Palestinian leaders to tell their people that the war with Israel was over, that the Jewish state was a permanent reality and Palestinian national aspirations were now being confined to Gaza and the West Bank. The maps of Palestine in Gaza's schools continued to absorb Israel; for the Palestinian leadership, independence in Gaza and the West Bank became a means, not an end. Every Israeli withdrawal was taken by Palestinians as a sign of weakness rather than conciliation. The dream of Gaza remained the destruction of Israel; we had left, but Gaza longed to pursue and dispossess us.

And now Eliyahu and I would enter Nuseirat, alone and unarmed, in search of a Sufi sheykh.

"Gaza is wonderful," Eliyahu insisted. "People are very warm. You have to learn to let go of your fears."

"Gaza isn't just a state of mind," I said, trying to control my annoyance. "I'd be less nervous waving an Israeli flag in downtown Teheran than going back to Nuseirat. For me the world is flat and it ends in Gaza."

"Don't worry," said Eliyahu, smiling his expansive Sufi-Hasidic-Sikh smile. "Sheykh Abdul-Rahim will protect us."

Here we go again: my fear versus his faith.

Ibrahim phoned Sheykh Abdul-Rahim, who said we were welcome to visit any time except Thursdays, *zikr* night. Eliyahu was disappointed. He'd hoped that Abdul-Rahim would allow us entry into the prayer circle. But Abdul-Rahim's fears were understandable. It was one thing to host us for a private meeting, quite another to admit us into a public gathering. Being welcomed into a mosque in Nuseirat was extraordinary enough; to try to join a *zikr* was straining God's generosity.

Months passed. We repeatedly delayed our trip, in part because I was covering the Israeli election campaign of spring 1999. I wondered whether I was using work as a pretext to evade Nuseirat. Indeed, each delay felt like a reprieve. But then, in early June, Eliyahu was about to leave for an extended stay in the United States, and we finally set a date for Gaza.

Ibrahim made the arrangements. "You are American friends," he told me. "American friends of Sheykh Ibrahim." In other words, he hadn't told Sheykh Abdul-Rahim that Eliyahu and I were Jews. Ibrahim was trying to ensure our entry into Abdul-Rahim's court and also to protect us. Still, I didn't like the subterfuge; it wasn't how I'd wanted to return to Nuseirat.

As the day approached, I became increasingly anxious. Nightmares troubled my sleep, and even when I couldn't recall their details, my first waking thought was Nuseirat. Still, I knew I had to return, that it wasn't mere bravado but a necessary confrontation with my deepest fears of Islam and the Middle East. I suspected it was no coincidence that my journey into the faiths with whom I shared the Holy Land was now leading me, despite myself, back to Nuseirat.

2

The Erez terminal, dividing Israel from Gaza, resembled a stockyard. A maze of high fences formed narrow queues through which Palestinian day laborers passed; they were surrounded by concrete lots where trucks were inspected for hidden bombs. No effort was made to remove the prodigious litter, which was simply swept into piles. Once Erez had been an almost symbolic checkpoint, but the Intifada and the suicide bombings had turned it into one of the world's most controlled borders, whose purpose was to manage an uprooted, unwanted, and potentially lethal population.

Approaching Erez from the vast parking lot through which an army jeep slowly circled, my old dread of Gaza returned. Not just fear for my physical safety, but the deeper fear of contagion, of being infected by rage and despair. Gaza was the most profane place in the Holy Land. Entering Erez meant leaving behind every dream of Israel as a worthy and meaningful place; the only dreams that Gaza allowed were of hatred and revenge.

Ibrahim was unable to join us, but he sent along his teenage son, Yusuf, as our escort and translator. Yusuf, sweet-natured and gangly and barely mustached, had grown up as his father's companion and attendant, arranging his schedule and accompanying him to exorcisms and *zikrs*. The youngest of Ibrahim's seven children, he'd been a boy when his mother died of cancer, and he'd been raised by Ibrahim, whom he described as "my father, my mother, my teacher, my friend." Yusuf was used to being ignored, happily listening to the conversations of the adults around him. His mouth would sometimes drop open, as if waiting for others to fill him with words. Like his father, he called me often just to say that I was his brother and that he loved me. He was the essence of harmlessness. Only a refined spiritual tradition could have produced such modesty and patience in so young a person.

Any Israeli entering Gaza had to be accompanied by Palestinian police. Neither side wanted dead Israelis on Yasser Arafat's watch while negotiations were proceeding over Palestinian statehood. But as a journalist, I was exempt from the forced escort. And Eliyahu, an American citizen, could likewise enter freely. He was used to traveling around Gaza without protection. He was a peacemaker, protected by God; why should he need men with guns?

Eliyahu and I went to a cubicle office where foreigners and Israeli journalists received their passes into Gaza from soldiers who acted with a courtesy rare at the checkpoints of the Palestinian-Israeli divide. Yusuf had to go through the regular Palestinian queue, where the treatment was far more abrupt. Since the suicide bombings of the mid-nineties, Palestinians seeking to cross between the West Bank and Gaza through Israel required military permission. And so just before coming to Erez we'd stopped at an army base near the West Bank town of Ramallah to get a pass for Yusuf. The officer who issued the pass had a photograph on the wall across his desk of kerchiefed Palestinian women traveling by bus to visit their husbands in Israeli prison, to remind himself, he explained to us, that every permit has a face behind it and not allow himself to become an insensitive bureaucrat.

Yusuf found us at the office in Erez and we walked through the vast concrete emptiness toward the final Israeli checkpoint. A soldier, noting Eliyahu's long black beard and baseball cap, called out, "Hey, Fidel!" Eliyahu, instantly entering the joke, raised his fist and replied, "*Viva la revolucion!*" The soldiers laughed, raised their fists in return, and shouted, "Viva Fidel!" And that is how we entered Gaza.

An arch that could barely accommodate a single row of cars greeted us, painted in black, red, and green, the implacable colors of Palestine. In the hutlike passport office, mustached men with submachine guns watched us sullenly. Behind them hung the map of Greater Palestine, including the territory otherwise known as Israel. They're concealing nothing, I thought; we Israelis just can't bear to face the truth.

A young man named Taiseer was waiting for us in a red sports car just beyond the passport office. Taiseer belonged to Gaza's tiny circle of coexistence activists whom Eliyahu befriended, arranging permits for them into Israel as part of his religious dialogue work. I had met several of them one night in Jerusalem. Children of Gaza's new elite, they wore leather jackets and Gap clothes, spoke fluent English, and were fascinated by West Jerusalem, the closest they'd seen to a modern city. I'd been struck then by the dichotomy between Eliyahu and his Gaza friends: He was hoping through them to advance his religious dialogue with Palestinians, but these secular young men were interested in Eliyahu because he was as far west as they could touch.

Taiseer, pudgy with slicked hair, helped run his family's ceramics factory. His manner was appropriately cynical: He was a young man with lots of money and connections but trapped in Gaza; for him, Erez was the outer wall of the prison courtyard.

I asked Taiseer if he intended to stay with us at Sheykh Abdul-Rahim's.

"I don't have time for sheykhs," he said.

Eliyahu retrieved from his pocket a *hamsa,* a hand-shaped piece of metal that is the Middle East's good-luck sign and on which was imprinted the Hebrew prayer for travelers. He quietly prayed, "Deliver us from the hands of every enemy and lurking foe, from robbers and wild beasts on the journey, and from all kinds of calamities that may afflict the world."

Taiseer opened the car's sun roof. "The prayers will reach heaven faster," he said dryly.

We drove past empty lots, half-built houses, a lone olive tree offering grudging shade, a pile of gutted cars—probably stolen from Israelis for spare parts: an incoherent landscape. Taiseer drove with reckless speed; he barely slowed even when we entered the narrow streets of Gaza City, honking with frustration as he weaved through the old Peugeots and donkey-driven carts. One of the most moving memories I carried from my reserve duty in Gaza was of young people along the shore flying kites, vicariously experiencing flight; Taiseer's kite was his little red sports car.

And then, suddenly, Nuseirat. The same streets of sand, rivulets of sewage between the little houses with corrugated roofs held down by cinderblocks, a painting of a Star of David pierced with swords dripping blood. I asked Yusuf to translate the graffiti, and he said, "*Shaheed*, our eyes weep for you." Mass murder as melodrama: *Shaheed* were the holy martyrs, the suicide bombers. We were gone, but Gaza hadn't forgotten us.

The Palestinian Authority had received billions in foreign aid yet had chosen to spend that money not on refugee relief but on arming its numerous security forces. Palestinian leaders deliberately maintained their people's misery, to keep alive the demand for the "right of return," euphemism for demographically destroying the Jewish state by inundating it with hostile refugees. So long as Palestinians were kept in refugee camps by their own leaders in their own land, peace would remain a fantasy.

On closer look, Nuseirat wasn't entirely the same. A bridal shop— in Nuseirat!—displayed elaborate white gowns; a photo shop featured pictures of American movie stars and distant pastoral scenes.

On a wall someone had painted a big red heart that contained the word *mabruk*, good luck, a defiant innocence.

A marble monument, unfinished and without an inscription, stood in an unnecessary traffic circle. Perhaps the monument was meant to commemorate Nuseirat's victory over the Israel Defense Forces, the routing of myself and my friends from here; but the listlessness of Nuseirat subverted any triumphalist statement.

We came to the outdoor market, where I'd been hit with a stone. There was the corner bakery. And here I was, unarmed and defenseless. I had to remind myself to breathe. If these people knew who I was, I thought, they would burn me alive.

Yusuf said, "The sheykh's mosque is right near the market." God's joke: I wasn't just returning to Nuseirat but to the precise place of my trauma.

Sheykh Abdul-Rahim's *zawiyeh*—or Sufi mosque—was a little building on a dead-end side street. The green flag of Islam hung outside, as though the building were an embassy; yet it was so modest that it lacked even a minaret. Taiseer dropped us off and sped away. No steps led into the *zawiyeh,* whose doors were opened to the street. Inside were two parallel rooms, both long and narrow with high ceilings; one functioned as a mosque, the other as a sitting room. A little hallway filled with shoes separated the two areas. We removed our shoes and entered.

Sheykh Abdul-Rahim was preparing for midday prayers, washing his feet at a low sink near the entry. His long white beard was thin, almost transparent. He kissed each of us three times on either cheek, slowly and deliberately. But that gentleness was misleading: He stared into you from black-rimmed eyes, as if from great depths, the misery of Gaza framing his vision. Sheykh Abdul-Rahim, I suspected, was not an easy man.

Speaking through Yusuf, the sheykh told us to wash our feet and join him for prayers. We quickly complied and entered the adjacent mosque. The room was an exuberant clutter of green flags and thin prayer rugs and chandeliers made of porcelain flowers and glittery streamers hanging in arcs. Each of the diamond-shaped brown and white tiles along the walls was imprinted with the word *Allah*.

About a dozen men lined up. They eyed Eliyahu and me with neutral curiosity. If the sheykh had invited us to pray, then we were welcome into their line. I stood beside Yusuf, who positioned me so that my feet and shoulders were aligned with the others. His father, I recalled, had done the same for me at the Ramle mosque. In Muslim prayer, surrender begins by accepting the supremacy of the line. Clearly, I wouldn't have made a good Muslim. I had trouble conforming to the laws of Judaism, insisting on my own idiosyncratic observance.

The prayers were led by an enormous man with a thick black beard, swathed in green robe and turban—an implacable mass of green, evoking the televised images of a Hamas or Taliban fanatic. I felt the enormity of my trespass into a Gaza mosque, even one belonging to Sufis.

I tried to subsume my panic into the movement of prayer. Kneel, prostrate, kneel, prostrate, kneel, stand, kneel. *"Allahu akbar,"* God is great. *"La illaha ill'Allah,"* There is no god but God. I didn't repeat the last part of the phrase, "Muhammad *rasul* Allah," Muhammad is His messenger. In fact, I had no qualms about appreciating Muhammad as a messenger of God, along with Jesus and Buddha and the other founders of the great faiths, but not as *the* messenger, which is obviously what Muslims meant. I could join Muslims in prayer to God; the rest was best resolved in silence.

And that is precisely what happened next. We sat on our knees in silence. I closed my eyes and felt impelled to raise my palms, asking God to fill me with courage. When I opened my eyes, I saw that everyone in the room had likewise raised palms in supplication. Instinctively, I'd joined the rhythm of the line. Just relax, I told myself, and trust the guidance of the heart.

All this time Sheykh Abdul-Rahim, wearing a starched white robe and a green felt pyramid-shaped hat, sat on a stool, watching us. He pressed the joints of his fingers, recalling with each motion another of Islam's ninety-nine Names of God. Watching him transform his fingers into vicarious names of God, I was reminded of tefillin: We bound the strap on our hand in such a way that the bent fingers were supposed to recall the Hebrew letters that spelled *Shaddai,* one of the names of God. We shared the same impulse with Islam: to transform the hands, our means of interaction with the world, into an instrument of God's will.

After the service, which lasted perhaps fifteen minutes, we entered the sitting room next door. It resembled the *zawiyeh* in Ramle: Two lines of mattresses faced each other across the narrow room. The walls were dense with hand-written quotes from the Koran, as well as text offering Sheykh Abdul-Rahim's spiritual lineage: "This *zawiyeh* belongs to the holy saint Sheykh Ahmed er-Rifa'i." Above the lines of green and red script hung a row of cymbals and drums, and above them a row of gilt-framed photos of white-bearded sheykhs, including several of Abdul-Rahim. But this was, after all, a shrine to ecstasy, and that careful order contained the promise of imminent rupture, as if the drums and cymbals were about to leap from the wall and amplify the dancing Arabic letters proclaiming God's presence.

Only a few men from the prayer service remained to drink bitter coffee with Sheykh Abdul-Rahim. Among them was the prayer leader who, it turned out, lived in Canada and spoke fluent English. He was, he explained, a Rifa'i born in Palestine, and he had come to Gaza to visit his sheykh, Abdul-Rahim. "In Canada everyone calls me the Green Sheykh," he said, enjoying the joke on himself. "You can call me that, too."

He smiled constantly at Eliyahu and me, as if to reassure and welcome us. Clearly I had misjudged him, equating Islamic piety with fanaticism.

Sheykh Abdul-Rahim sat cross-legged in a corner, smoking a

water pipe and frankly staring at Eliyahu and me through black-circled eyes. He didn't convey calm but a restless probing. Barefoot boys in stained T-shirts, the sheykh's grandsons, poured unsweetened coffee into little cups and distributed them to the men in the room, followed by heavily sugared tea that dispelled the coffee's bitterness, like a ritual enacting the passage of the soul from this world of sorrow to paradise. Every time the boys made eye contact with Eliyahu or me, they giggled and fled.

"Please tell the sheykh that we are honored to be in his presence," I said to the Green Sheykh.

Abdul-Rahim replied, "All those who love the prophets are welcome here. And Muhammad is the greatest of all prophets." He smiled, revealing a mouth full of gold caps, a hard, metallic smile.

He invited us to ask questions.

"How does one purify the heart from fear?" I asked. For me, sitting in a mosque in Nuseirat, that was the most urgent question.

"The Sufi heart constantly recalls the Name of God," he replied. "We silently repeat the words, *La illaha ill'Allah*. The key to opening the heart is prayer to the Prophet Muhammad, peace be upon him, our beloved in heaven and earth. And the most beloved of all the prophets."

"How do we open our hearts to each other?" I persisted, trying to ignore his repeated insistence on Muhammad's preeminence, as if he were baiting us.

"By having gratitude toward God," he replied.

The phone beside the sheykh rang. He answered firmly, "Allah," as though his being were an extension of God.

The *zawiyeh* functioned as a combination prayer hall and male social club. Men in gray robes entered, drank coffee, and left, their places on the mat taken by newcomers. Where else in Nuseirat could they recover their dignity, not with the false pride of religious or national fanaticism but with simple spiritual fellowship?

Every man who entered kissed the hand of the sheykh and then kissed everyone in the room, including Eliyahu and me. No one showed surprise at our presence: If we were in the *zawiyeh*, we obviously belonged. Their ease helped me relax. We were guests of the sheykh, under his protection.

The sheykh's grandchildren laid out a plastic tablecloth on the thin brown carpet and brought out massive platters of couscous and pumpkin and lamb. Everyone gathered around. Eliyahu explained to Sheykh Abdul-Rahim that he and I were vegetarians, so one of the boys returned to the kitchen and retrieved a large platter of couscous and pumpkin without lamb. "Do we have to eat the whole thing?" I whispered to Eliyahu, wary of offending our host. "I hope not," he replied grimly.

Eliyahu and I were given plates, but the others ate with large spoons directly from the platters. Sheykh Abdul-Rahim fiercely tore pieces of lamb and tossed the bones on the tablecloth, forming balls of couscous with grease-covered fingers. He ate like a refugee whose hunger could never be satisfied. I admonished myself not to judge. I reminded myself of bar mitzvah celebrations I'd attended as a boy in Hasidic synagogues of Holocaust survivors: Men whose personalities had become imprinted by hunger stood on benches and tried to grab trays from the waiters. Still, I couldn't help myself; I was repelled.

"You barely ate," Abdul-Rahim noted disapprovingly. We returned to our cushions and drank intensely sweetened tea, as if to compensate for Gaza's sense-deprived environment. Abdul-Rahim puffed on his water pipe and filled the room with apricot smoke, a singed sweetness. The sheykh looked at me, expectantly. *"Il hamdul'allah,"* I said, thank God, awkwardly offering one of my few Arabic phrases. *"Il hamdul'allah,"* he repeated solemnly.

A young man with a white knitted skullcap that entirely covered his shaved head sat beside Sheykh Abdul-Rahim. Eliyahu asked him in hesitant Arabic where he was from, and he replied, "Baka al Garbiyeh," an Arab town in Israel.

"So you're an Israeli," I said, delighted. And then I added, in Hebrew, "So am I."

No one seemed surprised or upset. I felt relieved. Ibrahim's well-intentioned ruse was over. If I was to make peace with Nuseirat, it could only be as an Israeli. And after we'd prayed and eaten together, I trusted the benevolence of this place.

The young man told us that he was a Sufi sheykh who now lived in Jerusalem, and he invited us to visit him.

"You wanted to meet Sufi sheykhs?" Eliyahu, delighted, said to me. "This is Sufi Grand Central Station."

I asked the sheykh from Jerusalem about his spiritual practices, but Eliyahu whispered to me, "We should address our questions to Sheykh Abdul-Rahim. It's the honor of the sheykh."

He was right. We'd been ignoring our host. And so I asked Abdul-Rahim, "Ya sheykh, how do you get close to God?"

"The only way to get close to God," he replied, "is through the Prophet, peace be unto him."

"Can the sheykh teach me something of remembering the presence of God through daily life?"

"Repeat, 'La illaha ill'Allah, Muhammad rasul Allah.'"

He wouldn't let go.

"Until you accept the Prophet," he continued, "you will never reach God. Muhammad, peace be upon him, is the medium for all religions, not just Muslims."

He leaned back, smoked his narghile, pleased.

This was Ibrahim's beloved master, the greatest of Palestinian Sufis?

I said, "Ya sheykh, what you say about the Prophet Muhammad, many Christians say about Jesus: that he is the only way to true intimacy with God."

"Every prophet comes for his nation," he replied. "But the Prophet Muhammad comes for all nations."

The sheykh smiled slyly at me, held up a forefinger and instructed me to do the same. "Now repeat after me," he said. I held up my forefinger and repeated, *"La illaha ill'Allah,"* There is no god but God. Then he said, "Muhammad *rasul* Allah," Muhammad is His messenger. I paused. Eliyahu whispered to me, "Unless you want to become a Muslim, you'd better stop now." Repeating the *Shahadah,* the creed of Islam, before three Muslim men was considered an act of conversion.

I lowered my finger. "I'm a Jew," I said to the sheykh. "But I revere the followers of the Prophet."

The sheykh was not appeased. "How can you revere the followers of the Prophet when you don't revere the Prophet himself?"

What was the point of telling him that I did revere the Prophet, but in my way, along with the saints of all faiths who were helping humanity evolve? I revered Muhammad in precisely the opposite way that he did: as an affirmation of religious pluralism, not triumphalism.

Now he tried his luck with Eliyahu. But Eliyahu smiled, shook his head, and said, "I'm also a Jew."

"Let's go," I said to Eliyahu. "Nothing is going to come out of this."

He tried to soothe me. "In my experience with sheykhs, first they have to declare their loyalty to orthodox doctrine, then you have a breakthrough of the heart. Each side has to state its basic beliefs, and then you can get to the real encounter."

And so I tried to circumvent theology through the heart. I said, "Ya sheykh, I'm grateful for you welcoming me into this house of God."

"The Divine Presence appears to anyone who comes here," said the sheykh affably.

"How can Jews and Muslims make peace?"

"That is God's secret. On the Day of Judgment, Jews and Christians will weep because they didn't accept Muhammad, peace be upon him."

Eliyahu countered with a quote we'd learned from Ibrahim: "Allah said in the Koran that He created human beings into different tribes to get to know each other. Otherwise he would have created us as one religion."

The sheykh puffed on his water pipe and didn't respond.

The Green Sheykh leaned across to me. "Perhaps later we can talk about these issues," he said, and I detected a tone of embarrassment.

I said to Abdul-Rahim, "We came here because we honor and love the followers of the Prophet."

"Congratulations for that," he replied. "You came very far for the love of the sheykh. But the sheykh's love is in Muhammad."

Eliyahu asked desperately, "Would the sheykh honor us with a zikr, to purify our hearts?"

Sheykh Abdul-Rahim motioned to his grandchildren to retrieve the drums from the wall. The men began a song of praise to Allah. But after a few minutes, it abruptly stopped. Eliyahu had hoped for a dance, but this was all the zikr the sheykh was prepared to offer.

We sat in uncomfortable silence. The sheykh smoked his water pipe, watching us.

"How does the awareness of our own death help us get closer to God?" I asked.

"Look across the street," he replied. "What do you see?"

I looked through the open doors of the zawiyeh to the cemetery across the road. The tombstones, thin and rounded, seemed like minarets pointing to the ascent of the soul.

"I built the zawiyeh deliberately at this spot, so that everyone who comes here could look out and see where he is going. The Prophet Muhammad, peace be upon him, said that when your heart feels heavy, you should visit a cemetery."

I recalled the technique I'd learned from the mad sheykh, Abu Falestin, and watched my breath, imagining that each exhalation contained my final moment of life. Sheykh Abdul-Rahim puffed on his water pipe, exhaling smoke, as if he were a cremation ground.

"When the sheykh looks at the cemetery," I asked, "what does he think about?"

"The grave is divided into two parts," he replied. "According to what a person did in life. If he loved people, prayed, and tried to get close to God, his grave is like paradise. And if he did the opposite? His grave is like fire."

He looked at me and offered his metallic smile. "What do you prefer?"

I smiled but didn't reply, assuming the question was rhetorical. But no; the sheykh was watching me, waiting for my answer. Now the dozen men in the *zawiyeh* and even the children were all staring at me. What did this Jew want, paradise or perdition?

"I'll take paradise," I said. Right answer. Everyone smiled with relief.

"Would the sheykh agree to take us to the cemetery?" Eliyahu asked.

Immediately, as if he'd been waiting to be asked, the sheykh rose, took Eliyahu by the hand, and led us across the street. Yusuf and the Green Sheykh followed. The cemetery gate was covered with laundry, perhaps from the sheykh's family, who lived upstairs from the *zawiyeh*—the intimacy between death and life.

The sheykh led us through the sandlot graveyard to a stone mausoleum, unlocked the door, and urged us to enter, like a spiritual teacher inviting his disciples to glimpse God's splendor. Inside, the heat and the mildew seemed to banish the air, as if death had transformed the whole room into a grave. I wanted to flee. There was no place here for the living. But the sheykh had shut the door.

In the center of the little room was a humped stone tomb, covered with the green banner of Islam. The walls, too, and even the ceiling, were covered with green cloth. Elsewhere, green was the color of life, renewal; here it meant acceptance of mortality.

I looked at the sheykh. He seemed happier than I'd seen him all day. He had no fear of this place; he was home. I sensed his strength. He tried to infuse every moment with the transience of life and the permanence of God.

The man who was buried here, he explained, was his teacher, Sheykh al-Qatwari. He proceeded to recite al-Qatwari's lengthy lineage, all the way back to the Prophet Muhammad.

When he finished, he turned to me and smiled. "Repeat after me," he said. I listened to the words; though I couldn't understand them, I knew they weren't the *Shahadah*. I asked the Green Sheykh what Abdul-Rahim was saying, and he explained, "It's a prayer asking God to lead you on the straight path." I repeated the words, asking God to show me the way to Him in Nuseirat. The sheykh extended his hand toward mine; we touched over the grave.

Outside, as we stepped between the stones, the Green Sheykh said to me, "He's a very kind man but not experienced in the world. Gaza has been his whole life. He doesn't know about other religions, other ways."

Back in the *zawiyeh*, Sheykh Abdul-Rahim withdrew into watchful silence.

Still, I sensed that something had changed between us. We had made the peace of the grave. Perhaps Palestinians and Israelis would stop fighting over the land once we acknowledged that it would ultimately claim us.

He was sitting diagonally across from me, a mere few feet away; I leaned toward him. "Ya sheykh," I began hesitantly. "I want to tell you something that's hard for me to say. This isn't my first time in Nuseirat. I was here during the Intifada, as a soldier. Not far from this *zawiyeh* I once got a rock thrown at my head. I've come back seeking God's peace between us."

"No, Yossi Halevi!" cried Yusuf. "You are an American friend! Don't mention this!"

The sheykh nodded but didn't speak. He seemed distracted, distant. But several of the men sitting on the mattresses looked at me with what I thought was horror.

I immediately regretted my confession; I felt like a fool. What right did I have to expect any understanding from these refugees?

This was Nuseirat, not southern California; here the word *closure* didn't mean healing some wound from the past but placing a population under curfew to restrain suicide bombers.

I asked for the sheykh's blessing for healing between our peoples.

"*Allah karim,*" he said only, God is generous.

That's it, I thought; the door has closed.

The Green Sheykh broke the long silence. "You are very brave for coming here," he said to me in English. "You had to overcome fear and hatred, and I respect that. I also had my struggles." He spoke with a soft lisp, as if to undermine his intimidating presence.

He told me that he'd grown up in one of the houses that Arabs had built along the Western Wall. When Israel returned to the Old City after the 1967 Six-Day War, it destroyed those houses and replaced them with a plaza, relocating their residents elsewhere in Jerusalem. I knew the story and felt sorry for the Green Sheykh's suffering, but I also understood Israel's motives. The Arabs had shown contempt for Jewish holy places, not only building houses by the Western Wall but throwing garbage onto the site, forbidding Jews to pray there, and turning the Old City's synagogues into stables and latrines.

But there was no need for a defensive polemic on my part; the Green Sheykh wasn't accusing. "For many years I felt great hatred for the Jews," he said. "But no more. Now, when you pray at the Wall, my heart is with you. I am grateful that prayers are being said where I once played."

I looked at him with wonder. What effort must have gone into forcing gentleness from this massive, seething man.

He continued, "Look how the God works in our lives. For you, a former soldier, to come searching for peace here, and for me to be expelled from my home and to come with a message of love. It's easy to be a man of peace when you come from a peaceful world. But to come from war, from real life, and to be a peaceful man . . ." He laughed quietly. "That is the real thing. To seek for light and harmony and humility. The God created us from dust. We exist for each other.

"You know, it's very strange," he continued. "I hadn't expected to come here today at all. I thought I would come another day. But when I woke up this morning, it was as if someone had whispered in my ear, 'Today you go to Sheykh Abdul-Rahim.' The God pushed me to come here to meet you."

"I'm sure of it," I said, deeply moved. "I'd been planning this trip with Eliyahu for months, and just on this day we happened to come."

He said, "We have to live the story of this time. The question isn't anymore to be or not to be a Muslim or a Christian or a Jew. Now it is about direct experience of the God. Not to *believe* in the God; to *know* the God. The story of religion is soon going to take a different turn. The God Himself will bring us to Him. Everyone will know that the God is real. The duty of Muslims, Christians, and Jews is to prepare the world for this divine revelation of harmony and unity and love."

Everything about this man was grand, not just his physical presence but also his vision.

"How do you know this?" I asked.

"It's not time to talk about that," he said enigmatically. It seemed to me he was speaking from some form of personal experience.

He held me in a massive embrace. "I feel like we knew each other a long time," he said. "Call me in Canada. If I am not present, speak to my wife. She is your sister. I will come back to Palestine in a month and a half. Then I will call you."

In Sufi time, "a month" usually meant an intention to reconnect sometime in the future, a wish rather than a commitment. The extra "half month" seemed to me an ominous addition. I wondered whether I would ever see him again.

"I know the God will bring us together," he said, as if reading my mind. "*Salaam aleikum,* my brother. Together, we will go toward the God, without fanaticism, our free way to the God."

Eliyahu, Yusuf, and I left Nuseirat in a taxi with torn upholstery and a framed photograph of a young mustached man on the dashboard whom I'd assumed was a martyr of the Intifada but Yusuf said was a popular singer. As we drove toward the Erez checkpoint, Eliyahu and I tried to make sense of our experience. Who was Sheykh Abdul-Rahim? And what exactly had happened to us in his *zawiyeh?*

I admitted to Eliyahu my disappointment in the sheykh, especially his crass attempt to convert us. It seemed to me, I said, that my real pilgrimage had been to the Green Sheykh. In Nuseirat of all places, where Islam was at its most wounded and aggrieved, I'd been offered a Muslim vision of a world beyond religious triumphalism.

Eliyahu said, "You came to Sheykh Abdul-Rahim looking for heal-ing from your experiences in Nuseirat, and you got it. Maybe not directly but from one of his disciples. Sheykh Abdul-Rahim sits in Gaza; he has to follow the orthodox doctrine. But even if the sheykh in his earthly place has to take a hard line, the sheykh on the higher plane provided the connection you needed. We want things to come *dugri*"—he used the Arabic word for "direct," which Israelis had incorporated into Hebrew—"but the Sufi way is roundabout."

Perhaps Eliyahu was right. The sheykh had rebuked me with one hand but embraced me with the other. What right did I have to expect more from this man? Though surrounded by Hamas, he'd opened his *zawiyeh* to us. And he'd been the instrument, however unconscious, of a remarkable encounter. Whatever limitations had been imposed on him by circumstance, he had attracted followers, like Ibrahim and the Green Sheykh, who were bringing universalist ideas into Palestinian Islam.

Still, I was unsure of where I stood with Sheykh Abdul-Rahim. Had our closeness in the mausoleum compensated for my refusal to repeat the *Shahadah*? Had my indiscreet revelation about being a sol-dier in Nuseirat undermined our graveyard reconciliation? Our part-ing had been unsatisfying: He'd been distant, perfunctorily kissing us on either cheek. He hadn't invited us to return.

But perhaps that, too, was the Sufi way: A connection with the teacher was meant to be arduous, as a test of the disciple's serious-ness. Though I could hardly consider myself a disciple of Sheykh Abdul-Rahim's, I had been pulled into his world. Perhaps it was no coincidence that I'd been hit with a rock in the head just down the block from the sheykh's *zawiyeh*. If God had set this process in motion, I had no choice but to see it through.

3

The prediction of the Prophet Moses to Sheykh Ibrahim became reality: Jews from all over Israel began gathering in his home in the West Bank village of Karawa.

Eliyahu was largely responsible. He introduced the sheykh to Israel's tiny interreligious community as well as to Israel's much more vigorous New Age scene. Eliyahu took Ibrahim to a New Age festival in the Galilee, and among the thousands of young Israelis massaging each other and chanting in Sanskrit, the sheykh erected a "Sufi tent of love and peace" and performed a *zikr*. He distributed a "Sufi mani-festo" in Hebrew, inviting Jews to visit him in Karawa. His half-built mosque became filled with spiritual seekers in dreadlocks and "chan-nelers" claiming to be in touch with angels, as well as professors of religion and peace activists and Orthodox Jews hoping to renew the medieval dialogue between Judaism and Islam. The Palestinian sheykh who spoke of prophetic visions of love between Muslims and Jews became a sensation among Israelis desperate for any sign that peace with Islam wasn't an illusion and that we weren't stranded in a region whose deepest religious vision was our disappearance.

At first the attention baffled and humbled him. With each new success he would call me, grateful to God for the opportunity to spread the message of religious peace. "Yossi Halevi! My brother from heaven! Do you know where the Sufi sheykh of love and peace was today? At the Bar-Ilan University! Fifty Jewish students heard the Sufi sheykh speak!"

Then the attention escalated. He even became, for a while, an international media star. It was the end of the millennium, and journalists were looking for the Moderate Muslim to interview along with the Moderate Christian and the Moderate Jew. I was responsible for the first interview: I mentioned the sheykh to a friend who worked for Israeli TV, and he dispatched a crew to film him. Not surprisingly, the handsome sheykh with the dimple, who laughed when he spoke of love and invoked peace with the forcefulness usually displayed by fanatics, was a hit. Sometimes two TV crews a day descended on the forlorn village of Karawa.

As the attention grew, the village sheykh lost his innocent charm and became a showman. The people wanted miracle stories, and he obliged. He told an interfaith audience that every time he entered the forest near his home, a deer ran into his arms and placed its head on his shoulders. "I just got a message from the angels," he intoned at another interfaith gathering. "Not from the Internet! Not from the fax! From the angels!" Even his voice began to change: It deepened with self-conscious authority, alternately mysterious and bombastic. He became convinced that he was a holy man, rather than a good man with a connection to God and a potential for holiness. He exchanged his simple brown robe for a gold-embroidered white one and wore matching white socks and white shoes.

At first I didn't want to admit what was happening. Ibrahim was my entry into Islam; without him, I was stranded. Maybe, I thought, I was overreacting, jealous over sharing "my" Sufi sheykh with the world. And what was he doing, after all, if not fulfilling the instructions he believed he'd been given by Moses: to open his house and make peace with the Jews?

But the arguments weren't working. I felt increasingly alienated from the sheykh. I even began to doubt his love. He called far less frequently now, and only, it seemed, when he needed a favor, like trying to help one of his sons get a visa to study in America. Finally, I confessed my concerns to Eliyahu, who admitted that he, too, was feeling distant from the sheykh. "His words don't sound like they're coming from the heart anymore," he said. "It sounds rehearsed."

And what, after all, had I learned in all my months with Ibrahim? I read longingly about Sufi disciplines for controlling human flaws and techniques for divine intimacy. But Ibrahim offered only increasingly stale rhetoric and improbable miracle stories.

One night the sheykh invited me to a *zikr* in a community center near Tel Aviv. Even as he hugged me in greeting I felt his attention wandering, scanning the crowd for anyone important whom he should be acknowledging. Then the *zikr* began, and it resembled a show more than a prayer. Dozens of secular Israelis watched Ibrahim and two of his sons breathe and chant and prance. One couple interpreted the sheykh's exhortations to love by making out. At one point he pulled me into his dance; I felt sullied.

"Were we taken in by a farce?" I asked Shoshi, an Israeli woman who'd been close to the sheykh and now shared my disillusionment.

"God has given him a test," she replied. "Can he be true to himself outside the village? So far, he's failed. But he really does have something; we know that. There's no reason to be angry at him or to judge him. To be a Sufi means to love unconditionally. In the end, we're only responsible for our own spiritual failures."

In fact, I still believed that "something" had happened to Ibrahim at Nebi Musa, some revelation that had transformed an ordinary man into a preacher of God's peace. And the sheykh had been my door into Islam, God's instrument to help me confront my fears. Through him I'd experienced Muslim prayer and had even returned to Nuseirat. Nothing could cheapen his gifts to me.

One night I dreamed that I was back in Sheykh Abdul-Rahim's *zawiyeh*. Its facade, as well as the walls within, were made of rippled sheets of silver. I was greeted by Sheykh Ibrahim and the Green Sheykh. I looked outside; the cemetery across the way had disappeared.

When I awoke, I considered the symbolism. Silver represents the moon, which is Islam. The cemetery had disappeared because I had entered the land of no death. Through Abdul-Rahim and the Green Sheykh and Ibrahim, I had touched the Islam of the next plane of existence, the Islam of love. At the very least, I thought, I owed them love in return.

4

Lailat al-Miraj is the holiday of Muhammad's night journey from Mecca to Jerusalem and from this world to the kingdom of souls. "Glory be to Him Who carried His servant by night from the holy temple to the farthest temple—whose precincts We have blessed— that We may show him some of Our signs." That oblique Koranic verse is the basis of the Muslim tradition that the angel Gabriel flew Muhammad from Mecca to the Temple Mount, or, as Muslims call it, the Haram el Sharif, the Noble Sanctuary, from where Muhammad ascended to Heaven before returning to Mecca. Sufis understood the ascent as a mystical transcendence of the physical world.

This year, 1999, the one-day festival fell in early November. Ibrahim was planning to spend the night with Sheykh Abdul-Rahim, and he phoned to say that the sheykh had invited Eliyahu and me to join him. Eliyahu was in America, but I welcomed the unexpected opportunity to celebrate with Abdul-Rahim. I suspected that the real reason Ibrahim called was that he needed help in securing an army pass for Gaza. "People come from all over and dance the whole night!" Ibrahim said. I envisioned hundreds of ecstatics crowding the narrow street between the *zawiyeh* and the cemetery, celebrating Muhammad's transcendence of the mortal body. I hoped that my return, on Muhammad's day, would be a way of signaling to Sheykh Abdul-Rahim that I honored the Prophet who took on the difficult job of transforming desert tribes into monotheists and whose movement brought such a vast part of humanity to God.

Rabbi Menachem Froman, who was always seeking connections to Islam and a way to further his one-man campaign of religious peace, asked Ibrahim if he could join us, and the sheykh happily agreed. I was less enthusiastic. As an Orthodox rabbi, Froman would refuse to remove his *kipah* even in Nuseirat, which meant that we would travel through the camp openly identified as Jews. Obviously, with Froman present, I would wear a *kipah* too. There would be no point entering Nuseirat incognito if he was a target. Froman assured me we'd be safe. He was friendly with General Nasser Yusuf, head of one of the dozen or more rival secret services that Arafat had created to keep each other in check. General Yusuf always provided an armed escort for Froman in Gaza, and this time, too, Froman said, we'd be protected. I accepted the arrangement. But I wasn't calmed.

There remained the problem of appearing as blatantly religious Jews at Sheykh Abdul-Rahim's *zawiyeh* during a public festival. That could embarrass, perhaps even endanger, the sheykh. I asked Ibrahim to phone Sheykh Abdul-Rahim and explain the situation. Ibrahim phoned me back: "Sheykh Abdul-Rahim welcomes Rabbi Froman and Yossi Halevi to the *zikr* in honor of the Prophet Muhammad."

"Did you tell him that we'll be wearing *kipot?*" I asked, wary of Ibrahim's reassurances.

"Sheykh Abdul-Rahim knows that Rabbi Froman and Yossi Halevi are Jewish brothers, and he welcomes them to the *zikr* in honor of the Prophet Muhammad."

Now all that remained for me was to confront my fear. I would be returning to Nuseirat as a publicly identifiable Jew, just as I'd been when I patrolled the camp as a soldier, except that this time I'd be trusting the benevolence of the Palestinian police.

Early on the morning of the holiday, I picked up Sheykh Ibrahim. I admitted to him that I hadn't slept well the night before, fearful of returning to Nuseirat. "A jinn visited you, Yossi Halevi!" he exclaimed. "The same thing happened to me before I visited Rabbi Froman's house. The jinn said, 'Don't go! The settlers hate Arabs! They'll kill you!' And what did I find in Rabbi Froman's house? Hatred? Violence? No! I found peace and love. Peace? And love!"

I told Ibrahim about Sheykh Abdul-Rahim's attempt to convert me. He was uncharacteristically silent, perhaps trying to figure out how to differ with his teacher without criticizing him. Finally, he said, "If Yossi Halevi wants to become a Muslim, first he makes an application. First? He makes an application. Then the angel brings the application to heaven. 'Yossi Halevi wants to become a Muslim.' But in heaven they say, 'Yossi Halevi is registered here as a Jew.' As? A Jew! If Sheykh Ibrahim wants to become a Jew, the angel looks up the Jewish list. No good: His name is on the Muslim list. How can Sheykh Ibrahim become a Jew if his name is on the Muslim list? No one can make Sheykh Ibrahim a Jew. No one can make Yossi Halevi a Muslim. Only in heaven, not on earth."

We drove on a narrow empty road to the tiny West Bank settlement of Otniel, on the edge of the Judean desert, where Froman was teaching at a yeshivah for soldiers. We passed through one of the world's most politicized landscapes. The flat-roofed stone houses of Arab villages spread through the hills, while the red-roofed houses of Jewish settlements nervously clustered. In the past, whenever I'd tried to engage Ibrahim in a political conversation, he'd said only that the land needed prophets, not politicians. But I pressed him now: "Ya sheykh, you must be upset when you see the hills covered with settlements. How do you keep your love for Jews from being overwhelmed by anger?"

"Yossi Halevi, I'll tell you a secret that nobody in the world knows. A secret from heaven! Many years ago, before the first Jews moved near my village, I walked through my uncle's olive grove. Saints came from heaven and said to me, 'Ibrahim, soon the Jews will be coming to this hill. They will build a big town here.' I became very afraid. They'll take my land, they'll hurt my children! 'No, Ibrahim, don't worry. The Jews will come, but nothing will happen to you or your family.'"

"But aren't you angry that the Jews build roads through olive groves?"

"Against whom should I be angry? Against God? I don't know why He wanted the Jews back in this land, but He did. All the Arabs, the Europeans, the whole world can say no, and if God says yes, who can stop it? Even if Hitler came back—Hitler!—he couldn't stop it either. So why should I be angry?"

I didn't quite believe his story of yet another revelation, but it moved me anyway. Ibrahim knew this land needed divine revelation, and so he dared to offer it. Perhaps he hoped that if he repeated his miracle stories often enough, they would actually happen.

We picked up Froman at the electric gate at the entrance to Otniel. His black suit carried the dust of the Judean hills. Ibrahim got out of the car, and they repeatedly kissed each other from cheek to cheek. Froman was trying to soften the West Bank's hard desolation with love. If the settlement movement had been led by people like him, maybe it would have turned out differently.

We headed toward the Erez checkpoint. Froman sat alone in the backseat, quietly chanting from a pocket-sized Bible the Torah portion that would be read in synagogue the following Saturday, infusing the week with anticipation of Shabbat. The portion Froman was reading dealt with Sarah's burial in Hebron's Cave of Machpelah. As we approached the entrance to Gaza, that anti-Eden, the legend of the Machpelah as an opening to Paradise seemed more like mockery than promise.

I asked Ibrahim what Lailat al-Miraj meant to him. He said, "I ask the question, Why did God have to take Muhammad from Mecca to Jerusalem? The gates of heaven aren't open in Mecca? There aren't enough mosques in Mecca? Why did he have to go to Jerusalem? To make a link between the family of Ishmael in Mecca and the family of Isaac in Jerusalem. A link? Between Ishmael in Mecca and Isaac in Jerusalem."

We came to Erez. Froman raised his palms in supplication, perhaps in despair.

We went to the VIP office for our Israeli entry permits into Gaza. Though Ibrahim was supposed to be processed through the Palestinian queue, I insisted he come with us. "But I'm not a VIP," he said, nervously, no longer a sheykh but a Palestinian under occupation. "Sure you are," I said, teasing, "Very Important Prophet."

We crossed the Israeli checkpoint into Gaza, arms linked: an Arab in a robe and two Jews in all-white knitted *kipot*. (Froman and I had had the same impulse: to honor our hosts by wearing Sufi-style *kipot*.)

"May I ask you a question?" said an Israeli soldier in the concrete guard post. "What are you planning to do in Gaza?"

"We're building a new settlement," said Froman, and he laughed.

Two Palestinians with Kalashnikovs were waiting for us in a car with tinted glass: General Nasser Yusuf's escorts. I looked at their impassive faces and thought: These men would just as soon kill us as protect us. Wordlessly they drove us into Gaza City, through narrow streets crowded with robed men and veiled women mingling with old cars and flatbed carts. Froman resumed chanting from his little

Bible. Ibrahim pulled me close. "No fear!" he whispered in my ear; he pointed upward and laughed.

We came to Nuseirat. Even armed police escorts failed to calm me. Here we were, flaunting our Jewishness among people who saw Jews as the reason for their suffering and the source of evil. And how would Sheykh Abdul-Rahim and his followers receive me now, wearing a *kipah* and in the company of a settler rabbi?

A towering minaret near Sheykh Abdul-Rahim's *zawiyeh* glowed with blinking colored lights, ready for the festival. But at the little *zawiyeh* without a minaret, there were no holiday decorations. Our Islamic haven, the one mosque in Nuseirat, perhaps in all of Gaza, where we'd be welcome and safe, seemed so peripheral. If Froman and I were to try to enter any other Gaza mosque, we might not make it out alive. We had come to make peace with Islam, but Gaza allowed us no illusions.

We pulled in front of the *zawiyeh*. Our two guards got out and scanned the street with pointed Kalashnikovs. We entered the *zawiyeh*, and they got back into the car. "Call us when you want to return to Erez," one said, and they drove off. Wait a minute, I wanted to shout, where are you going? How can you leave us, two blatantly Jewish Jews, in Nuseirat? I turned to Froman, angry and desperate. "You said we'd have protection through our entire visit!" He shrugged and tried to reassure me with a smile. I thought of Amnon Pomerantz, the Israeli reservist who'd taken a wrong turn and been burned to death by a Gaza mob. The only prospect more frightening to me than being protected by Arafat's police in Gaza was not being protected by Arafat's police in Gaza.

I turned to God. "Now I'm really dependent on You alone." Maybe that realization was why I was here.

Sheykh Abdul-Rahim vigorously kissed my cheeks and peered

into me through black-rimmed eyes, a severe embrace. The *zawiyeh*'s happy clutter comforted. The inscriptions from the Koran and the photos of the distant-looking, white-bearded sheykhs and the drums and cymbals awaiting *zikr* all proclaimed God's pervading presence. The room tolerated no empty space, no intimation of the void just outside the *zawiyeh*.

Perhaps a dozen men were sitting on the mattresses against the wall. I followed Ibrahim's lead and kissed each man. Some remembered me from my last visit. I heard whispers of "Nasser Yusuf" followed by meaningful looks toward Froman and me. We were not only guests of the sheykh but protected by the general. We were welcome.

Ibrahim's son Yusuf, who had come to the *zawiyeh* on his own, greeted me with kisses and hugs and then more kisses. He wore a white robe and a square stiff green skullcap that covered his whole head. He and Ibrahim seated me between them, perhaps to help me feel safe.

A plastic tablecloth was spread on the floor between the two rows of facing mattresses. The sheykh had prepared a nonmeat feast in honor of his Jewish guests: humus and bitter olives, large platters of fried fish stuffed with chili peppers. Froman didn't eat, because the food hadn't been prepared with kosher utensils. My own observance was pared to what I considered the essence of keeping kosher: respecting the sacrifice of an animal's life by applying strict separation between eating dairy and meat. I rejected the strictures on kosher plates and utensils, which seemed intended to keep Jews and non-Jews from socializing and undermined the healing that needed to happen between us. If Froman disapproved of my joining the meal, he didn't say; he seemed to be that rare Orthodox believer who could accommodate diverse ways to God, or at least had learned to restrain his judgmental instincts.

Froman retrieved pita from his knapsack; he would eat nothing of gentile food. I was especially glad at that moment to be joining our hosts and not insulting the sheykh.

Froman recited the Hebrew blessing over bread while everyone listened quietly. Ibrahim responded with an enthusiastic "amen" in Hebrew. Then, realizing he may have revealed too much intimacy with Judaism, he quickly added, *"La illaha ill'Allah."* Everyone in the room repeated the phrase, pulled into devotion.

I knew their faces. These men with bad teeth and gray skin were our gardeners and waiters. But I'd never seen them in their white holiday robes and green caps, drinking tea from delicate cups and reclining like royalty. One of the sins of the occupation, it seemed to me now, was that it kept us from respecting the dignity of Islam.

An old man, whose sunken cheeks were covered with stubble, entered the *zawiyeh* and fell on my neck and wept, apparently overwhelmed to find a Jew coming to honor his religion and his sheykh. Ibrahim called out, "The Sufi mosque of love!"

Froman looked around the room, smiling in turn at every man. He had the ability to convey ease in an awkward situation; even in his black suit, long gray beard, and thick side locks, he seemed to feel at home here.

Now he addressed Sheykh Abdul-Rahim. "Ya sheykh, I am honored to be with our Muslim brothers who know the One God."

Abdul-Rahim replied, noncommittally, "We are all Adam. From *adama*, earth."

"Why do we say an elderly man is wise?" Froman continued. "Because he remembers that we come from the earth and return to the earth."

"The earth is close to young and old," said Abdul-Rahim. "Death comes to all." And then he added, "There is one God, and Muhammad is His prophet. Muhammad is the head of the prophets, of the heavenly host and the earthly host."

Froman sidestepped the challenge and tried to return the conversation to its initial theme. "It's true that death can come to young people, too," he said. "But young people don't think of death. The elders do, and that is the source of their wisdom."

The sheykh persisted. "Whoever believes in Muhammad is closer to God."

I'm going to let Froman handle this, I thought. I had resolved to return here in silence, without theological disputations or dramatic revelations. Simply to be present, as Sister Miriam of the Beatitudes had said to me at Yad Vashem. I closed my eyes and opened my palms, trying to suppress anxiety and accept whatever God wanted me to receive.

The call to prayer resounded from the minaret down the street so intensely that I felt myself within its reverberation, caught inside the mouth of prayer. *"Allahu akbar,"* I said involuntarily, intending only to think those words, not say them aloud. *"Allahu akbar,"* the men around me repeated appreciatively. Some sighed.

We moved into the adjoining prayer room. Froman stood to the side, slowly swaying. I joined the line. *Allahu akbar:* bow from the waist and straighten. *Allahu akbar:* kneel, prostrate, kneel. *Allahu akbar:* prostrate, kneel, stand. Again. Repeatedly, until you are no longer in control of your movements but animated by the will of the line.

When the prayer ended, Froman asked Sheykh Abdul-Rahim for a private place where he and I could say our Jewish afternoon prayers. Abdul-Rahim's son Nabhan, a young man with his father's penetrating eyes and who likewise wore the high triangular green-felt hat of a sheykh, wordlessly led us to a bedroom just behind the prayer room. All afternoon, I'd noticed, he seemed to be keeping his distance from us. But now he suddenly said, in fluent Hebrew, "Here you can pray quietly."

"You speak Hebrew?" I asked, surprised.

"I used to work as a welder near Tel Aviv." He smiled and left us alone. Perhaps he'd decided to speak to us in Hebrew because we were about to pray in it.

A double bed took up most of the space. A shelf was crowded with toiletries and medicines, plastic flowers, framed photos of sheykhs. Suitcases were piled above a dresser. In this room was the meanness of refugee life, cramped and random, the haste of upheaval from which it never recovered. Or perhaps the disorder reflected the sheykh's indifference to this world of exile, this refugee camp for the soul.

Froman and I stood pressed together between the bed and the wall and prayed the silent standing meditation. Perhaps I should have prayed for the courage to accept whatever God's will dictated for this night; but fear overtook me, and I prayed instead for protection.

The *zikr* began with cymbals and drums, so loud and relentless that my own thoughts became inaccessible, and that was perhaps the point: to empty the mind. Though no more than fifty people were gathered, the long and narrow prayer room was filled. Old men, working men, teenage boys and children held hands and formed a circle. Yusuf, quietly looking after me, took my hand. Froman joined the circle. Ibrahim and Sheykh Abdul-Rahim's son Nabhan stood in the center and led us.

"La illaha ill'Allah. La illaha ill'Allah. La illaha ill'Allah!" Slowly, then faster, until the phrase merges into one word, one breath. We sway in unison, a dance of controlled ecstasy balancing effusiveness and restraint, stripping away inhibition but avoiding hysteria, gradually losing ourselves into heightened alertness.

"Allah-hu," Allah is He. Bow to the waist and exhale, rise and inhale. Quickly, repeatedly, until your hands dangle uselessly like a marionette and you know yourself to be a mere instrument of a higher will. I forget to worry about being observed, the outsider trying to keep in step. I am no longer an Israeli with a *kipah* in a Gaza mosque but part of the great human wave of surrender.

Froman breaks from the circle, waving his hands and laughing. After all these years of lonely search for peace with Islam, he's finally embraced by Muslim prayer. "Allah!" he cries. "Allah! Allah!"

"Hai-Hai-Hai-Hai," the Living One. *"Haq-Haq-Haq-Haq,"* The True One. Exhale and leap, exhale and leap. Until you forget to inhale and there is only the relief of exhalation, emptying into God.

I'm on a trampoline, thrust higher with each leap. Above me is a fluorescent light, radiant, absorbing, pulling me in . . .

Yusuf grabs and steadies me, coaxes me back into measured leaping.

Ibrahim signals a break.

I opened my eyes. The room was spinning slowly. If at that moment someone had asked me my name, I'm not sure I would have known how to respond.

Then I noticed Sheykh Abdul-Rahim. He hadn't joined the circle but was standing to the side, impassive, watchful. The subtle impresario of our ascent, presiding over his congregation of broken ecstatics.

Inexplicably, I felt the sheykh summoning me. I had the overwhelming urge to kiss his hand. Like a sleepwalker, I headed toward him. He seemed to know my unspoken intention; he looked at me with a keen distance that showed no surprise, and he raised his hand to my lips. I'd never done anything like this before; I disliked and mistrusted demonstrative piety. I kissed his hand and returned to my place in the line.

I looked around the room. The *zikr* had distilled its participants to quivering open hearts. The sheykh's son was resting his head on the shoulder of a big bearded man, weeping. An old man was moaning, "Allah! Allah!" his head thrust back and his mouth agape. "There is a great light with him," Yusuf said to me. Here we were, experiencing Muhammad's ascent not from the Temple Mount, place of Islamic glory, but in a refugee camp, place of Muslim shame and defeat.

And then I noticed the faces in the window: neighbors drawn by the tumult, some curious, some smirking. Froman and I have been spotted. Exposed. The whole camp must know by now that two Jews are dancing with the holy rollers in Sheykh Abdul-Rahim's *zawiyeh*. The masked men marching with hatchets, the future *shaheed* parading in white shrouds: I know their faces; I've been in their bedrooms and led them bound and blindfolded to interrogations. And now they're just outside the door . . .

"La illaha ill'Allah. La illaha ill'Allah!"

Ibrahim resumes his place in the center of the circle, measuring with his palm the pace of our rapid exhalations. *"Allah-hu! Allah-hu!"* He places his palm on my chest, as if to embolden me. I feel an electrical current, sharp but painless, like the first time I met him in his mosque in Karawa, when he'd spoken the word *"ahavah,"* love, and I'd involuntarily entered meditation.

"Hu-Hu-Hu-Hu!" Through the fear, through the fear . . .

"Hu-Hu-Hu-Hu!" This body is Yours, protect or destroy it . . .

"Hu-Hu-Hu-Hu!" The freedom that comes from surrender . . .

The *zikr's* end startled me; I had no sense of time. Beyond ecstasy, the *zikr* had imparted the feeling that I'd found my natural rhythm and could keep spinning inexhaustibly.

Froman and I joined Sheykh Abdul-Rahim and the other men back in the sitting room. A few sullen young men lingered in the foyer, peeking in, but I didn't care: An open heart knows no fear.

We drank tea and more tea. "Allah," someone called out softly, and then everyone repeated and amplified the call. Whenever one of the men caught my eye, he'd greet me with the welcome of *"Ahalan wasahalan,"* no matter how many times we'd already greeted each other. *"Ahalan bik,"* I offered in response, evoking delighted smiles. We all shared the same impulse: to continue the intimacy of the *zikr,* with whatever meager words we could exchange. The Arabic phrases I knew as an occupier in Gaza, like knocking on a door and shouting *"Iftah, jeish,"* Open, army, were all commands. Now I was learning the decorous Arabic of the *zawiyeh*.

Froman tried his luck again with Sheykh Abdul-Rahim, perhaps hoping that the *zikr* had opened our hearts to each other and we could now move beyond theology. "Ya sheykh," Froman began, "why did I leave my wife and ten children and come to Gaza on this night? To learn from my Muslim brothers, the children of Ishmael, how to worship God. The Jewish people was exiled from this land because of our sins. And during the exile we forgot many things about how we served God in our youth, when we lived in the land. Now God has brought us back, to serve Him. God wants us to learn from our Muslim brothers how to serve Him with the joy of the *zikr*, as we once knew how to do when we were young."

It was an astonishing moment. Froman—a settler rabbi!—was telling these casualties of the Jewish return that our presence in this land was willed by God. But he spoke with such modesty and love for Islam that no one seemed offended. Froman's dare, that true peace would come only through religious reconciliation, suddenly seemed possible. Froman was implicitly offering this exchange: Jews would honor Islam, and Islam would honor the Jewish return.

Then I remembered: It was November 4, anniversary of the assassination of Yitzhak Rabin. In Tel Aviv's Rabin Square, thousands were now gathering for the annual memorial rally, with its elegiac songs and angry peace slogans. Meanwhile, in a little Gaza mosque, Muslims and Jews were praying and dancing and celebrating together, repudiating, however unintentionally, the religious assassin. But we were so peripheral; who would know or care that we existed?

A young man asked Froman, "Why do so many people around the world become Muslims but the Jews refuse?"

Froman smiled. "I don't have to become a Muslim because I already am one. Surrendering to God is Islam."

There were smiles of appreciation for the clever rabbi.

"We accept all the prophets," another man persisted. "Why don't you accept Muhammad, peace be upon him?"

Froman explained, "The Jews made a covenant with our father, Jacob, to be faithful to the Torah through all eternity. Doesn't the Koran say that the children of Israel have their way, and you have your way? We have sacrificed for thousands of years to preserve our way. But we never say that our way is for everyone. Others must have their own way to God. Satan knows that if the children of Ishmael and the children of Isaac make peace, he won't have any work left. That's why he's trying so hard to keep us apart."

Vigorous nods around the room. The rabbi knew how to touch the Muslim soul.

Since we'd arrived at the *zawiyeh,* I had maintained public silence, refraining from questions and arguments and proclamations. But now, using Ibrahim as a translator, I asked Sheykh Abdul-Rahim, "Can you say something about the significance of this night in relation to the Prophet Muhammad, peace be upon him?" In Hebrew the phrase had a soothing softness: *Hanavi Muhammad, alav hashalom.*

The sheykh replied, "This is the night when Muhammad, peace be upon him, and all the holy ones come to us. They were with us in the *zikr.* A green light came down to the *zawiyeh* tonight. The light went through everyone and connected us. First I felt it in my heart, then I saw it with my eyes."

Tonight, then, was also a night of descent: the descent of Muhammad into Gaza.

Then the sheykh asked me, "How did you feel tonight?"

I was taken aback. The only questions he'd ever posed to me were related in some way to converting to Islam.

I replied, "I felt that a person who truly loves God doesn't need to be afraid."

He placed a hand over his heart and smiled at me. He said, "Ever since you went with me into the tomb and put your hand into mine, I have considered you one of my own. I think of you all the time. All my students, Muslim or Jew, are in my heart."

I was overwhelmed. A sheykh in Nuseirat was praying for me, protecting me. *"Allahu akbar,"* I said, in gratitude. *"Allahu akbar,"* the men solemnly repeated.

Ibrahim said, "The sheykh's heart is like an ocean."

"And we are fish in it," I added.

Everyone laughed, including Abdul-Rahim.

The friendly disputation between Froman and the sheykh's disciples resumed. Muslim challenges, conciliatory replies, tense moments, laughter. I stopped following the arguments; even the voices seemed to recede. Instead I felt drawn back into the dance, imagining our words merging into a single exhalation, *"Ah-llah."* As if I could dispel this world of fragmentation and remain, just a little longer, in the oneness of God.

EPILOGUE

And then the madness came. Gaza and the West Bank turned into battlefields; travel in the Palestinian-controlled territories became a life-and-death danger for Israelis; and my forays into Islam abruptly ceased. Except for brief and awkward phone calls, I lost my connection to the Palestinians with whom I'd celebrated and prayed. Access to some of the Christian communities I'd grown close to—like the Beatitudes in Bethlehem—also was blocked. Inevitably, the sensation of transcending this fragmented reality receded. I had stood at the entrance and glimpsed the garden, but that was all.

The violence penetrated my daily life. There were shooting attacks on Israeli cars on the edge of my neighborhood, French Hill; a neighbor's son was killed in an ambush on a West Bank road. Two boys from Tekoah—Rabbi Menachem Froman's settlement, whose children Sheykh Ibrahim had blessed—went wandering in the desert caves below their homes and were stoned to death and mutilated so badly their faces were unrecognizable; my oldest son, Gavriel, knew one of them from baseball camp. A suicide bomber blew himself up in French Hill, as a bus passed not far from the nursery school of my youngest son, Shahar; though several passengers were wounded, only the terrorist was killed.

Thanks to my journey into the faiths of my neighbors, my grief could no longer be confined to one side of the border. Sheykh Abdul-

Rahim's grandson—one of the boys I'd met in the Nuseirat mosque, who had played a game with me of repeatedly saying "Shalom" and then running away, giggling—was shot in the head during a confrontation between Palestinian rioters and Israeli soldiers in Gaza. He emerged from a coma and is on his way to recovery. Even the Galilee, where decency between Arabs and Jews seemed possible, is no longer immune. Arab Israelis joined the Intifada riots in early October 2000, and Israeli police shot dead thirteen Arab citizens. The rioting approached the edge of Father Yaakov Willebrands's hilltop retreat of Lavra Natofa; Hararit, the little village of meditators bordering Lavra Natofa, was briefly under siege. In the nearby village of Arrabe—where I'd bought olive oil for the Shabbat meal with our Muslim friends, the Joulanis—a seventeen-year-old boy named Asel Asleh, an activist in Arab-Jewish coexistence, was killed by police while apparently trying to calm passions. Since those events, the alienation between Israel's Arabs and Jews has deepened. Arabs see the police killings as proof that the Jewish state considers them enemies rather than citizens; Jews regard the readiness of Arab Israelis to join in Palestinian violence as proof that they aren't a loyal minority but part of a hostile regional majority.

Despite the growing despair, Eliyahu McLean has continued his brave attempts at opening hearts. Every Friday he and a half dozen friends, Muslims and Jews, gather at a lookout in Jerusalem's Old City, opposite the Al Aqsa Mosque, and pray for peace. Yet even he has had to concede the danger of traveling through the Palestinian territories, and his contacts among Muslims are now largely restricted to Israeli Arabs.

Sheykh Ibrahim was forced back into anonymity by the Palestinian Authority. He was summoned to the headquarters of one of Yasser Arafat's security services and warned that his life was in danger from "Hamas extremists." For your own protection, an officer told him, we advise you to stop fraternizing with Jews. Ibrahim took the hint and disappeared from the interfaith circuit.

I phoned him on the night of the French Hill suicide bombing, desperate for a reminder of a benevolent Islam. The voice that greeted me was thin and remote; he sounded like a man on his death-bed. For Ibrahim, confinement to village life was indeed a kind of death sentence.

"Welcome, my brother," he said in English, avoiding Hebrew, perhaps out of fear. "I miss you, my brother. You are safe? I pray to my God every night to stop the fire and help us to make forgiveness."

There was no laughter in his voice; he no longer repeated phrases for emphasis, delighting in his own exuberance.

"This is the time of the fanatics," he continued. "I am crying all the night, but the angels last week they promised me, 'Don't worry, the peace is coming.' The angels tell me that the future is for us, the peacemakers."

"*Inshallah*," I said.

"Thank you, my brother. See you again."

But I couldn't imagine when that might be.

At difficult moments—when I am overwhelmed with fear for my children's safety and rage at the Palestinian leadership for rejecting compromise and despair at the Middle East for turning the Jewish homecoming into another form of exile—I try to recall what I learned from my teachers, the monastics and sheykhs of the Holy Land. I remind myself of Sister Johanna's warning against building barriers in the heart and excluding even one person from our love. And Father Yaakov Willebrands's insistence on relating to human beings as evolving souls destined for perfection. And Sheykh Abdul-Rahim's contempt for death and Sheykh Ishak Idriss Sakouta's steadiness that evoked the Divine Presence.

When I become too immersed in the political work of a journalist, I sometimes hear the admonition of Sheykh Ibrahim: "There are enough politicians in the land of the prophets. But where are the prophets in the land of the prophets?" I tell myself that it is precisely in times like these that the beautiful teachings of faith become either real or mere sentiment. More than ever, the goal of a spiritual life in the Holy Land is to live with an open heart at the center of unbearable tension. Still, I regularly disappoint myself, unable to exorcise, except for brief interludes, the jinns of fear and rage. The best that I can say is that I'm struggling, and that maintaining a painful awareness of the gap between what I've been taught and my inability to embody those teachings defines my spiritual life.

The one enduring transformation that I carry with me from my journey is that I learned to venerate—to love—Christianity and Islam. I learned to feel at home in a church, even on Good Friday, and in a mosque, even in Nuseirat. The cross and the minaret have become for me cherished symbols of God's presence, reminders that He speaks to us in multiple languages—that He speaks to us at all. Even if much of Arab Islam has descended into the kind of Jew-hatred for which Christianity is now trying to atone, I insist on revering Islam and its fearless heart. The fanatics will not deprive me of that victory.

This year, shortly before Easter, I took my two oldest children, Moriah and Gavriel, to the Church of the Holy Sepulcher. They'd never been there, and I wanted them, as citizens of Jerusalem, to experience that sacred place as part of their patrimony. The massive building was nearly deserted; few tourists or pilgrims were coming to Israel. We entered the little stone structure in the center of the great domed hall that Christians believe was the scene of the burial and resurrection of Jesus. As we stood before the marble slab covered with candles and icons and flowers, I told my children that, while we don't accept Christian theological claims, we should venerate a holy place sanctified by the prayers and expectations of pilgrims. I wanted them to understand that, even as this land showed its hardest face, we can still receive inspiration from another tradition's experience of God's presence.

It is late morning. I am sitting at my desk, looking toward the desert expanse outside my window. Somewhere in the blurred distance is Nebi Musa, the Muslim shrine to the Prophet Moses where Sheykh Ibrahim and I prayed together. I am suddenly aware of the muezzin, summoning me from the next hill. I get on my knees, press my fore-head to the floor, immobile with surrender.

Jerusalem

Shavuot, Pentecost, Mawlid an-Nabi (the Prophet's Birthday)

June 2001